B9   31

CW00525610

THE SCIENCE OF A LEGISLATOR

THE SCIENCE OF A LEGISLATOR

The Natural Jurisprudence of David Hume and Adam Smith

KNUD HAAKONSSEN

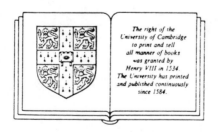

CAMBRIDGE UNIVERSITY PRESS

CAMBRIDGE

NEW YORK   PORT CHESTER

MELBOURNE   SYDNEY

Published by the Press Syndicate of the University of Cambridge
The Pitt Building, Trumpington Street, Cambridge CB2 1RP
32 East 57th Street, New York, NY 10022, USA
10 Stamford Road, Oakleigh, Melbourne 3166, Australia

First published 1981

First paperback edition 1989

Printed in Great Britain by
The Bath Press, Avon

British Library Cataloguing in Publication Data

Haakonssen, Knud
The science of a legislator.
1. Hume, David, 1711–1776 – Law
2. Smith, Adam, 1723–1790 – Law
3. Jurisprudence
I. Title
340'.109   BI499.L3   80–42001

ISBN 0 521 23891 9 hard covers
ISBN 0 521 37625 4 paperback

Contents

v

Acknowledgements

It is my great pleasure to acknowledge the constructive criticism and general support I have received during my work on this book from George E. Davie, Duncan Forbes, Jeremy F. G. Shearmur, and Donald Winch. I am grateful to the Editor of *Hume Studies* for permission to incorporate material from my 'Hume's obligations', *Hume Studies*, vol. IV, no. 1, 1978, pp. 7–17.

K.H.
Wellington
June 1980

List of abbreviations

David Hume:
E.   *An Enquiry Concerning the Principles of Morals*
T.   *A Treatise of Human Nature*

Adam Smith:
Anderson Notes   From John Anderson's Commonplace Book, vol. 1,
                 Andersonian Library, University of Strathclyde
Corr.   *Correspondence*
ED   Early draft of *The Wealth of Nations*
EPS   *Essays on Philosophical Subjects,* which include:
  Ancient Physics   'History of the Ancient Physics'
  Astronomy   'History of Astronomy'
  External Senses   'Of the External Senses'
FA   First fragment on the division of labour
LJ(A)   *Lectures on Jurisprudence*: Report of 1762–3
LJ(B)   *Lectures on Jurisprudence*: Report dated 1766
LRBL   *Lectures on Rhetoric and Belles Lettres*
TMS   *The Theory of Moral Sentiments*
WN   *An Inquiry into the Nature and Causes of the
                 Wealth of Nations*
See the Bibliography, p. 227, for details of editions.

LJ(A) references are to volume and page of the original manuscript; LJ(B) references are to page of the original manuscript. Both are given in the edition used here. References to Anderson Notes, ED, EPS, FA, TMS, and WN, use the *paragraph* system in the Glasgow Edition. All other references are to pages.

CHAPTER ONE

Introduction

The aim of this book is threefold: firstly to argue that Adam Smith developed a number of suggestions from David Hume into a new and original answer to the perennial philosophical question of how legal criticism is possible; secondly, to show how the answer was the basis for Smith's system of natural jurisprudence and as such the core of his political thought; and thirdly, to give a systematic account of Smith's natural jurisprudence.

There seem to have been two obvious avenues open to Hume after he had rejected the existing 'foundation-theories' of morality and law, according to which moral and legal evaluation had an ultimate and validating source in either the reasoning faculty or a moral sense: he could find an alternative 'foundation', or he could shift the problem away from the question of foundations altogether. It may be tempting to understand him in terms of the former strategy, especially in his theory of justice, if one interprets it on proto-utilitarian lines. There are, however, great difficulties in this, as we shall see, partly because of the meaning he gives the term 'utility', and partly because this interpretation would lead directly to the kind of legal positivism which he strongly criticizes. The suggestion to be pursued here, therefore, is that he somehow changes the problem. He does not do so by completely rejecting all talk of foundations, for he puts forward his well-known emotivist theory of the *origin* of evaluation. What changes the situation is his idea that it only makes sense to ask about the validity of evaluation in the particular social contexts which give concrete form to the expression of the emotions behind the evaluation. With the addition of these social and historical dimensions, the problem that emerged was: how are argument and criticism possible within a given moral and legal framework?

The theory of justice is of the greatest importance in Hume and although he never puts forward anything like a system of natural jurisprudence, it is quite clear that natural justice occupies a very central place – if not *the* central place – in his overall theory of politics. This is, however, not part of our interest here; it has recently been treated so thoroughly that it would be impertinent to go over the same ground again.[1] The intention in the following discussion of Hume is simply to present an

interpretation of the theory of justice in the *Treatise* and in the second
Enquiry which will make clear the nature of the philosophical task which
it set for Adam Smith in his legal philosophy. Accordingly we shall, of
course, also renounce the nearly inexhaustible fund of other points of
comparison and contrast between the two thinkers – interesting and
important though they are.

The subtitle of this book is thus not intended to indicate that Hume and
Smith will be treated with equal fullness, but to convey the suggestion
that it was Hume's speculations about justice which put the decisive
questions in answer to which Smith developed a whole new foundation for
a system of natural jurisprudence. As far as the system itself is concerned,
Smith was obviously very strongly indebted to the Continental natural law
tradition of Grotius, Pufendorf, and others, and especially to the form
which this tradition had been given by his teacher, Francis Hutcheson. He
was also heavily influenced by Montesquieu and by his old mentor, Lord
Kames. But these legacies do not, either individually or collectively,
produce the problem situation which gave Smith's jurisprudence its very
special character. This derived from Hume's question about the possibility
of legal criticism – or of how to avoid a complete relativism – if neither
naturally nor divinely given standards were available. It is therefore not
blindness to other important influences, but a judgement of priorities
which leads us to concentrate on the connection between Hume and
Smith in the present study.

While Smith was unhappy with the specific answer which Hume gave
to the problem posed, he followed his lead in how to approach it. This
approach was basically a matter of finding the principles which make it
possible to pursue ordinary human aims in whatever social situation we
are dealing with. But in order to formulate such principles in a way which
gives them a more than local and momentary importance, we shall need
three things: a general socio-psychological theory of motivation, a general
theory of the historical process, and specific historical knowledge of the
situation in which we are interested. Consequently, we find that Smith's
jurisprudence integrates a *history* of law with an *analysis* of the forces
which shape law, and that both are presuppositions for the possibility of
criticizing law. By separating the analytic, the critical, and the historical
sides of his argument, and by going through the various branches of the
jurisprudential system from each angle, we shall get a full view of how
his argument works in practice. At the same time we shall obtain a
methodical account of the system.

While the importance of Smith's ideas of natural jurisprudence have
been stressed in recent scholarship,[2] they have never been the subject of a
comprehensive study. This is perhaps not surprising in view of the state of
our sources until recently. Although Smith promised a 'discourse' on

natural jurisprudence fairly early in his career, he was still promising it when he died.[3] For over a century after his death the only clues to this part of his thought were his general treatment of justice in Part II of *The Theory of Moral Sentiments*, his very general outline of a system of natural jurisprudence in the final Part of that work, and material scattered throughout *The Wealth of Nations*.[4] But since the over-all context was missing, the full significance of this material was hard to appreciate. Much was gained when, in 1896, Edwin Cannan published a scholarly edition of a newly found set of student-notes from Smith's lectures on jurisprudence while he was professor of moral philosophy at Glasgow.[5] These notes have had an appreciable influence on Smith scholarship since, but they seemed too cursory to allow a systematic treatment of the subject.[6] This was greatly changed when, in 1978, yet another set of student-notes from Smith's lectures was published alongside the earlier set as part of the Glasgow Edition of Smith's works.[7] Although this set is incomplete in its coverage of Smith's course, leaving out something like a quarter, it is very full and detailed concerning the Justice part of the course – that is, the heart of the system of jurisprudence which we needed to know so much more about.[8] A small selection from yet another set of lecture notes has recently been discovered.[9] We shall also find much valuable material in a set of notes from Smith's *Lectures on Rhetoric and Belles Lettres*.[10]

Evidence from these student-notes from Smith's lectures must necessarily play a crucial part in the present attempt at interpretation. The risks in this are obviously very great, but they seem inevitable; and the best way to test the value of the notes for the interpretation of Smith is after all to accept them prima facie as expressions of his views, unless there are specific reasons not to do so.[11]

CHAPTER TWO

Hume's theory of justice

1 One theory or two?

When Hume refused to follow Francis Hutcheson's advice to preach morality at the same time as he explored its foundations,[1] he clearly implied that his task was a factual and descriptive one. But when he added that his own 'Metaphysician may be very helpful to a Moralist',[2] we can take it that he was aware of the principle that 'ought implies can', and that his view of the 'cans' was highly relevant for what view one should take of the 'oughts'. The roots of the latter are given us by nature in the form of the activating forces in our life, as passions. In this sense the foundation of morality is private and subjective. And yet morality as such is something public and objective: it is that which binds people together and makes a society possible, and in this function it is dependent upon the existence of a common moral language.

Hume's task in his moral philosophy is, therefore, completely analogous to his task in epistemology: to explain how a common world is created out of private and subjective elements. For, as he expresses it, ''twere impossible we cou'd ever make use of language, or communicate our sentiments to one another, did we not correct the momentary appearances of things, and overlook our present situation'; fortunately, 'Such corrections are common with regard to *all* the senses' (T. 582; my italics). In order to fulfil this task Hume takes an approach which is both psychological and social. On the one hand morality is a matter of the passions, and hence to be dealt with within the framework of his associationist scheme of the human mind. But at the same time the mind is seen not just as acting, but as inter-acting with other minds. For Hume, as well as for Smith, morality is not primarily accounted for in terms of the person acting and the subject of his action, but in terms of the reaction of the *observer* of men's dealings with each other. Morality thus arises out of such triadic relationships.

But before we outline how this happens, it may be useful to say a few words about the relation between Hume's two main texts on moral philosophy, the third book of the *Treatise* and the second *Enquiry*, as far as the fundamental features of his theory are concerned.

It has been argued that the two works are fundamentally different, and

4

that this shows a significant development of Hume's views.[3] In the *Treatise*, it is said, Hume's problem is how morality is *constituted*, that is, what forces are capable of forming morality, and the approach is accordingly psychological. But in the *Enquiry* morality is taken as a given social fact which has to be described and the function of which has to be explained. The approach is therefore distinctly social in the later work, and the whole cumbersome theory of the passions is left out completely. This is taken as a sign that Hume was in difficulties with his original programme and, more importantly, that he was beginning to realize the independence of the various disciplines which had hitherto been integrated in one comprehensive moral philosophy – disciplines such as psychology, morals proper, social and political disciplines, etc.[4] This alleged change from an interest in the individual and his actions to an interest in the social effects of his actions, is further seen as an important step towards the utilitarianism of Bentham and the two Mills.[5]

There is much to be said for this line of interpretation. First of all, it gives the *Enquiry* an independent value, which is in accord with Hume's own high opinion of it. Secondly, it makes sense of the obvious differences between the two works: the complicated theory of the passions is left out, and is explicitly declared unnecessary.[6] Accordingly, the concept of sympathy is no longer used in a strictly technical sense, but is now and then used interchangeably with fellow-feeling – although we know from the *Treatise* that it is not a feeling at all – and fellow-feeling seems nearly to include the moral evaluation itself. Finally, the concept of utility seems to be stressed much more strongly in the *Enquiry*.

These points, however, seem to exaggerate the difference between the two works. Firstly, it is a fatal mistake to overlook the fact that morality is already clearly treated from the 'social' point of view in the *Treatise*, and that Hume's whole moral psychology is incomprehensible if the individual is not seen in a social context. This has already been indicated above, and it will become even clearer when we come to treat of justice. Secondly, although it is true that Hume deliberately left out the theory of the passions in the *Enquiry*, this is certainly not a sign of a complete change in the substance of his theory. For in the very first Section of the *Enquiry* he states that his aim is to show the relative roles of reason and sentiment in our moral evaluations; and Section v, 'Why Utility Pleases', and Appendix I, 'Concerning Moral Sentiment', show clearly that ultimately they are passions. In this fundamental question there is thus no change. And presumably Hume was not all that dissatisfied with the theory of the passions in itself, since he republished it in shortened form, as *A Dissertation of the Passions*, some years after the *Enquiry* had appeared.

But although the neglect of the theory of the passions in the *Enquiry* is real enough, I think that it is a complete illusion to see the later work as an approach towards the utilitarianism of a later age. Certainly the word utility is used more frequently, but it means the same as it did in the *Treatise*, and – as will be argued below – this meaning is rather different from what Bentham and the Mills meant. And the verbal change itself is presumably the kind of difference we need in order to distinguish an essay from a treatise.

However, it remains a fact that the theory of the passions *is* left out in the second *Enquiry*, and that one of the most central concepts in this theory, namely sympathy, seems to lose its original and somewhat technical meaning. This is the most significant clue we have to finding an explanation of the differences between the two works. It is, however, a clue which we cannot fruitfully follow up till much later in the present treatment of Hume's moral theory, for what I wish to argue is that it is in connection with a special group of virtues that Hume's sympathy mechanism fails, namely the artificial virtues.

My tentative conclusion is, then, that Hume came to see that he could achieve his most basic purpose with a theory of morality which did not invoke the full detail of his theory of the passions: he could explain how morality is the cement of social life, in spite of the fact that it is 'merely' a natural growth, and not a set of abstract truths, instituted by the reason of God or man and the subject of a calculating science. Consequently, he emphasized the social perspective at the expense of the psychological for the purposes of the *Enquiry*. And this may well have been reinforced by the difficulty already mentioned as to how sympathy can provide the connecting link between the passions and the artificial virtues. But it is difficult to believe that Hume should have given up completely his theory of the passions and their connection with morality. It seems to me that a false alternative is being presented when Hume is said to be *either* reducing morality (and social life) to psychology *or* innovatively treating morality as a social phenomenon *sui generis* and the object of an independent social science. For the real methodological importance of Hume, as well as of Smith, would seem to be that they began to treat the theory of the human mind, including the psychology of the passions, as part of a social science, the object of which is the individual in his social context. This is the reason why the other person and the spectator, plus their actions and their language, are of such importance in Hume's theory of knowledge as well as in his moral theory.

While the difference between the *Treatise* and the *Enquiry* can thus be taken as a clue to the true nature of Hume's theory of the passions rather than as evidence of its abandonment, it does make the later work less valuable for our present purposes. For when he to some extent disregards the constitution of the various parts of morality, he takes away an aspect which – as we shall see – is particularly important for our understanding of justice. The following account is, therefore, mainly based on the *Treatise*, although the *Enquiry* will not be forgotten.

2 Moral evaluation

Whenever we, as spectators, observe other men we have only their actions, their behaviour, to go by, but we take this as a clue to their motives, and we are more interested in their motives because they are more firmly connected with their character or person.[7] And in the end the objects of our moral evaluations are persons and their permanent characters.

Our reactions to our fellow men and their activities can be divided into two broad categories of negative and positive reactions; the first reaction being pain, the second pleasure. This of course also applies when we 'observe' our own behaviour. Pleasure and pain are impressions, and they give rise by association to some impressions that resemble them. The new impression is pride, if the original impression was one of pleasure, *and* if the person concerned, that is, the *object* of the passion, is oneself. If the object is someone else, the new impression is love. And if the original impression was one of pain, the new impressions are humility or hatred, respectively. Finally, an association of ideas takes place between the idea of the original *cause* of pleasure or pain, and the idea of the *object* of pride or humility, love or hatred – that is, between the quality judged of, and the person concerned (oneself or some other person).

Pride and humility, love and hatred, belong to the so-called indirect passions, and their formation by means of pleasure and pain is one of the necessary links in the chain of causes which forms our moral feelings of approval and disapproval. Another vital ingredient is a certain natural *rapport* between men, a mechanism by which they come to take some interest in their fellow men. Unless such a thing exists, it is impossible to understand how that 'objectivity', in the sense of 'inter-personality', which is a distinguishing characteristic of morality, can come about. This is what Hume calls sympathy, which is *not* a passion, but a 'principle of communication'.[8] The central feature of sympathy is the conversion of an idea into an impression. Whenever the behaviour of some other person gives us an idea of his present feelings, this idea is liable to be turned into an impression, that is, into an actual feeling of a kind similar to the other person's. This conversion is liable to happen because we always have a strong and lively impression of our own self; and any feelings of which we have initially nothing but an idea are therefore easily connected with the self and made our own, that is, turned into impressions. It is, however, important to understand the place of sympathy in Hume's account of our evaluation of people: sympathy does not convey to us the motive or character trait of the person who is the object of our evaluation; what we sympathize with is the *effect* which this motive tends to have on other persons (or on the person himself). This effect, or tendency to have certain effects, is the *utility* (or disutility) which Hume stresses as a main determinant of our evaluations – and which is particularly dominant in the second *Enquiry*. It is thus sympathy with the utility, that is, the tendency, of a quality of a character that is the *cause* of the passion which constitutes our evaluation; but it is the person with the quality who is the *object* of the evaluation.

This concept of utility is obviously of great importance for our understanding of Hume's moral theory. It is, however, more easily understood in the context of his theory of justice, where it becomes even clearer that it is significantly different from the idea of utility which we find in the later utilitarians.

It is not sympathy with utility, in the sense given above, that as such creates moral approval. There are further complications. Thus, although it is normally the *actions* of a person, the actual *effects* of his personal qualities, that bring about our sympathy, this is not a necessary condition. We can sometimes sympathize with the *imagined* effects of such qualities, although they may never be allowed to show themselves in *action* because of external hindrances. Our imagination is able to tell us what the effects of the qualities in question would have been, if the hindrances were removed; this starts the machinery of sympathy, and that again creates our evaluation of the qualities concerned. But although it is possible in this way to judge a person independently of his actual action, or lack of action, it would in practice be extremely difficult for men to do so to any large extent, if they were not supported by general habitual *rules* about the connection between motives and behaviour. Such general rules are amongst the most important means of creating an objective and intersubjective morality, which is independent of the accidental features of the given situation.[9]

The other important accidental influence on our evaluations – and indeed on all our impressions and ideas – is the particular situation in which we happen to be. As with all the senses, we have to make allowance for our particular and limited perspective when we judge morally. We are naturally inclined to have a more lively sympathy with those close to us in some respect than with other people. But we must remember that human nature is essentially uniform, and it is therefore possible to sympathize with any given person. It is this side of sympathy that is the foundation for our ability to learn how to judge objectively, in the sense of interpersonally. For experience will soon teach us, not only that the same thing appears different to ourselves at different times and from different viewpoints, but also that our own evaluations vary from those of others, and that unless we approach each other's standpoints, it is difficult or impossible to communicate. Under pressure of the influence of actual spectators, everybody is thus forced to approach the standpoint of an independent spectator, or a general rule – and this even applies to our judgement of our own behaviour.[10]

I think this account is sufficient to enable us to state the essentials of Hume's ideas of moral approval and disapproval, vice and virtue. Moral virtues and vices are those qualities in a person which have a tendency to create such effects as by means of a sympathy, unbiased by the actual success of or personal relation to the person judged of, cause a pleasure or pain in the observer – a pleasure or pain which by association of impressions calls forth *calm*, as opposed to violent, versions of love or hatred; and the *idea* of the person with those qualities, by association of ideas from the idea of the cause of our pleasure/pain, is called forth as the *object* of those two calm passions just mentioned; and those two passions are what is properly called moral approval or disapproval, according to Hume.

There are, of course, innumerable qualities in persons that are subject to moral evaluation, but they can all be reduced to four broad, non-exclusive groups: those which are immediately *agreeable* to ourselves (that is, to the person with the quality), or to others; and those which are *useful* to ourselves, or to others.[11] Hume is not in doubt as to which are the most important: 'I am...of opinion, that reflexions on the tendencies of actions have by far the greatest influence, and determine all the great lines of our duty.'[12] The last group of qualities, those useful to others, is especially important, because it comprises the so-called artificial virtues, including justice.

3 The motive for justice – a dilemma

As already noted, actions have a strong influence on men's moral evaluations, but ultimately they refer to the motive, and through the motive to the person, behind the action, as the real object of evaluation. This doctrine of Hume's means that any action at least partly derives its moral quality from the motive behind it, and he must therefore be able to show in each individual case what the motive is, and that it is subject to moral approval or disapproval, in the manner described above. This task leads to some prima facie difficulties with certain actions that are normally characterized as virtuous. Those are the virtues Hume – for reasons to be explored later – calls artificial. They constitute an enormous complication of his moral theory, and the explanation of what at first sight seemed an exception, becomes an outgrowth that dominates the rest of the tree.

Hume clearly indicates the importance of the artificial virtues, and especially of justice. The treatment of them takes up more than half of the third Book of the *Treatise*, and in the *Enquiry* he virtually uses them as an

introduction to the whole of his theory of the Principles of Morals; and
the second Part of *Treatise*, Book III, deals with all of the artificial virtues,
but it is called 'Of Justice and Injustice'.

Hume opens his treatment of justice[13] as we would expect him to, given
the background of his general moral theory, by asking what the motive
behind just acts is. For since we commonly regard such acts as virtuous,
there must be a motive behind which is the real object of our judgement
(or rather, which makes us judge the person with the motive virtuous). The
most common motive referred to is, of course, a sense of duty or honesty
and Hume explicitly allows that that *is* the common motive.[14] But as duty
can only be understood in terms of justice, and thus presupposes that justice
is a virtue, it is a circular justification of justice: we are back where we
started, looking for a motive which has such a tendency as will, by means
of sympathy with its supposed beneficiaries, give rise to moral approval
(and its absence, disapproval).

Hume considers various alternative kinds of motives as possibly underlying just behaviour – and he rejects them all. They are: self-love; regard
to public interest; benevolence towards mankind as such; and finally,
benevolence towards the person to whom justice is being shown. Let us
take them one by one.

First, it is clear that self-love *per se*, or unregulated, is directly contrary
to justice. Or, as Hume has it, ''tis certain that self-love, when it acts at its
liberty, instead of engaging us to honest actions, is the source of all injustice and violence'.[15] As to a regard to public interest, this is ruled out as
a motive to justice by the following three arguments. First, that there is no
natural connection between public interest and observance of the rules of
justice; they are only connected, as Hume says, 'after an artificial convention for the establishment of these rules'[16] – though what exactly is meant
by that can only be seen at a later stage of the argument. Secondly, many
acts of justice are only a matter between individuals, without any public
interest involved at all. Hume's example is a secret, private loan.[17] Thirdly,
it is a matter of fact that men only rarely have the public interest in mind,
'when they pay their creditors, perform their promises, and abstain from
theft, and robbery, and injustice of every kind'.[18] It may be remarked that
this last argument seems somewhat beside the point; for although public
interest may not be the motive behind acts of justice in a society, where
you can already talk of creditors, promises, etc., it might still in some
sense be an original motive to justice.

The idea of a regard to public interest will not carry the weight of being
the original motive of just behaviour even if we broaden the idea to one
of general benevolence towards mankind – for the simple reason that there
is no such thing as a benevolence to mankind. Hume here introduces a
useful distinction between sympathy with mankind, and sympathy with

any given man. As all men are fundamentally alike, we have an ability for the latter, and thus for coming to feel benevolence towards any man. But he has to be a concrete man. We cannot sympathize with abstract mankind as such.[19] The last class of possible natural motives for just behaviour that Hume considers is 'private benevolence, or a regard to the interests of the party concerned',[20] that is, the person to whom justice should be shown. This is obviously implausible, since it is a characteristic of justice that it is shown to friend and foe alike, regardless of personal relations. Furthermore, benevolence is variable from person to person,[21] whereas justice is embodied in a general rule that does not take into regard who the persons involved are.

The result of this first Section on justice in the *Treatise* is a dilemma. Justice exists as a moral fact, for we do consider just acts as virtues. It is a social fact as well, for it is articulated in rules, which we consider obligatory. And it is a psychological fact too, for we do at least sometimes behave justly with nothing but a regard to justice as our motive. But the existence of all these facts presupposes as their origin a natural motive, which is morally approved of, in the manner described at the beginning of this chapter – and such a motive cannot be found:

> From all this it follows, that we have naturally no real or universal motive for observing the laws of equity, but the very equity and merit of that observance; and as no action can be equitable and meritorious, where it cannot arise from some separate motive, there is here an evident sophistry and reasoning in a circle. Unless, therefore, we will allow, that nature has establish'd a sophistry, and render'd it necessary and unavoidable, we must allow, that the sense of justice and injustice is not deriv'd from nature. (T. 483)[22]

This is a rather dramatic place in the *Treatise*. To say that something is not derived from nature seems tantamount to saying that Hume's naturalistic programme for a science of human nature has broken down. And yet Hume thinks that his theory of the artificial virtues, especially justice, can avoid this difficulty. For he continues the passage just quoted by saying that the sense of justice 'arises artificially, tho' *necessarily* from education, and human conventions'.[23] When something arises necessarily, it can also be explained by means of that which necessitates it, and that is exactly what he intends to do.

If we look upon this first Section on justice in isolation, we can see, as I have pointed out elsewhere,[24] that it is of some methodological importance. It amounts to an argument against what we should now call a psychologistic explanation of one of the most central social institutions. And in keeping with this, we see that Hume prefaces his further discussion with a remark to the effect that we have to take social phenomena into consideration in order to find a satisfactory explanation – namely, what he broadly describes as 'education, and human conventions'. Given the

structure of the *Treatise*, with its elaborate theory of the passions as the
background for the moral theory proper, it is only too easy to see Hume's
approach as wholly psychological. And, indeed, much of the problem-
situation he inherited was psychological; I am thinking of Hobbes, and to
some extent also Hutcheson. But this must not lead us to overlook the fact
that the moral sentiments are accounted for from the outset by means of a
minimum of social framework, namely the spectator situation described
earlier in this chapter. And it is this social or institutional framework that
is greatly added to when Hume comes to the artificial virtues. For whereas
his original problem was to show how values emerge in a world of natural
facts (namely, as a certain set of passions), the difficulties in accounting
for the artificial virtues, represented at first and mainly by justice, forces
him to go one step further back to ask how certain *social* phenomena can
emerge in this world – for he needs those social phenomena to explain
the emergence of part of the values. As far as this institutional aspect is
concerned, Hume was undoubtedly very much influenced by modern
natural law theories in Grotius, Pufendorf and others.[25] But his real genius
was to combine the strands of his inheritance into a completely new sort
of natural law theory – for, indeed, he is quite willing to use that label,
provided we let him fill in the contents himself.[26] And that is what he
begins to do in the following Section, 'Of the Origin of Justice and
Property'.

4 The origins of justice

Given that justice is not established as a moral virtue by means of a
natural motive, Hume, then, takes the approach, that first it must be
shown how justice comes into existence as a social practice, or institution,
and *then* he will show how we acquire the proper passion, and thus the
moral obligation, to adhere to it. In other words, he distinguishes between

two questions, viz. concerning the manner, in which the rules of justice are
establish'd by the artifice of men; and concerning the reasons, which determine
us to attribute to the observance or neglect of these rules a moral beauty and
deformity. (T. 484; the passage is italicized in Hume.)

The former question, which is one of our main concerns, takes up nearly
the whole of the present Section, while the latter is not finally answered
till the first Section of Part III, where he makes the transition from the
artificial to the natural virtues.

It is important to remember that the whole of Hume's discussion of how
justice arises as a social institution is itself set in a social framework from
the outset. He simply points out that man, considered individually, does
not have any ecological niche, and that he is only able to acquire one by
living *some* kind of social life. The extant members of the species are thus

necessarily social.[27] The bare minimum of social life is the family; and that is held together by sexual and parental feelings. This latter fact might be taken as an attempt, after all, to reduce the minimal social institution to psychological principles. But that clearly will not do, for these passions are themselves to be accounted for inter-personally; and they are only socially formative in a more or less hostile *environment*.[28]

This minimal social life, which men must necessarily lead, is sufficient to allow justice to emerge, and it is justice that creates the possibility for the development of social life on a larger scale. But Hume never makes it absolutely clear to what extent justice is established within the family, and to what extent it only comes about as a relationship between families. On the one hand he says that 'every parent, in order to preserve peace among his children, must establish the rule for the stability of possession'.[29] But on the other hand he points out that families naturally develop a tribal morality, which includes a strong partiality against other such societies (all men are governed by self-love and a confined generosity – confined to the family). And it is this friction between tribal societies that justice has to overcome.[30] The obvious solution, of course, is, that the faint beginnings of justice in the small society have to be transplanted to a larger scale.[31]

Justice is an absolutely necessary ingredient in any kind of social life. At least some minimum of it must be present, for, as already indicated, justice is

a remedy to some inconveniences, which proceed from the concurrence of certain *qualities* of the human mind with the *situation* of external objects. The qualities of the mind are *selfishness* and *limited generosity*: And the situation of external objects is their *easy exchange*, join'd to their *scarcity* in comparison of the wants and desires of men. (T. 494)

It will be seen that for Hume the origin of justice is to be accounted for in terms of challenges to the possession of *external* goods. The reason he gives for this is simply that the other kinds of 'goods', as he calls them, namely 'the internal satisfaction of our mind' and 'the external advantages of our body',[32] cannot be of any use to another person, and they are therefore not matters of dispute. This seems a little odd, for it appears to restrict Hume's concept of rights that are protected by rules of justice to property rights. Now, there is of course no reason why he should not be able to account for our more personal rights by simply saying that our concept of right is extended to include personal rights as people become more and more civilized. Nevertheless, it is of some importance that he does not do so, and that he deliberately concentrates his theory of the origin of justice around the concept of external goods – and with a reference to what can be of use to people. For it is exactly those points that Adam Smith takes him to task for. According to Smith, men are quite likely to try and dominate their fellows just for the sake of dominating. This seems to show a certain difference in their ideas of what kind of creature man is: is he primarily concerned with bettering his lot, or with dominating his fellows? Be that as it may, Hume and Smith would undoubtedly find common ground in pointing out that bettering one's lot is in fact one of the main instruments for dominating one's fellow men.

The background for the emergence of justice and society is a combination of the qualities of the human mind, and the external situation in which men find themselves. Hume underlines this argument strongly by showing that if we imagine that either of the two, the qualities or the situation, were changed materially, then justice would not arise. In other words, justice is not naturally relevant to man; it only becomes relevant to him because of his particular circumstances.

Those imagined situations are presented both in the *Treatise* and in the *Enquiry*, but like so many of the more spectacular and dramatic elements in Hume's argument, they are dealt with more extensively and systematically in the latter work. First Hume asks us to imagine that our external situation has been changed to one of complete abundance in everything:

It seems evident that, in such a happy state, every other social virtue would flourish, and receive tenfold increase; but the cautious, jealous virtue of justice would never once have been dreamed of. For what purpose make a partition of goods, where every one has already more than enough? Why give rise to property, where there cannot possibly be any injury? Why call this object *mine*, when upon the seizing of it by another, I need but stretch out my hand to possess myself of what is equally valuable? Justice, in that case, being totally useless, would be an idle ceremonial, and could never possibly have place in the catalogue of virtues. (E. 183–4)

A few things, such as air and water in most parts of the world, are so abundant that this situation does in fact arise.[33]

Equally if we suppose that human nature has been transformed, so that the human mind is completely dominated by generosity and general benevolence to every other man,

it seems evident, that the use of justice would, in this case, be suspended by such an extensive benevolence, nor would the divisions and barriers of property and obligation have ever been thought of. (E. 185)

And again this is a situation which is approached in the real world in the relations between friends and members of the same family; and it is an ideal which has inspired 'fanatics' with such 'enthusiasms' that they have tried it on a larger scale – only to be taught a lesson by experience about the 'selfishness of men'.[34]

Finally, Hume invites us to imagine the direct reverse of the two situations quoted above.

Is it any crime, after a shipwreck, to seize whatever means or instrument of safety one can lay hold of, without regard to former limitations of property? (E. 186)

And

suppose likewise, that it should be a virtuous man's fate to fall into the society of ruffians, remote from the protection of laws and government; what conduct must he embrace in that melancholy situation?...He...can have no other expedient than to arm himself, to whomever the sword he seizes, or the buckler, may belong:...his particular regard to justice being no longer of use to his own safety or to that of others, he must consult the dictates of self-preservation alone, without concern for those who no longer merit his care and attention. (E. 187)

And as the quotations show, those two situations are certainly instanced in the world in which we live – not least in a civil war.[35]

Taken together, the two first imagined situations amount to a description of 'the *poetical* fiction of the *golden age*' whereas the two latter give the elements of 'the *philosophical* fiction of the *state of nature*'. Both are, of course, 'an idle fiction',[36] but they serve Hume well to underpin his point,

that 'tis only from the selfishness and confin'd generosity of men, along with the scanty provision nature has made for his wants, that justice derives its origin. (T. 495; cf. E. 188)[37]

All these reflections lead up to the main problem: *how* does justice arise from the combination of human nature and its particular environment? Hume's answer is, in a sense, very simple. He points out that men in general are not so stupid that they do not see that most of the trouble in the world arises when one man makes free with what is in somebody else's possession. Only 'slight experience' with this, and 'the least reflection'[38] on it, are required to make men abstain from such violence. But what does this more particularly mean in terms of the operation of the passions? It simply means that when men see that it is self-defeating (in the world as it is) to act on a combination of self-love and confined benevolence, they are led to restrain these 'interested passions' – but in the sense that they redirect them. For those passions will be satisfied much more easily in a social situation:

Instead of departing from our own interest, or from that of our nearest friends, by abstaining from the possessions of others, we cannot better consult both these interests than by such a convention; because it is by that means we maintain society, which is so necessary to their well-being and subsistence, as well as our own. (T. 489)

Whatever else men may be inspired by, we know that they are at least under the guidance of the interested passions, and

'tis certain, that no affection of the human mind has both a sufficient force, and a proper direction to counter-balance the love of gain, and render men fit members of society, by making them abstain from the possessions of others...There is no passion, therefore, capable of controlling the interested affection, but the very affection itself, by an alteration of its direction. (T. 492)

Although Hume does not say so explicitly in this context, we must undoubtedly understand this idea − of the interested passion restraining itself by finding a new direction or outlet − in terms of his theory of the calm passions. For the passion keeps its identity, but it gets another emotional strength, through 'the least reflection' on our situation, reflection being one of the things that can make a passion calm *and* strong, but not violent.[39] That he does have this theory in mind is also given some support from the fact that he draws it in when he returns to the problem of how to ensure that the rule of justice is observed, in the Section 'Of the Origin of Government'.[40]

'Slight experience' and 'the least reflection' lead us to abstain from our neighbours' possessions, by making us enter a *convention* about this,

a convention enter'd into by all the members of the society to bestow stability on the possession of those external goods, and leave every one in the peaceable enjoyment of what he may acquire by his fortune and industry. (T. 489)

But Hume's idea of a convention must be attended to with much care. For 'this convention is not of the nature of a *promise*: For even promises themselves...arise from human conventions.'[41] It is difficult to say exactly what Hume means by entering into a convention, but let me first quote his own description, and afterwards see what can be made of it. The convention

is only a general sense of common interest; which sense all the members of the society express to one another, and which induces them to regulate their conduct by certain rules. I observe, that it will be for my interest to leave another in the possession of his goods, *provided* he will act in the same manner with regard to me. He is sensible of a like interest in the regulation of his conduct. When this common sense of interest is mutually express'd, and is known to both, it produces a suitable resolution and behaviour. And this may properly enough be call'd a convention or agreement betwixt us, tho' without the interposition of a promise; since the actions of each of us have a reference to those of the other, and are perform'd upon the supposition that something is to be perform'd on the other part. (T. 490; cf. T. 498 and E. 306)

And Hume then goes on to liken this to situations where two men are rowing a boat, and to the conventions about language and money.

The most natural way to read the passage just quoted is that men actually express their common interest verbally. But on the other hand, this would come pretty near to a promise. And, furthermore, Hume says explicitly that it is the individual *actions* of abstaining from the other person's property that have a reference to each other. This reading is also supported by at least the first of the parallel examples he mentions, namely the rowing of a boat. So on the whole the most reasonable reading seems to me to be that it is the individual actions that function as signs or expressions of the common interest.[42] The parallel passage in the *Enquiry* does not offer much help: both expressions and actions have disappeared in any recognizable shape:

> if by convention be meant a sense of common interest; which sense each man feels in his own breast, which he remarks in his fellows, and which carries him, in concurrence with others, into a general plan or system of actions, which tends to public utility; it must be owned, that, in this sense, justice arises from human conventions. (E. 306)

At first sight this is a rather trifling difficulty in Hume's idea of the conventional origin and character of justice. But if we attend more closely to it, important problems will open up to us. When Hume begins his account of the convention in the passage just quoted from the *Treatise* above, he talks of 'a general sense of common interest; which . . . *all* the members of the society express to one another' (my italics); and this requirement of universality tallies with Hume's often expressed view that it is of the essence of justice that it is a general rule.[43] But the fact that the passage just quoted suggests verbal expression – indeed, something very close to a promise – and the fact that it requires universality, are both hard to reconcile with Hume's repeated insistence that justice is a slow growth, something developing through the ages.[44] For if justice is only justice when it is universal within a society, then it seems as if its institution must happen as one single event, such as our passage seems to suggest. Yet Hume does within the same paragraph say the following:

> Nor is the rule concerning the stability of possession the less deriv'd from human conventions, that it arises gradually, and acquires force by a slow progression, and by our repeated experience of the inconveniences of transgressing it. (T. 490)

No, quite; but then the convention, from which it derives, can hardly be an event where 'all the members of society express a general sense of common interest'. It is, however, exactly in the light of this difficulty that it is interesting to see Hume, later in our passage, go on to account for the actual moves in the convention in terms of individual *actions* between given persons, as pointed out above. For actions do not carry any implications of universality. They can act as 'an example to others'.[45] And if justice is understood to develop by imitation of examples of it in action, *then* we can understand why Hume says that 'it arises gradually, and acquires force by a slow progression'.

From what I have said so far, it should be relatively clear that in this passage about the convention concerning justice, we in fact have the indications of two widely different views of the origin of justice. On the one hand what may fairly be called a rationalistic and contractarian view and on the other hand an evolutionary view. On the former view justice is instituted as a general rule by all the members of a society. On the latter view it grows out of a practice which slowly becomes more and more general. The rationalistic view immediately strikes one as rather un-Humean, and the evolutionary one seems to be the one borne out by the whole trend of Hume's discussion. Against the background of such an impression one might try to account for the rationalistic view of the convention as a mere methodological device for Hume. On such an interpretation Hume is really saying that the qualities of universality and conventionality make justice a phenomenon, which exists *as if* it had been instituted by men as such a thing, whereas its real origin must be accounted for by an evolutionary theory.

This is an attractive interpretation, but there is rather little to support it in Hume's text. First of all, Hume does not say that the convention is to be taken only as a methodological device, such as he does with the state of nature. And Hume was in general not a person to miss a chance to drive home a methodological rule. Secondly, Hume does give the above mentioned rationalistic indications, as well as others to be described below, in stating the efficient causes that lead to the institution of justice. And thirdly, we should like to see some kind of bridge explicitly established between, on the one hand, the efficient causes of the evolutionary strand of the theory and, on the other hand, the 'final causes' (that is, the functions of justice) imaginatively accounted for by a rationalistic convention. But no such bridge is explicitly established, and this speaks against Hume's consciously using the rationalistic convention as a mere methodological tool.

In order to get any further in this matter, I will first describe what I am convinced would be Hume's considered view of the origin of justice. I will then discuss in what sense this justice is artificial for Hume. This will enable us to discuss, and maybe to some extent explain, what I have called his rationalistic indications.

Hume's considered view of the origin of justice must be evolutionary. He says so emphatically in the *Treatise*, as we have seen above; and in the *Enquiry*, which is otherwise not very specific in these matters, we have his sketch of how justice and society develop together.[46] But let us characterize this theory more closely. As we have seen already, it accounts for the development of justice in terms of individual acts, which are imitated more and more widely. If we pay attention to the nature of these actions, we will see that they are exceedingly simple, being in reality pieces of inactivity – namely, the 'abstaining from the possessions of others'.[47] All this tallies with Hume's often repeated insistence that the role of reason is very modest in the institution of justice (and thus of society): 'Vulgar sense and slight experience are sufficient.'[48] For if the rule for the stability of possession

> be very abstruse, and of difficult invention; society must be esteem'd, in a manner, accidental, and the effect of many ages. But if it be found that nothing can be more simple and obvious than this rule; that every parent, in order to preserve peace among his children, must establish it; and that these first rudiments of justice must every day be improv'd, as the society enlarges: If all this appear evident, as it certainly must, we may conclude, that 'tis utterly impossible for men to remain any considerable time in that savage condition, which precedes society; but that his very first state and situation may justly be esteem'd social. (T. 493)[49]

This idea that only a very low degree of rationality is involved in the origins of justice is extremely important, for it allows Hume to point out a nearly paradoxical disparity between causes and effects. The causes are a presumably immense number of individual actions, which are all done out of a combination of restrained, or enlightened, self-love with confined benevolence. But the end effect is a set of universal or general rules which are absolutely vital for the very existence of society, and thus for the individual, and which in that sense have as strong a 'natural tendency' to the public good as could be imagined, but which may yet very easily be directly contrary to both private and public good in their application to individual cases.

> Judges take from a poor man to give to a rich; they bestow on the dissolute the labour of the industrious; and put into the hands of the vicious the means of harming both themselves and others. The whole scheme, however, of law and justice is advantageous to the society, and to every individual. (T. 579)[50]

The long-term effect of individual men's 'selfish' actions is thus something very far removed indeed from what they did have, and could have, in mind. The idea of justice 'wou'd never have been dream'd of among rude and savage men'.[51] Justice, in the form of institutionalized general rules, is the *effect* of individual human actions, but they are not *intended* effects. And this is not just a doctrine which is implied in what Hume has to say about justice: it is an explicitly stated idea:

> Those rules, by which property, right, and obligation are determin'd...have all of them a direct and evident *tendency* to public good, and the support of society. This last circumstance is remarkable upon two accounts. First, because, tho' the cause of the establishment of these laws *had been* a regard for the public good, as much as the public good is their natural tendency, they wou'd still have been artificial, as being purposely contriv'd and directed to a certain end. Secondly, because, if men had been endow'd with such a strong regard for public good, they wou'd never have restrain'd themselves by these rules; so that the laws of justice arise from natural principles in a manner still more oblique and artificial. 'Tis self-love which is their real origin; and as the self-love of one person is

naturally contrary to that of another, these several interested passions are oblig'd to adjust themselves after such a manner as to concur in some system of conduct and behaviour. This system, therefore, comprehending the interest of each individual, is of course advantageous to the public; *tho' it be not intended for that purpose by the inventors.* (T. 528–9; my italics)[52]

If we take first what is implied by the use of the subjunctive mood in the first point in this quotation, we find that the cause of justice is not a regard for the public good,[53] although that is the effect it naturally tends to. In the latter half of the citation we are then told that the individual 'interested passions' have to 'adjust *themselves*', and thus form a '*system* of conduct and behaviour'. And finally, it is explicitly underlined that the whole outcome is 'not intended. . .by the inventors'.

Later in the *Treatise* we find Hume adding a clarifying marginal note. In the text he says that justice, allegiance, the laws of nations, etc., 'are mere human contrivances for the interest of society', and then he adds

The Inventors of them had chiefly in view. . .their own Interest. But we carry our Approbation of them into the most distant Countreys & Ages & much beyond our own Interest. (T. 577)

In other words, how justice is established is one thing, our relationship to it once it is established is another.

To see justice in this way, as an unintended consequence of individual human actions, must be one of the boldest moves in the history of the philosophy of law. And it is as ingenious as it is bold. For it allows Hume to avoid any excessive rationalism, of a Hobbesian kind;[54] although justice is a result of human activity, it is not deliberately constructed by men.[55] And in this sense Hume avoids the pitfalls of legal positivism, and keeps the options open for some kind of 'natural law', or basic law, standing above all positive law. On the other hand, Hume is able to keep the origin of justice well within the natural world: he is able to identify the specific causes that bring it about, namely the actions (and interactions) of individual men. He, therefore, has no need for any divine interference – or, for that matter, for any special moral sense. True to his general empiricist leanings and to his Newtonian rules of philosophizing he can account for the origins of justice in terms of well-known and very general human passions (restrained self-love and confined benevolence), actions (prudent abstention from the possessions of others), and interactions (*mutual* abstention and imitation).

The idea of social institutions as the unintended effects of human actions is in itself a negative doctrine. It merely says what is *not* the cause of the institutions concerned. It therefore merely broadens our quest, for we then have to ask not only what actions in fact caused which institutions but also what motivated those actions. For if we can find those motives, we may find an explanation of why the intention of creating the institution in question could *not* be part of those motives.

Now it is a significant fact that Hume's theory satisfies us on this point. For he only reaches the conclusion that justice is an undesigned and unenvisaged institution, after having scrutinized the causes and after having found what a modest role constructive reasoning has to play in the process.

The idea that some social phenomena are the unintended effects of human actions is not original with Hume: it is in modern times clearly anticipated by Bernard Mandeville. But Mandeville uses the idea in a rather general way, without too much attention to the details of the links between the individual causes and the over-all effect. He also uses the idea mostly in an economic context, which was of course the context in which the idea was to become especially famous with Adam Smith. But the particular boldness in Hume is that he uses it in accounting for one of the traditionally most central, and in a way most 'sacred', elements in social life, namely fundamental law itself, our very 'sense of justice'. It is one of the most important parts[56] of his philosophical justification for replacing traditional natural law with a secular and empirical conception of fundamental law, which makes it truly 'natural' in the sense that it can be accounted for within his science of human nature and thus be accounted a full member of his Newtonian universe. And yet it does, in common with traditional natural law theories, find the roots of justice beyond any rational human deliberations, and far beyond our present society.

In this last respect Hume's theory is obviously in line with the Common Law tradition and with Burke. And he would find further common ground with those thinkers in the stress on the historical development of justice. But this must not make us blind to the very decisive difference there is. For Hume would never say that the antiquity of law in itself justified it. Its historical development would be of the very highest importance for our understanding of it, and for our chances of changing (or preserving) it. But it would never be one of our principles of evaluation. The exact nature of these principles will be explained below; but it should be pointed out here that this balance between the history of law and its theory is one of the most important themes to be developed by Adam Smith.

5 Nature and artifice

Throughout his treatment of justice Hume is concerned with its metaphysical status. As we have seen, one of his main points is to show that it has natural causes, and yet he calls it an artifice or contrivance, instituted by men conventionally. The distinction between nature and artifice seems, from the very structure of the *Treatise*, Book III, to be of fundamental importance in Hume's moral theory. Part II deals with the artificial virtues, while Part III opens with his account of the natural virtues, and then goes on to gather up the threads of the theory as a whole. But let us see whether it really is of such importance.

In the first Section of Part II, where Hume has asked 'Justice, whether a Natural or Artificial Virtue?', and where he has come down firmly (as we have seen) in favour of the latter, he concludes with the following clarification of 'natural' and 'artificial' as applied to justice:

I must here observe, that when I deny justice to be a natural virtue, I make use of the word, *natural*, only as opposed to *artificial*. In another sense of the word; as no principle of the human mind is more natural than a sense of justice; so no virtue is more natural than justice. Mankind is an inventive species; and where an invention is obvious and absolutely necessary, it may as properly be said to be natural as anything that proceeds immediately from original principles, without the intervention of thought or reflexion. Tho' the rules of justice be *artificial*, they are not *arbitrary*. Nor is the expression improper to call them *Laws of Nature*; if by natural we understand what is common to any species, or even if we confine it to mean what is inseparable from the species. (T. 484)

Two things stand out in this passage; that artificial phenomena are the result of the intervention of 'thought and reflexion' and that they, paradoxically, are natural in the sense that they exist with the same necessity as everything else in this world – which, of course, means that they are brought about by natural causes. These two points presuppose that 'thought and reflexion' can be accounted for in terms of such causes. We of course know that to be Hume's position, and he explicitly refers to it the first time he discusses the distinction between natural and artificial in connection with moral qualities:

Nature may also be opposed to artifice, as well as to what is rare and unusual; and in this sense it may be disputed, whether the notions of virtue be natural or not. We readily forget, that the designs, and projects, and views of men are principles as necessary in their operation as heat and cold, moist and dry: But taking them to be free and entirely our own, 'tis usual for us to set them in opposition to the other principles of nature. (T. 474)

In other words, Hume invokes his methodological determinism[57] to say that although justice and the like are artificial phenomena, because they are brought about through the intervention of men's rational powers, they are yet securely within the orbit of the natural world, because the activity of the rational powers can in itself be explained by means of natural causes. And as we have seen, this means that men's situation in the world is such that 'vulgar sense and slight experience' necessarily bring the 'interested passions' to restrain themselves and thus our behaviour towards our neighbour, etc.

This theme, that artificial phenomena have their specific character because our rational powers are involved in their causation, and that those powers and their activity are in themselves a link in nature, turns up again and again. Thus:

The remedy [for men's plight in the world]...is not deriv'd from nature, but from *artifice*; or more properly speaking, nature provides a remedy in the judgement and understanding, for what is irregular and incommodious in the affections. (T. 489)[58]

On closer examination it therefore turns out that the distinction between natural and artificial which Hume seemed at first sight to take as fundamental, is in one respect not regarded by him as fundamental at all. Artificial things have causes as natural as any others, and the distinction is, therefore, in this view, rather verbal. It is accordingly not at all surprising to find Hume warning us in the *Treatise*, that 'there is none more ambiguous and equivocal' than 'the definition of the word Nature';[59] and in the *Enquiry*, that 'The word *natural* is commonly taken in so many senses and is of so loose a signification, that it seems vain to dispute whether justice be natural or not.'[60]

It is with a sense of relief that one reads in a footnote, that 'all these disputes are merely verbal'.[61] We must conclude that Hume, as we would expect, is absolutely intent on keeping nothing but purely natural, efficient causes in his universe, and in accordance with this we see him declare in a letter to Francis Hutcheson, to whom he had sent the manuscript of the third Book of the *Treatise*:

I cannot agree to your Sense of *Natural*. Tis founded on final Causes; which is a Consideration, that appears to me pretty uncertain & unphilosophical...I have never call'd Justice unnatural, but only artificial.[62]

It is clear that Hume is engaged in a discussion of a distinction that is nearly as old as Western philosophy, the distinction between nomos and physis, the conventional, or artificial, and the natural,[63] and I think it likely that Hobbes was his immediate inspiration for embarking on this question.[64] The negative side of his discussion of it, which we have now been presented with, seems to lead to the conclusion that it is really a nondistinction. Nevertheless, Hume keeps using the distinction, and if we take this as an indication that there is *some* use for it in one sense or another, we are not altogether wrong.

In at least one place Hume takes a somewhat abstract view of artificial phenomena, represented by justice, not only from the point of view of their origin, but also from the point of view of their characteristics, once they are created:

Those rules, by which property, right, and obligation are determin'd, have in them no marks of a natural origin, but many of artifice and contrivance. They are too numerous to have proceeded from nature: They are changeable by human laws: And have all of them a direct and evident tendency to public good, and the support of society. This last circumstance is remarkable...because, tho' the cause of the establishment of these laws had been a *regard* for the public good, as much as the public good is their natural tendency, they wou'd still have been artificial, as being purposely contriv'd and directed to a certain end. (T. 528–9)

It is on the third and last mark of artificiality mentioned here that I want to concentrate. As pointed out earlier (p. 20 above), the subjunctive mood clearly implies the point which Hume makes explicitly a little later, namely that the 'aim' of the rules (the public good) was not an *intended* aim. But he then goes on to say that even if this had been the case, the rules 'wou'd still have been artificial, as being purposely contriv'd and directed to a certain end'. In other words, it is the fact that the rules of justice have a *purpose* or an *end*, that makes them artificial. But although the passage clearly implies that there is a difference between an *intended* aim and an 'aim' that is just a '*natural tendency*', Hume never brings this out clearly in his reasoning about the distinction between natural and artificial. This is a pity, for Hume is as close as could be to a very important revision of the distinction between natural and artificial. If he had worked out what he implies in the passage quoted above, and in his whole theory of justice, as an 'unintended consequence' phenomenon, he would have seen that there is a third category between natural and artificial, which shares certain characteristics with both. The things in this category resemble natural phenomena in that they are unintended and to be explained in terms of efficient causes, and they resemble artificial phenomena in that they are the result of human action, including of course rational human action. But it remains a fact that Hume did not work out such a theory, although he virtually stated the idea, as we have seen, and although he gave a superb example of this third category in his idea of justice.[65]

In a couple of comparisons Hume is again, in effect, pointing out that justice, as an artificial phenomenon, has a rather special status in this world – but again without saying the decisive things. He compares property with 'the imaginary qualities of the *peripatetic* philosophy', and then points out that the only difference is that property is able to cause moral approval – and it is only able to do so because it serves a certain function.[66] And in the *Enquiry* he compares justice and various 'vulgar superstitions', with the result that the former 'is absolutely requisite to the well-being of mankind and existence of society', whereas the latter 'is frivolous, useless, and burdensome'.[67]

It is clear that what really impressed Hume in what he took to be artifices was their goal-directedness, the fact that they had a certain function. Now, if we take this fact, and add to it the fact that the traditional conception of artifice was that it involved some kind of constructive reason, and add the further circumstance that for Hume 'the intervention of thought and reflexion' did in fact play a decisive role in the origination of justice – although *not* as constructive reasoning aiming at rules of justice, but *only* as the 'vulgar sense and slight experience' which is sufficient to restrain and redirect the interested passions of self-love and confined benevolence in concrete situations – if we take all these facts together, I think it becomes somewhat more intelligible why Hume fairly frequently slipped from the evolutionary theory of justice, which we presented above, into the indications of a rationalistic view.[68] The troublesome concepts are those of reason, goal-directedness, and utility. The level of reason involved in the origin of justice is low, but its operations *result* unwittingly in an institution which looks as if it had involved a very high level of rationality because it is directed towards a certain goal, in the sense that it has a definite function. The individual actions in which justice originates have one conscious end, namely a safer satisfaction of the 'interested passions', that is, self-interest, but they result in the rules of justice which have *public* interest (or utility) as their 'end'. And this public interest, of course, comprises each individual's private interest; but *qua* public interest it could originally be nobody's *aim* and, indeed, it is properly nothing but a 'natural tendency'. I suggest that it is the failure to keep these tangled relationships quite clear (plus the lack of clarity about the natural/artificial distinction) that in some individual cases leads Hume to say things that are patently inconsistent with his theory of justice. I will take the more obvious cases: 'The whole scheme...of law and justice is advantageous to the society and to every individual, and 'twas with a view to this advantage, that men, by their voluntary conventions, establish'd it.'[69] But surely men could not have had the *public* advantage in view beforehand – only the individual (so it is significant that Hume added in the margin the words 'and to every individual').

In discussing the moral character of justice, Hume adds: 'Now justice is a moral virtue, merely because it has that tendency to the good of mankind; and, indeed, is nothing but an artificial invention to that purpose.'[70] And elsewhere: 'These rules [of justice]...are artificially invented for a certain purpose.'[71] Here the same comment applies.

Finally, in the *Enquiry* appears what is perhaps the most rationalistic-sounding passage of all – precisely in Hume's discussion of the sense in which justice may be said to be artificial:

Natural may be opposed, either to what is *unusual, miraculous,* or *artificial.* In the two former senses, justice and property are undoubtedly natural. But as they suppose reason, forethought, design, and a social union and confederacy among men, perhaps that epithet cannot strictly, in the last sense, be applied to them. (E. 307–8, note)

It is rather difficult to square 'reason, forethought, design', as well as the previously quoted long-ranging views and purposes, with that 'vulgar sense and slight experience', that 'least reflection', which we otherwise meet in Hume when he is concentrating on the origin of justice.

If we turn our attention to the closely connected problem of where public interest (or utility) comes in, we will also find the occasional confusion: is it actually part of the original motivation for instituting justice, or is it only a 'natural tendency' of justice, once established? Thus Hume says quite clearly that ''tis only from the selfishness and confin'd generosity of men, along with the scanty provision nature has made for his wants, that justice derives its origin'.[72] But only half a page later he allows confusion to slip in: ''Twas therefore a concern for our own, and the *public interest*, which made us establish the laws of justice.'[73] Equally he declares at the outset of his Section 'Of Justice' in the *Enquiry* that he wants to show 'that public utility is the *sole* origin of justice'.[74]

There can hardly be any doubt, however, that passages such as these are the result of carelessness, for elsewhere Hume is perfectly clear about the relation between private and public interest in his theory:

Thus self-interest is the original motive to the *establishment* of justice: but a *sympathy* with public interest is the source of the *moral approbation*, which attends that virtue. This latter Principle of Sympathy is too weak to control our Passions; but has sufficient Force to influence our Taste, & give us the Sentiments of Approbation or Blame. (T. 499–500)

It is here disclosed that public interest comes in when Hume accounts for the moral quality of justice – a theory which we have yet to describe – while private interest is reaffirmed as the force behind the origin of justice.

All these occasional tensions between Hume's evolutionary theory of justice and various rationalistic ideas do, I think, in the end stem from the difficulty I mentioned at the outset:[75] on the one hand, Hume can only recognize justice as justice in the form of absolutely general rules, for if there were any exceptions the system would break down. But on the other hand, if justice is created piecemeal by individual actions and imitation of such actions, then an intermediate state must be possible where individual acts, that are later recognized as being just, are able to gain ground *without* justice existing in the form of general rules, for those rules are the *outcome* of the individual acts of that particular kind gaining ground.

We are thus referred back to the individual actions that lie behind the origin of justice. Hume took these to be the acts of *redirected* self-interest (self-love and confined benevolence), but in order to show that people would actually be able and willing to imitate such 'enlightened' self-interest Hume would need to put even more stress upon the point that the imitation takes place between family groups rather than between individuals.

6 Property

Hume has tried to account for the origin of justice by means of the idea of external possessions. Originally, justice is, as we now understand, the kind of behaviour men exhibit when they keep away from the possessions of others. This gives these possessions a certain stability, and stable possessions protected by justice is what we call property. Thus the idea of justice gives rise to the idea of property.[76] The question is, however, *which* possessions are turned into property under the protection of justice. In his usual dialectic way, Hume only reaches his own conclusion by way of a couple of impossible alternatives: since the ultimate justification for the rules of justice, as we shall see later (pp. 40–3 below), is the kind of public utility which is able to call forth our moral approbation, it might be thought that the possessions which justice protects, and thus turns into property, would be those which would yield the maximum public use, that is, those in the hands of men who would be best suited to use them for the common good.[77] But this cannot possibly be the case; for first of all it is not an unequivocal criterion which would single out a particular person for particular pieces of property; and secondly, men's ideas of who are fit for what possessions are 'liable to so many controversies, and men are so partial and passionate in judging of these controversies, that such a loose and uncertain rule wou'd be absolutely incompatible with the peace of human society',[78] and thus with the very 'purpose' of the rules of justice.

The second possibility that Hume considers is that 'real' justice only protects possessions when they are *equally* distributed among men, as the Levellers claimed.[79] But this is also impossible. First of all, men are by nature so different that even if equality had at some point been reached, inequality would immediately crop up again. And secondly, as far as the origin of justice is concerned, one could not imagine anyone having sufficient power to distribute property equally. And as to the normative side of the Levellers' doctrine, it would be highly dangerous to try and make a reality of it, for it would inevitably require a tyranny.[80]

The outcome of Hume's discussion of this point is, then, that the possessions which justice is introduced to protect cannot be required to be redistributed in any way, for that would require a power which nobody, in fact, can have, and/or a unanimity which is not present. And if anybody tried to act on the opposite assumptions, it would wreck the possibility of any society.

Hume's own solution is that the introduction of justice cannot possibly do more than ratify *de facto* possession. Apart from the negative arguments given above, Hume points out that men are slaves of habit and custom, so that they develop a greater affection for what they in fact have in their possession than for anything else. And this makes it seem rather obvious to them that the rules of justice should protect this *de facto* possession. In a long footnote he makes his meaning a little clearer. Although there are 'motives of public interest for most of the rules which determine property' and although, as we know, 'vulgar sense and slight experience' is enough to give men such motives, Hume still finds reason to 'suspect, that these rules are principally fix'd by the imagination, or the more frivolous properties of our thought and conception'. He then goes on to invoke his principles of association, pointing out that the relation between a man and his possessions is such that the mind naturally tends to connect them, and the new relation called property is therefore nothing but an underpinning of an already existing relation:

As property forms a relation betwixt a person and an object, 'tis natural to found it on some preceding relation; and as property is nothing but a constant possession, secur'd by the laws of society, 'tis natural to add it to the present possession, which is a relation that resembles it. (T. 504–5, note; and cf. E. 195–6)

Present possession is thus the circumstance that explains the original emergence of property through the introduction of the rules of justice, and it remains also in developed society one of the sources of property. Hume then calls it occupation.[81] But as he points out, this is obviously too impracticable and inflexible a rule to be the only source of property in a changing and developing society, and the principles of prescription, accession and succession therefore naturally develop. In all these the rules have a background in the natural operation of the imagination, but what the imagination yields is frequently rather vague and contradictory from case to case, and there is thus bound to be a strong element of arbitrariness in such rules. Where obvious analogies or considerations of utility fail, civil law comes in and supplements natural law.[82]

In these short sketches it is clear that Hume is not only concerned with explaining some fundamental principles underlying law as it is found in present society. He is quite as much interested in showing that, given man's nature and situation, fundamental law must be a phenomenon with an evolutionary background. For the reasons already given, some kind of stability of possession must be developed. This in itself gives rise to a new situation which requires the articulation of this fundamental rule in the more specific rules about prescription, etc., which again requires interference by civil law and statutes. In the same manner necessity and convenience naturally lead to the rule about the transference of property by consent,[83] and to the institution of promises and contracts.[84]

In what follows we shall see how Adam Smith takes up these areas of law as part of his system of jurisprudence. But he develops their basis in the imagination into a spectator account, and this makes the social setting and hence the historical development more obvious as necessary elements in the explanation.[85]

7 Promises

In the *Treatise* Hume makes a special study of promises, the aim of which is to show that just like 'justice in general'[86] promises constitute an artificial institution, and that the attendant virtue of keeping one's word is in that sense an artificial virtue. This is an extremely important discussion, for it is one of the few indications of Hume's views on obligation, and thus on the moral quality of the laws of justice in general, that is, their character as 'natural law'.

Precisely as in the case of justice, Hume begins by pointing out that there is no natural motive for keeping promises.[87] The general motive is a sense of duty or obligation, but that presupposes a promise by which the obligation is incurred. What precisely this means cannot be seen till we come to treat Hume's theory of obligation (pp. 31–5 below). Till then we must take it as a premise for his further argument, which is that we shall first have to explain how promises can emerge as a social institution, and then show how our moral obligation to keep promises arises out of that.

His account of the emergence of promises is closely parallel to his account of how the fundamental law of justice arose, as he himself points out.[88] On the one hand the reign of the interested passions over men's minds makes it very difficult for them to come to trust each other. But on the other hand their situation is such that it is necessary for them to do so. For although they may have developed a certain stability of property, and even the idea of transferring it by consent, it will still not be possible for them to transfer such property as is *'absent* or *general'* without the institution of promises and contracts. 'One cannot transfer the property of a particular house, twenty leagues distant; because the consent cannot be attended with delivery, which is a requisite circumstance.'[89] And equally the exchange of services is impossible. Under the pressure of this situation, individual men will in particular circumstances see the advantage of taking the risk of trusting another man, and this other man will very likely see it as in his interest to prove himself trustworthy. For if he does not, he cannot expect ever to be trusted in the future and he would therefore cut himself off from a co-operation that is necessary for him. This danger arises because promises have to be expressed and this verbalization of one's resolution makes it public:

When a man says *he promises any thing,* he in effect expresses a *resolution* of performing it; and along with that, by making use of this *form of words,* subjects himself to the penalty of never being trusted again in case of failure. (T. 522)[90]

It is thus not the resolution that creates a promise, for that is just our natural motive. It is the use of signs, or expressions, to publicize the resolution that creates the promise[91] because it creates a new motive, namely the fear of not being trusted by our fellow men in case of non-performance. And as the signs used are artificially invented by men, we see that promises are artificial phenomena as well.

As in the case of justice, there are certain rationalistic elements in Hume's much shorter account of the origin of promises. Thus he talks of the 'institution' of promises and he clearly thinks of promises as created deliberately for a certain purpose. But on the other hand he stresses that the purposefulness and deliberation is of the kind involving very low rationality, such as only emerges from concrete situations. It is also clear that the emergence of promises is just another step in the gradual articulation of the laws of justice, for it is only the logic of situations where property already exists and where slightly more complicated social relations are under way, that creates a real need for the institution of promises. It must, however, be made quite clear that in his treatment of the origin of promises, Hume does not give us the kind of clarifying comments that he does in connection with the origin of justice about the relation between men's *intentions* and the over-all *result* of their actions. What we should have expected him to point out is that men unwittingly create a new institution when they take the chance often enough, in individual instances, of trusting their neighbour's word out of self-interest, and that this new institution is such that it automatically creates a new self-interested motive for keeping one's word, namely the fear of 'never being trusted again in case of failure'. Although he never says this explicitly, it is clear that he has all the materials for saying so. And against the background of what he does say in the parallel case about the origin of the fundamental idea of justice, there can hardly be much doubt that this would be his opinion, if challenged on the point.

Promises form the core of contract law, as Hume makes clear, and in that context Smith takes over Hume's account, formalizing and emphasizing the spectator principle which is here so obvious in Hume. And as with Hume, this provides the key to the theory of obligation.[92]

8 Obligation

As we noted at the beginning of the present treatment of Hume's theory of justice, this theory is really made up of two parts: a theory of the origin of justice, and a theory of the moral quality of justice. So far we have only dealt with the former. Not until we have gone through the latter and seen how it is integrated in Hume's general account of moral evaluation, will we be in a position to appreciate how important the fundamental division of the theory of justice into the two parts is.

Hume's general theory of morals is mainly concerned with explicating moral good and bad, virtue and vice. And so it is not surprising to find that when, at the end of his Section 'Of the Origin of Justice and Property' in the *Treatise*, he turns to the question of the moral quality of justice, he formulates it as 'Why we annex the idea of virtue to justice, and of vice to injustice'.[93] He does, however, have a theory of obligation as well, which is completely in accord with his general theory. And although he does not say very much about it, his theory of obligation is both so clear and so important that I think it most convenient to approach his ideas of the moral quality of justice (including promises)[94] through this theory.

Hume opens one of his most important paragraphs on obligation by stating the principle that *ought* implies *can*: 'No action can be requir'd of us as our duty, unless there be implanted in human nature some actuating passion or motive, capable of producing the action.'[95] We can only be under an obligation to do actions the motives for which are within the range of natural human motivation. He then goes on to spell out what this means for our idea of obligation:

This motive cannot be the sense of duty. A sense of duty supposes an antecedent obligation: And where an action is not requir'd by any natural passion, it cannot be requir'd by any natural obligation; since it may be omitted without proving any defect or imperfection in the mind and temper, and consequently without vice. (T. 518)

In other words, we have an obligation to perform an action (1) if the motive for this action is a natural human motive (this is the principle that *ought* implies *can*, and it is a necessary condition for obligation), and (2) if our non-performance of the action is a sign that we lack a quality in our character (and consequently a motive for the action) which it is a 'defect or imperfection in the mind and temper' not to possess. What Hume means by 'defect or imperfection' is strongly indicated on the previous page:

All morality depends upon our sentiments; and when any action or quality of the mind, pleases us *after a certain manner*, we say it is virtuous; and when the neglect, or non-performance of it, displeases us *after a like manner*, we say that we lie under an obligation to perform it. (T. 517)

The imperfection, of which the non-performance of an obligation is a sign, is thus a quality that is subject to a certain kind of displeasure, namely a displeasure which is similar to the pleasure which accompanies our perception of virtue. But now we know from Hume's general exposition of the emotional background to moral evaluation, that this latter pleasure arises in conjunction with a peculiar indirect passion which is closely akin to, and in a way nothing but a corrected version of, love, and which we call moral approbation.[96] This, of course, leads us to expect that the displeasure in question here arises in conjunction with the indirect

passion which is akin to hatred and is known as moral disapprobation.[97]
That this is what Hume intends is strongly supported by a short treatment
of obligation much earlier in the *Treatise*:

When any virtuous motive or principle is common in human nature, a person,
who feels his heart devoid of that principle, may *hate himself* upon that account
and may perform the action without the motive, from a certain sense of duty...
(T. 479; my italics)[98]

If we put all these pieces together, we can see fairly clearly what Hume's
theory of obligation was. Obligation has to be seen against the background
of the natural and common qualities of human character and the
accompanying motives. If a man either lacks a certain quality, or in a
particular situation does not have the common or natural motive, he may
yet perform the action which this quality and motive would have led him
to do if he had possessed it. For he may see that if he looks upon the
situation as men commonly and naturally do, that is, as an impartial
spectator, then he will come to hate himself (in the sense of disapproving
of himself) if he does not perform the action. Whereas on the other hand,
he will be pleased with, that is, approve of, himself if he does perform it.
And in this consists the sense of duty:

A man that really feels no gratitude in his temper, is still *pleas'd* to perform
grateful actions, and thinks he has, by that means, fulfill'd his duty (T. 479)

Tho' there was no obligation to relieve the miserable, our humanity wou'd lead
us to it; and when we omit that duty, the immorality of the omission arises from
it being a proof, that we want the natural sentiments of humanity. A father
knows it to be his duty to take care of his children: but he has also a natural
inclination to it. And if no human creature had that inclination, no one cou'd lie
under any such obligation. (T. 518–19)

It will be noticed that I have above interpreted Hume's obligation as
making up for motives which are natural and *common*. This latter description was used to indicate Hume's view that the natural principles in the
human mind have conventional expressions and that these can vary from
time to time, and from place to place.[99] In this way it becomes possible for
him to reconcile the idea of a basically uniform human nature with the
facts of historical and geographical differences.[100] We must not be led to
believe that the regard for what is natural and common in our idea of
obligation makes obligation the same as respectability. Although our idea
of obligation is *formed* under social pressure, it only becomes moral obligation proper when the situation is viewed objectively and impartially –
exactly as in all moral evaluation in Hume. This is a vital step in Hume's
argument, but its full import can only be appreciated after we have
analysed the role of history, and the idea of utility.

What we have presented so far, however, is only part of Hume's theory of obligation. For it is evident that as the theory stands, it can only explain how a sense of duty can make up for natural motives, and thus why we have an obligation to practise natural virtues. But what we are particularly interested in is the obligation to practise artificial virtues. One can formulate the problem about these virtues in the following way. There are no natural motives for practising them, that is, no motives which do not presuppose their existence as social practices, as we have seen. But this means that not practising them does not indicate any natural 'defect or imperfection in the mind and temper'. Accordingly, one does not naturally come to hate oneself for not practising them, and therefore there does not naturally arise any sense of duty to practise them. It is this situation which forces Hume to embark upon his detailed theories of how the rules of justice (including the institution of promises) emerge from men's individual, self-interested actions and how, once in existence, they are maintained through the same self-interest – though redirected. And from this basis he is to explain how we come to attach a moral value to them. We can thus see how the whole plan is well suited to convey the idea of justice as something *developing*, as a *natural* growth, in the sense that it is non-arbitrary and has natural causes in man's nature and situation; and as an *unintended* growth, in the sense that it is not rationally planned in any of the major turns of its development.

How do people come to hate themselves – and, of course, others – for not acting in accordance with the rules of justice, and thus develop a sense of duty on top of the interest they have in such behaviour? In one central paragraph Hume invokes his principle of sympathy. He first points out that as society grows larger, the self-interested motive to observe the rules of justice grows fainter for the individual, where his own affairs are concerned: a single exception to such a wide-ranging rule does not seem to do much harm. But this tendency is countered by the sympathy we have with others when they are being treated unjustly by some third person, as well as by the resentment we feel when we ourselves are the subject of injustice (this latter could, of course, be construed as spectator-sympathy with ourselves):

Tho' in our own actions we may frequently lose sight of that interest, which we have in maintaining order, and may follow a lesser and more present interest, we never fail to observe the prejudice we receive, either mediately or immediately, from the injustice of others; as not being in that case either blinded by passion, or byass'd by any contrary temptation. Nay when the injustice is so distant from us, as no way to affect our interest, it still displeases us; because we consider it as prejudicial to human society, and pernicious to every one that approaches the person guilty of it. We partake of their uneasiness by *sympathy*; and as every thing, which gives uneasiness in human actions, upon the general survey, is call'd Vice, and whatever produces satisfaction, in the same manner, is denominated

Virtue; this is the reason why the sense of moral good and evil follows upon justice and injustice. (T. 499)

By and by, those individual cases of sympathy, and consequent moral approval/disapproval or just/unjust actions, grow into a general rule which 'we fail not to extend...even to our own actions'. And this extension is supported by the fact that 'we naturally *sympathize* with others in the sentiments they entertain of us'. With this last point Hume is undoubtedly thinking of our ability to become spectators of our own actions and thus to evaluate them (or, rather, their motivation) by sympathy with their effects (or, more correctly, their tendency). All this seems very clear and we readily allow Hume to draw his general conclusion: 'self-interest is the original motive to the *establishment* of justice, but a sympathy with public interest is the source of the *moral approbation* which attends that virtue'.[101] But if we ask how we are to derive the moral *obligation* to justice from this account, we encounter difficulties. For exactly *what* motive is missing if we behave unjustly? What motive do we come to hate ourselves for not having? It cannot be the sympathy with public interest, for sympathy is nothing but a principle of communication and not a motivating force, as we have seen.[102] The obvious answer is that the motive is the one which we come to approve of through sympathy with its effect (or tendency). Now, the effect (or tendency) is the public interest. But the motive? Well, as long as the sense of duty is not yet established the only motive is self-interest. But as we know that the motive is only taken as an indication of a quality of character when we evaluate morally, and as it is hardly likely that Hume thought self-interest, as a general character trait, morally approved by men (which, of course, does not entail that it is generally disapproved), the conclusion must be *that there is no motive* which we could come to hate ourselves for not having. It thus seems as if Hume fails to give us the motive which could form the link between the interested motivation for just behaviour and the moral obligation to such behaviour. He does not, however, fail us completely. For if we turn to his treatment of promises again, we shall find sufficient indications to allow us to fill in what is missing to make the theory coherent:

The difficulties, that occur to us, in supposing a moral obligation to attend promises, we either *surmount or elude*. For instance; the expression of a resolution is not commonly suppos'd to be obligatory; and we cannot readily conceive how the making use of a certain form of words shou'd be able to cause any material difference. Here, therefore, we *feign* a new act of the mind, which we call the *willing* an obligation; and on this we suppose the morality to depend. (T. 523; first italics mine)[103]

If we draw on what we know from the case of justice, we can put the following interpretation upon this. When promising, motivated by self-interest, becomes regular behaviour and when through sympathy with its beneficial tendency we come to approve of this behaviour, then the natural tendency in men to see behaviour as an expression of motives and motives as expressions of qualities of character, leads them to *imagine* that there is a natural motive (and thus a character trait) behind promises – namely the willing of an obligation. And it is this *imagined* motive that, through sympathy, they come to approve of. And when they find that, for very good reasons, they do not have this motive themselves, they come to hate themselves, and this self-hatred creates the sense of duty to fulfil their promises. In other words, certain actions done out of a morally *neutral* motive (self-interest) have on the whole such good consequences and seem so clearly aimed at those consequences, that men naturally come to imagine that there is a specific motive for the actions which directs them towards those consequences. They naturally come to approve of this non-existing motive and to hate themselves for not having it. And this self-hatred is the magic formula, for it constitutes the real moral motive to do justice and fulfil promises, viz. our sense of duty.

Let me stress that this suggestion about the imagined motive is a construction of mine. I put it forward for the following reasons. (1) It is needed at a vital turn in Hume's argument, namely the development of moral obligation out of interested motivation. (2) There is the quoted indication of such a view – and it seems quite a strong indication, when read in this context. (3) The idea is in line with Hume's general position, that moral approbation is about motives and through them about persons. And (4) it is in line with his general idea of obligation as self-hatred for lack of a motive.[104]

9 Two difficulties

The whole preceding account of the moral value and obligation of the artificial virtues in general and of justice in particular makes one significant presupposition. It is taken for granted that Hume's theory can account for how we sympathize with those who benefit from the useful tendency of these virtues, once they have been established as social institutions in the way described earlier. But it seems to me that this is precisely what Hume's theory is not able to do. It is self-evident from Hume's description of the sympathy mechanism that we can only have sympathy with specifiable individuals. It may be virtually any man, however strange, but it has to be a concrete, individual man. But this condition is clearly not fulfilled with the artificial virtues, and particularly not justice. Here the usefulness is for a group with a changing membership of non-specific persons, and it may not even be present for those whom one knows as concrete persons. This is the whole point in the distinction between the natural and the artificial virtues: whereas the former are useful in each individual case, the latter need not be.

This failure in the theory of sympathy to provide a necessary step in the theory of moral evaluation is not only of significance in itself. It also seems to me to be the most obvious reason Hume could have for leaving the technical concept of sympathy behind when he came to write the second *Enquiry,* and instead bring in the broad concept of fellow-feeling which 'solves' the problem precisely in that it does not require the concreteness of object which the sympathy of the *Treatise* does. As indicated earlier in this chapter (pp. 5–6 above), this difficulty – serious as it is – should hardly therefore be taken as a more or less complete breakdown of Hume's original theory of the connection between the passions and morality, but rather as the occasion for renewed speculation. And the *Enquiry* constituted some such speculation.

Whether Hume was content with this speculation we do not know, but Adam Smith was not. Although we do not have direct evidence for this, I suggest that it is a fruitful perspective on Smith to see his ideas of situational propriety, which we will discuss in the following chapter, as an attempt to connect the two strands of Hume's theory of justice – the origin of justice and the moral value of justice – into one theory and thereby solve the difficulties in each of these two parts. The difficulty in the former part, the origin of justice, is the one we pointed out on p. 26 above, viz. that Hume fails to spell out the details of how the spread of just behavioural practice is psychologically possible. And the difficulty which Smith saw in the latter part of the theory, the moral value and obligation of justice, can, I suggest, be formulated as the following dilemma. Either moral value and obligation have to be accounted for in terms of sympathy (*Treatise* solution), though that requires a concreteness of object which is just not present in the case of justice in the 'anonymous' society, that is, the society beyond the family group; or they are accounted for by means of 'fellow-feeling' (*Enquiry* solution), which avoids this difficulty, but which is so optimistically forward looking, and in that sense rationalistic, that it is not to be found in ordinary men, but is rather a philosophers' speculation. How Smith retained the concreteness of the *Treatise* without running into Hume's difficulties, and how he thus avoided the second horn of the dilemma, the excessive reliance on the '*tendency of affections*',[105] will be part of the theme of the next chapter.

10 The role of history

'Men are mightily addicted to *general rules*',[106] 'they cannot even pass each other on the road without rules'; yes, 'it is impossible for men so much as to murder each other without statutes, and maxims, and an idea of justice and honour'.[107] This ability and tendency to create rules by following a uniform pattern of behaviour is a basic feature of human life, and we have now seen how it gives rise to some of the most important rules of all, namely the fundamental 'laws of nature'. These laws are not in any way *derived* from statements about human nature, they are *caused* by certain elementary features of human nature, when the latter is placed in a world like the present one. And because men have an ability to balance long-term interest against short-term interest, they come to be bound by the rules they themselves happened to bring into being, and the rules, therefore, in a sense win a certain independent status. This is further increased when the rules acquire a moral quality. This moral quality is also not 'derived' in any mysterious sense from descriptions of man's nature. It consists of a set of indirect passions, which men (in contrast to animals)[108] have a natural ability to come to feel when they are exposed to certain causal circumstances. What Hume is proposing, therefore, is an (intendedly empirical) hypothesis about a possible sequence of causes and effects, the end-result of which is far beyond the plans and intentions that any individual could have. As laws, they are laws without a legislator. As social institutions, they carry all the marks of being an 'artificial invention' in spite of their wholly 'natural' causes. They are universal, or general, in the sense that they do not allow of any exceptions. They are thus 'impersonal', because they do not take into regard the individual merits in a given case.[109] This is again just another way of saying that they do not allow of any overriding values – a point to be explored more closely below. The same is shown by the fact that, unlike the natural virtues, they do not allow of any degrees. They are absolutely precise and sharp and 'property, and right, and obligation [and therefore justice] admit not of degrees'.[110] The result of following these rules is the establishment of an over-all order, called society. For justice and society are coincident; indeed, justice is 'of all circumstances the most necessary to the establishment of human society'.[111]

But although Hume arrived, through his theory of justice, at the basic idea of social order arising spontaneously and without the intervention of deliberate constructions, it is at least doubtful whether and to what extent he carried this into his general social philosophy in the *Essays* and the *History of England*. Certainly one can hardly read a thoroughgoing social evolution into his texts and see this as his central interest.[112] Caution on this point would be of importance if we were concerned with a general interpretation of Hume's social and political philosophy, and it is of importance here because it forces us to face the following two decisive questions. What is the relation, in Hume's theory, between justice and historical evolution? And what is the relation of justice to other values that men could invoke – or in other words, in what sense is justice a fundamental law for men?

I have argued that Hume's conception of justice was evolutionary, but this must not be understood to mean that he put forward a theory of how justice did in fact evolve. His argument is firmly rooted in his theory of human nature. But on the basis of this he shows that justice is such a phenomenon that it must necessarily have an evolution behind it. In a way his argument could be said to be negative: he tries to show that justice is neither the effect of a separate faculty in the human mind, nor a deliberate construction of human reason, and he does this by showing that it is a necessary by-product of men's natural responses to their situation in the present world. He is thus not writing the history of justice, but he is show- ing that, given the ever-present features of human nature (self-love and confined benevolence) and the equally universal features of the world (relative scarcity), justice must have a history and this history must be a purely natural one. But the theory clearly does not say anything about what course this development takes in particular cases.[113] Thus not only the question of who owns what is contingent,[114] but one would also imagine that the very idea of what *kind* of things could count as property would be variable and subject to development.[115]

The same point – that Hume's theory is of such a design that it fairly clearly points out the place of history, without itself being a historical theory – is brought home to us when we attend to the moral quality of justice. This arises through sympathy from the utility of just acts, as is the case with all the social virtues.[116] But if we look at this concept of utility, it turns out to be a general principle, rather than an idea with a specific content:

Usefulness is agreeable, and engages our approbation. This is a matter of fact, confirmed by daily observation. But, *useful*? For what? For somebody's interest, surely. Whose interest then? Not our own only: For our approbation frequently extends farther. It must, therefore, be the interest of those, who are served by the character or action approved of. (E. 218)

But obviously this interest is extremely variable, and the concept of utility must be equally so. This is an important point, for it shows the room for improvement in morals and thus the role of knowledge. The better people understand human nature and its situation, the better they will be able to see what men's true interests are (given their basic passions of self-love and confined benevolence), and to evaluate accordingly. One of Hume's finest examples of such revaluation in the light of improved knowledge is the case of luxury:

Luxury, or a refinement of the pleasures and conveniences of life, had long been supposed the source of every corruption in government, and the immediate cause of faction, sedition, civil wars, and the total loss of liberty. It was an object of declamation to all satirists, and severe moralists. Those, who prove, or attempt to prove, that such refinements rather tend to the increase of industry, civility, and arts regulate anew our *moral* as well as *political* sentiments, and represent, as laudable or innocent, what had formerly been regarded as pernicious and blameable. (E. 181)[117]

We must agree that 'Hume's "general psychology" is concerned with the function and mechanism, not the content of mind, which is various and supplied by social and historical circumstances.'[118] And this conclusion allots to philosophy, criticism (in the broad, Humean sense), and history their proper functions. What I have been concerned to show is *how* the 'general psychology' itself leads to a demand for historical evolution in the case of justice. Whether Hume's historical and 'sociological' writings fit the bill is not part of my proposed problem here.

11 Utility and natural justice

We have already been brought a long way into the second large problem that was suggested above, namely, in what sense justice is a fundamental law for men. There are certain difficulties with such an interpretation which we must now face. We know that justice gains its moral character through sympathy with its utility and that this leads Hume to maintain that the force of the obligation to be just tends to be proportional to the utility. This clearly indicates that justice is not so fundamental that it cannot be overruled by other values. And it thus appears that Hume comes down firmly on the side of utility, with justice as more or less an epiphenomenon, a mere function of utility. The matter is, however, much more complicated than that. For we must remember that the utility in question is the *public* utility, which on an enlightened view comprises each individual's private utility and which the individual takes part in by means of sympathy. This means that justice can only be overridden if it is no longer of public use. But as justice is the very cement of social life, this can only happen in the most extreme cases, where society is threatened with dissolution from 'external' pressures:

Is it any crime, after a shipwreck, to seize whatever means or instrument of safety one can lay hold of, without regard to former limitations of property? Or if a city beseiged were perishing with hunger; can we imagine, that men will see any means of preservation before them, and lose their lives, from a scrupulous regard to what, in other situations, would be the rules of equity and justice? The use and tendency of that virtue is to procure happiness and security, by preserving order in society: but where society is ready to perish from extreme necessity, no greater evil can be dreaded from violence and injustice; and every man may now provide for himself by all the means which prudence can dictate, or humanity permit. (E. 186)

In other words, only where the public interest cannot be affected can other motives, like prudence or humanity, take over from justice.[119] The connection between the general rules of justice and the public utility they create is so close that only in very few circumstances does it allow of exceptions. But the connection is obviously an empirical matter, or at least that is Hume's intention, and the task for his philosophical politics is to show men this connection. With a better understanding there follows a stronger obligation and in this way Hume's new science fulfils much the same function as political propaganda and parental indoctrination[120] for those who can understand it. And these latter become the 'moderate men' in whom Hume invested so much hope for the future. Only when men are not so informed do they become 'a kind of political fanatics', like the Levellers,[121] and start acting against the laws of nature on the basis of their own evaluations.

If we now look closer at the kind of utility that is involved – that is, the public utility – we will see that Hume's view on this point also is rather complicated and unusual. When he presents his account of how justice gains its moral quality, he does so by showing how *in*justice is a vice.[122] Men have a strong tendency to sympathize with the effects of injustice and accordingly to disapprove of it. This apparently implies that just behaviour is what is left when injustice is ruled out. Justice, so to speak, is a negative virtue and 'We may often fulfil all the rules of justice by sitting still and doing nothing', as Smith was later to express the idea. Only when justice is done under difficult circumstances do we directly and actively approve of it as more than the absence of injustice. This negative form of the rules of justice means that, in a way, they say something only about what is *not* to be done – don't encroach on anybody else's property; don't break promises, etc. – but nothing is said about the rights that are protected in this way. The property and the contract that are protected and only exist by means of the rules of justice can be used for any purpose one wants, as far as justice is concerned. Of course such actions can be subject to further general moral evaluation, but that is outside the scope of justice. Now this means that the interest that justice promotes and protects is not any concretely specifiable one. It is simply the sum total of individual interests that are compatible within a society, that is, which are not unjust. And *this* is the public interest (which, through sympathy, is the ultimate cause of our moral approval of justice):

as the self-love of one person is naturally contrary to that of another, these several interested passions are oblig'd to adjust themselves after such a manner as to concur in some system of conduct and behaviour. This system, therefore, comprehending the interest of each individual, is of course advantageous to the public. (T. 529)

This again means that the laws of justice are *useful* in the sense that they serve as a *means to an end*, the end being the public interest. But this idea of 'means-utility', as we could call it, is clearly different from the idea of utility which we find in the later utilitarian theorists. For them utility is more or less identified with pleasure or happiness of a kind, and it is thus the *end* towards which actions should aspire.

This distinction between means-utility and end-utility is extremely valuable,[123] but it is very doubtful how clearly Hume himself saw it. If we stick narrowly to the way in which he uses the concept of utility, it may appear as clearly the 'means' sense. When he talks of the public interest as useful to the private, the content of the latter is clearly irrelevant. It may, of course, be pleasure or happiness; but that is another matter which lies outside the utility-justification of justice. For as far as justice is concerned, all that can be said about the individuals' ends is that they must be compatible, that is, that they are not unjust: that is the public interest. And it is not simply in connection with justice that Hume uses the 'means' sense of utility. When we approve morally of a character trait because of its tendency to promote the interests of another person, in the way described above, this is clearly means-utility. 'Usefulness is only a tendency to a certain end.'[124] It is obviously this means-utility which makes possible the 'correction' of our impressions, so that we as 'a judicious spectator' can judge morally, that is, impartially, about our servant as well as Marcus Brutus, and aesthetically, that is, impartially, about the fortifications of *any* city. But all this clarity is rather blurred by Hume's constant reference to the happiness which these various 'means' tend to create. There is, of course, nothing wrong in talking of means and ends together. But in the absence of a direct clarification of the concept of utility it does make one wonder how clearly Hume saw the consequences of his dual use of it. And when we come to deal with Adam Smith we shall still be kept wondering about this problem.

However, in view of the strong presence of the 'means' sense of utility, it is clearly misleading to say that Hume's moral theory in general, and his theory of justice in particular, is utilitarian, for this label is unambiguously connected with the end-utility of Bentham and the Mills. For Hume the moral justification of justice, or the cause of our approval of it, is that it creates a 'system of conduct or behaviour' which allows the optimal pursuit of individual interests which is compatible with living together in a society. Exactly what relevance the content of these individual interests has for his argument is the doubtful point.

But it must be stressed that this does not prevent us from making further moral evaluations of just acts, since all those individual interests which pass the test of justice, that is, which are not unjust, may cause all sorts of other moral feelings. We may find that although an action is just, in that it does not transgress the laws of justice, yet it may be wanting in benevo-

lence, or, on the contrary, that an action is unjust, and yet humane. But
the point is that such further moral evaluations are irrelevant as far as
justice is concerned and therefore outside the law, because they do not
affect the public interest as this has been defined above. Only when the
public interest is out of the picture, 'where the society is ready to perish
from extreme necessity',[125] can other moral and non-moral evaluations
replace justice.

When is an action just, according to Hume? The simple psychological
answer is, when it is the expression of a character trait which on the whole
has a tendency to be useful as a means towards another person's interests
which we can appreciate through sympathy. But the circumstances under
which this sympathy can operate is the really important and interesting
thing. It can only operate from an impartial point of view, that is, it must
not be dependent upon the particular persons involved. But this again is
tantamount to saying that the action must be in accordance with a general
rule: anybody should be able to be willing to do it. This, however, is just
another way of saying that the action, or at least the motive behind it,
should be compatible with the highest possible number of other aims in
the society or group concerned, otherwise not 'anyone', or as near as
possible to 'anyone', would be able to be willing to do the action. This is
the significance of our 'correcting' the particular perspective from which
we judge in each case the actions of other people as well as our own
actions, so that we can take our stand in the shape of 'anyone', or the
judicious spectator, as Hume more elegantly expresses it.

This way of formulating the central points in Hume's theory of justice
allows us to shed a ray of light on the role of history in a would-be
Humean discipline of natural jurisprudence. If one of the central tests of
justice is the maximization of compatibility of aims, in the way outlined
above, then clearly knowledge of the 'aims' which pervade a society at
any given time will be of decisive importance. Such knowledge would be
contained in a natural history of the society, and particularly a natural
history of its law. It is exactly in this sense that we can read Hume's point
about the importance of *de facto* possessions in the establishment of the
rules of justice. If *de facto* possessions were not respected as they happened
to have developed in a given society, then many more persons' aims would
be thwarted than was in fact the case with the rules of justice. This does
not, of course, mean that people actually calculated in this way. What it
does mean is that if anyone came to doubt the justice of the rules, then
knowledge about the existing conditions (*de facto* possessions) would be
decisive in order to settle his doubt. What I suggest is that we can read
this as Hume's model for determining any question of justice. And it
would seem that this model extends well beyond problems of justice: it
explains Hume's respect for the importance of the given situation for the

evaluation of any social phenomenon, whether a past, a present, or a proposed future one.

All those reformulations of Hume's points lead us to show how his extraordinary combination of descriptive and normative disciplines completely bypasses the usual 'is/ought' problems as far as justice is concerned.[126] The whole point in Hume's denying that there is a state of nature is that man's aims and aspirations always exist in a context of other men's aims and aspirations. This means that the normative question of what to do always arises, so to speak, piecemeal: what can I do, given all the other things which I and everyone else want to do? Moral justifications can never be ultimate; they must take their starting point from a given social value-system. Such a system must always be present where men are: at the very least there must be the will to live and propagate and the confined benevolence amongst the members of a family. But when this is the case the normative question of what to do will never arise as a question of ultimate justification. It is impossible for us to say whether an action or rule of action is just in an absolute sense. All we can do is to check its justice, given all the other aims and values we hold – and each of these can again be checked in the same piecemeal fashion. In a sense this is a coherence theory of moral validity, but it should be remarked that a very firm link to nature is provided by the natural 'aims' or strivings of human nature.[127]

We can now see that the evolution behind justice and law does not as such lend it any further weight. The antiquity of law does not in itself make it obligatory. It is, therefore, misleading to see any close relations between Hume's theory and the traditionalist justification of law which we find in, for example, the Common Law theoreticians, the Whig tradition, and in Burke, as has been suggested.[128] In a sense Hume is closer to the modern natural law theoreticians in claiming that there are certain universal tests for justice. But he is quite unlike them in letting the given system of values in a society play an important role in these tests. Hume's theory is built around a distinction between the origin and the moral value of justice, and if his treatment of the former suggests a superficial affinity with the traditionalist approach, his treatment of the latter suggests an affinity with natural law which is almost as superficial.

The alternative of historical justification or natural law is not the only one which becomes obsolete in Hume's theory. The same applies to natural law versus a positivist foundation for law, as has already become clear. Natural justice is neither a set of eternally valid, substantial laws; nor is it a deliberate human construction. It is, rather, a few universal test-principles, which necessarily refer to the existing value-system in a society. The implication of this view would seem to be that justice is neither wholly relative (to society, age, class, or whatever), nor absolute in the sense that it is spelled out in definite rules – although, given the world and human nature as they nearly universally are (relative scarcity and confined benevolence), the basic rules of justice will take the form explained by Hume: 'the stability of possession,. . .its transference by consent, and. . . the performance of promises'.[129] But natural justice as such seems to be a kind of directive ideal, rather analogous to the way in which truth can be said to be a directive ideal in our search for knowledge. And the search for justice becomes a process without any natural end point – at least as long as mankind remains an 'inventive species' with ever new kinds of behaviour to be tested for their justice.

CHAPTER THREE

Smith's moral theory

1 Hume and Smith on sympathy

Turning from Hume's major philosophical work, the *Treatise*, to that of Smith, *The Theory of Moral Sentiments*, is a somewhat confusing experience. On the one hand there are all the similarities in the problems dealt with and the theories proposed, in the criticisms and alignments of predecessors, and there are the recurring, more or less clear references to Hume himself. On the other hand there is a significant change in the tone and style of the discourse. While one could say that Hume is constructing an abstract theory with its own language, and trying to accommodate common experiences and their linguistic expressions within it, Smith is trying to accommodate an abstract theory within the conceptual framework of ordinary language – or at least with a minimal stretching of it. And this is presumably one of the reasons why Hume scholars find it difficult to see much profundity in Smith, and why Smith scholars may tend to think that Hume's profundity was bought at the cost of empirical content and relevance. Nor is the difference confined to language and style. For it is precisely Smith's complaint against Hume that his theory of morals was a philosopher's construction which did not catch human morality as it is[1] – a complaint which we shall have occasion for returning to in the present chapter.

Smith's use of the word 'sympathy' is a prime example of the advantages and of the dangers in using ordinary language for theoretical purposes. On the one hand we all understand it to some extent, but precisely because of this it is difficult for us to get at the technical twist Smith gives it. As with Augustine's difficulties with time, we seem to know what it is as long as we don't ask Smith. Nevertheless, there seems to be some considerable consensus on one point, namely that Smith's concept of sympathy, whatever it may be, is radically different from that of Hume. It is, therefore, with some hesitation that I suggest that there are some striking structural similarities between the theories of sympathy in our two philosophers and that the equally striking differences come about because Smith broadens and generalizes Hume's idea.[2]

One key to the problem of sympathy in Hume and Smith is to see it as a problem of causation. When we have two similar passions and one is said to be the effect of sympathy with the other, or the sympathetic reflection of the other, what does 'sympathy' stand for? Hume narrows his answer to a fairly simple psychological process in the first instance: when a man perceives the expressions of a passion in another man, he forms an idea of this passion on the basis of his own earlier experience, and this idea is turned into an impression, that is, into a passion similar to the original one in the other person, by the enlivening presence of the impression of the spectator's self. This psychological process is the starting point for all evaluation, but in order to create a proper moral or aesthetic evaluation, the sympathetically created passion has to be 'corrected' in the light of the *situation* in which the original passion and its expression occurred. As we have seen in the previous chapter, this is the way in which objective evaluations come about.

What Smith does is simply to broaden the causal factors in the creation of the sympathetic reaction of the spectator to *include* the situation in which the original passion and its expression occurred. According to him the situation is not just a secondary and corrective factor. It is not just the perception of the expression of another man's passion that sparks off our sympathy. It is true that this may be the case to some extent with fairly simple passions which do not point beyond the person who has them, such as joy or grief, but even in those cases the sympathy is rather imperfect until more is known than the mere passion (or, rather, its expression). Certainly more is required in the case of the morally more relevant passions which point towards, or involve, other men.[3] The cause of sympathy is, rather, the whole set of circumstances in which the passion occurs: 'Sympathy...does not arise so much from the view of the passion, as from that of the situation which excites it.'[4] This is extremely important, for it shows a distinction between the *object* of sympathy, which is another man's passion, and the *cause* of sympathy, which is the whole situation that gives rise to the original passion. And this again shows that the original passion is only a contingent part of the whole process. The causes may, for some reason, have failed to produce the original passion and yet they may produce the sympathetic passion in the spectator. Hence the possibility that the spectator can say what the original passion *should have been* according to his view of the situation. Smith illustrates this very important idea by some well-known non-moral cases: the sympathy we can feel with the affliction of being an idiot, although the idiot may be perfectly happy;[5] the sympathy a mother will feel for her sick baby's future, although the child does not have the slightest possibility of knowing anything about its future; and, the most extreme case of all, our sympathy with the dead, although every possibility of feeling any passions at all is ruled out for them.[6]

Now, this account of the causes of sympathy is clearly different from

Hume's, but it is equally clearly compatible with it. For all Smith is doing, so far, is to point out that the cause Hume singles out, the perception of expressions of passion, is insufficient in itself and far from universally present when the effect, namely sympathy, is present. Hume's theory makes actions and their motives in a sense forward-looking, and accordingly we judge of them from this viewpoint. Motives and actions are seen as aiming at certain results, intentionally or unintentionally, and moral judgements consist of estimates of their merit in this regard. By contrast, actions and their motives are backward-looking for Smith; they are *re*actions to a situation. And it is in this view we judge of them, as proper or improper to the situation. This change is of consequence not only for the contents of moral theory but also for its epistemological status or, rather, for the epistemological status of moral judgements. On Hume's own epistemological terms moral judgement must take its *beginning* from an illusion, for it starts with imagining the essentially private and in-accessible reaction of one man to the action (or motive) of another. It is based upon a kind of analogical 'inference' called sympathy; and it is upon this that the situational 'corrections' are superimposed, thus creating moral (or aesthetic) judgement proper.

This is significantly changed in Smith, for in taking moral judgement as *primarily* a problem of fitting the action judged of to its situation, Smith switches the problem of knowledge on to the situation. To be able to judge is to be able to know the situation, and hence the ideal of the impartial and informed spectator. This is obviously an advance in the explanation of the communal character of our moral world; for at least parts of the situation will normally be open to the public view, and the whole exertion of sympathy makes as much of the situation as possible common between spectators and the person principally concerned. In other words, in Smith's view moral judgements have already a much broader empirical basis as their starting point than they have for Hume.

Smith is able to put this to good theoretical use, for the view of the situation as the primary basis for moral judgement allows him to make a rough division of situations and their attendant sentiments according to their normal accessibility to spectators through sympathy. This is what he is doing in Part I, Section ii of *The Theory of Moral Sentiments*. Thus it is difficult for us to enter, for example, into passions arising from another's body, and it is more difficult with those which have internal causes, than with those which have external causes which we can see. Equally, it is difficult for a spectator to gain sympathetic understanding of passions which are somehow unique for the person concerned, such as love. But though we are unable to go along with the particular passion, we know its general type and this enables us to enter into all the surrounding or attendant passions. Love 'interests us not as a passion, but as a situation that gives occasion to other passions which interest us'.[7] Smith then goes on to discuss three much more important categories of passions: the unsocial, the social, and the selfish. These we can all enter into, that is, understand, by sympathy, and his main theme is the extent to which we can sympathize with them in the sense of approve of them as proper.[8]

Hume's explanation is in terms of the chain of association. Smith uses the broader 'imagination'. But obviously it would have been quite possible for Smith to explain the functions of imagination by means of association. Presumably he did not do so because for his purposes it would have been an unnecessary detail in the general theory. Be that as it may, there are some striking parallels in the further details of the two theories. For Hume, the sympathetic feeling arises when we expose ourselves to the influence of the expression of the original feeling; and although it resembles the original, the sympathetic feeling is our *own* as spectators, since it comes about through the enlivening influence of the impression of the self. Whether or not this can be described in modern psychological terms as empathy[9] is rather irrelevant. The main point is to notice that it is a simple condition for sympathy that the sympathetic feeling exists as the spectator's.

According to Smith, the sympathetic feeling arises when the spectator exposes himself to the influence of the circumstances which gave rise to the original feeling. This can only be done by means of the famous imaginary change of situation: we imagine that we are in another man's shoes in order to see what our reactions would be under such influence. And the feelings that we, as spectators, come to have by this use of imagination are the sympathetic feelings, 'sympathy, or the correspondent affection of the Spectator'.[10] The point which has always caused difficulties is, of course, how we are to understand this imaginary change of place for the spectator. What is it he changes: just the situation, or himself as well? It seems to me that there is not and cannot be any clear general answer to this. It necessarily varies with a number of factors, such as the personalities of both spectator and agent (the man who has the original feeling), their mutual relationship, the nature of the situation and the feeling concerned, etc. But there are a couple of points to be made about it. First, the personality of the agent is in itself a very important part of the total situation and, therefore, the better the spectator is able to identify in imagination with this personality, the better will be his understanding of the situation and the more accurate, therefore, his sympathetic feeling.[11] But secondly, it must be pointed out that for Smith, just as for Hume, the act of sympathizing must necessarily be accompanied in the spectator by a consciousness of his own self. The whole drive behind all sympathizing is, as we shall see, a basic wish to relate or compare our *own* reactions to those of *others*. It is only this 'tension' between persons that gives rise to all evaluations of persons, of which the act of sympathy is the necessary first step.

It is therefore necessary and, in my view, rather a matter of course that Smith right from the beginning of his discussion of sympathy makes it plain that the spectator's own consciousness always in some degree accompanies the act of sympathy and that however successful he may be in approaching the actual state of the agent, what he feels

will, indeed, always be in some respects different from what [the latter] feels,... because the secret consciousness that the change of situations, is but imaginary, not only lowers it in degree, but in some measure varies it in kind, and gives it a quite different modification. (TMS, i, i, 4, § 7)[12]

Indeed, one can say that it is only on condition that Smith retains the spectator's self-consciousness in all acts of sympathy that he will be able to use the sympathy mechanism as the foundation for evaluations at all. For, as we have already seen, we are perfectly able to sympathize, and thus evaluate, even where there is either no one, or only a completely subnormal and unreachable person to sympathize with – that is, where there is absolutely no other person with whom to 'identify'. In short, the spectator can take the place of the agent in his imagination in many degrees, but there is a point beyond which he cannot possibly go in his identification: he must retain some consciousness of his own self as that which sympathizes.

2 Sympathy and moral approval

Smith opens *The Theory of Moral Sentiments* by pointing out the reality of sympathy as a principle in human beings, even in the worst of them. But it is important to remember that he does not let the matter rest there. He makes it clear in various places that sympathy is put to work by an even more fundamental principle in human nature, the desire to agree, to be in accord with our fellow men. Thus he says, for example:

The great pleasure of conversation and society...arises from a certain correspondence of sentiments and opinions, from a certain harmony of minds, which, like so many musical instruments, coincide and keep time with one another. But this most delightful harmony cannot be obtained unless there is a free communication of sentiments and opinions. We all desire, upon this account, to feel how each other is affected, to penetrate into each other's bosoms, and to observe the sentiments and affections which really subsist there. (TMS, vii, iv. § 28)

This nearly compulsory interest in other men is extremely important. On the one hand it leads men to let themselves be led by others; on the other hand it makes them try to lead others. And it is basically this continuous exchange that underlies all human culture. It probably underlies language; through vanity it is the foundation for all distinctions of rank in society; in the form of bartering it is behind any economy; and through the mechanism of sympathy it gives rise to human morality.

The seeking of agreement, however, only requires sympathy when the object about which agreement is sought is somehow closely connected with one person but not with the other(s), so that the former will be influenced in a significantly different way, that is, will be in a different situation. This is not the case with, for example, the objects of 'science and taste'. Here, all

look at them from the same point of view, and we have no occasion for sympathy, or for that imaginary change of situations from which it arises, in order to produce, with regard to these, the most perfect harmony of sentiments and affections. (TMS, i, i, 4, § 2)[13]

But if the object is such that one man is particularly affected by it (it might be, for instance, another man's resentment against him), everybody else – that is, all spectators – can understand and evaluate his response only by means of sympathy, by trying to let the object and the whole situation affect them in imagination.[14] It is this difference in situation which, together with the desire for understanding and agreement, leads to sympathy.

However, the spectators' feelings are nothing but sympathetic reflections of the original feelings and agreement will therefore be difficult. 'The person principally concerned is sensible of this, and at the same time passionately desires a more complete sympathy.'[15] This leads *him* to sympathy with the situation of the spectator. It is thus only by a mutual sympathy in this sense that the maximum degree of agreement can be reached. This will never be complete because of the spectator's own accompanying consciousness but it can be quite 'sufficient for the harmony of society'.[16]

Sympathy in the sense now explained is the means for all judgement of other men and, as we shall see later, also of ourselves. The basic act of evaluating or judging consists simply in a comparison between the original reactions of the person principally concerned and the sympathetic reactions of the spectators. If they are in agreement, the spectators approve of the man concerned; otherwise they disapprove:

To approve of the passions of another. . . as suitable to their objects, is the same thing as to observe that we entirely sympathize with them; and not to approve of them as such, is the same thing as to observe that we do not entirely sympathize with them. (TMS, i, i, 3, § 1)

Here is clearly implied that distinction between sympathy and approbation resulting from sympathy which Smith had to clarify for Hume in a later footnote:[17]

It has been objected to me, that as I found the sentiment of approbation, which is always agreeable, upon sympathy, it is inconsistent with my system to admit any disagreeable sympathy. I answer, that in the sentiment of approbation there are two things to be taken notice of; first, the sympathetic passion of the spectator; and, secondly, the emotion which arises from his observing the perfect coincidence between this sympathetic passion in himself, and the original passion in the person principally concerned. This last emotion, in which the sentiment of approbation properly consists, is always agreeable and delightful. The other may either be agreeable or disagreeable, according to the nature of the original passion, whose features it must always, in some measure, retain. (TMS, I, iii, I, § 9, note)[18]

This has the abstract clarity reminiscent of Hume which many scholars would like to have seen more of in Smith. There is, however, enough of it to enable us to see the following distinctions in Smith's theory of sympathetic evaluations. First there is the imaginary change of situation by which the spectator tries, as far as possible, to expose himself to the same causal influences as the man originally concerned. We will often find this process alone called sympathy in Smith. Secondly, there is the result of the influence of this cause, namely the reaction of the spectator. This too is called sympathy, or the sympathetic feelings, sentiments, etc. Thirdly, there is the comparison of the original and the sympathetic sentiments. And fourthly, there is the emotion arising from this comparison, which is either a kind of pleasure called approval when the original and the sympathetic sentiments coincide, or a kind of pain called disapproval when they do not coincide. This pleasure is often called sympathy, while the pain ought to be, and occasionally is, called antipathy. It is clear that when Smith uses sympathy in the first two senses it is neutral and may result in antipathy as well as in sympathy in the last mentioned sense. This usage is technical and presupposes an understanding of his theory, while the last sense seems to be closer to the ordinary sense of the word where it implies some kind of positive attitude. What is most confusing of all, however, is that Smith frequently uses sympathy to denote all three of the senses mentioned plus the comparison – that is, he often talks of sympathy as the whole process including its result, which in that case can only be 'positive' (approval).[19]

I mentioned that approval and disapproval for Smith are special kinds of pleasure and pain, namely those arising from the comparison of original with sympathetic sentiments. This needs some justification. Smith never treats this very explicitly but, first of all, he does in the footnote already quoted call the positive case, approval, 'agreeable and delightful'. Furthermore, he has a whole chapter, called 'Of the Pleasure of Mutual Sympathy', in which he points out that sympathy has its own distinctive pleasure, both for the man who receives the sympathy, and for the man who gives it; and it is quite clear that sympathy here must mean, or include, approval.[20] In the same chapter he also deals with the negative

case, that is, what we should like him to call antipathy or disapproval, in
a parallel way. The conclusion must be that in this basic question of the
character of approval, Smith was in virtually complete agreement with
Hume: they would both maintain that approval and disapproval consist
of distinct emotions or passions.[21] Their whole argument is over the chain
of causes leading to those passions.

3 The mutuality of sympathy

I have already indicated more than once that sympathy for Smith is
something *mutual* between men. This feature of sympathy is, I suggest,
crucial for Smith's whole moral theory and, indeed, his idea of sympathy
is in itself hardly intelligible without it. Yet it is easy to undervalue the
importance of the mutual character of sympathy because of the way in
which the *Theory of Moral Sentiments* is composed. For although in the
second chapter of the book he treats 'Of the Pleasure of Mutual
Sympathy'; although as early as the fourth chapter[22] he gives a fairly
good description of the idea; and although one cannot get an adequate
understanding of Parts i and ii without presupposing it, it is not till
Part iii that the reader is presented with a thoroughgoing treatment. One
can say that in Parts i and ii Smith tells us how sympathy is *given*, whereas
in Part iii he shows how it is taken or *received*. But as one of Smith's
perhaps most original points is that the moral sentiments which he wants
to explain are the outcome of *both*, the first two Parts lose much of their
significance if they are not read in the light of Part iii.

Smith always takes it as a matter of course that man is social, that he is
bound to be together with his fellows. This means that he will always
literally have to look upon them; he is forced to watch them and see what
they are like, physically and morally, that is, as to behaviour:

Our first ideas of personal beauty and deformity, are drawn from the shape and
appearance of others, not from our own...In the same manner our first moral
criticisms are exercised upon the characters and conduct of other people.
(TMS, iii, i, §§ 4, 5)

Irrespective of the fact that men are naturally searching for agreement
with their fellows, as mentioned earlier, they are forced by their social
circumstances, by their merely being together, to *give* sympathy in the
neutral sense of trying to understand each other. But the important thing
is, that men will immediately discover by this means that their fellows are
watching them in the same way. 'We soon learn, that other people are
equally frank with regard to our own [character and conduct].'[23] Once we
realize this, we become aware for the first time of ourselves as persons with
a certain physical and, more importantly, moral appearance which can be
the subject of evaluation. The awareness of other people's observation and

evaluation of us makes us see that there is something to be observed and evaluated, and we naturally try to imagine what it can be, or how we suppose we look to other people.[24] It is thus the perception or, in my earlier terminology, the reception of other men's sympathetic endeavours that makes us conscious of our own mind. And if man, *per impossibile*, grew up outside society, such consciousness simply would not develop.[25]

Once this awareness of ourselves as subjects of judgement has been awakened in us, the desire of agreement drives us to try to judge ourselves as we imagine others would. This means that we have to act as spectators of ourselves at the same time as we are the agents who are judged of:

> When I endeavour to examine my own conduct, when I endeavour to pass sentence upon it, and either to approve or condemn it, it is evident that, in all such cases, I divide myself, as it were, into two persons; and that I, the examiner and judge, represents a different character from that other I, the person whose conduct is examined into and judged of. The first is the spectator, whose sentiments with regard to my own conduct I endeavour to enter into, by placing myself in his situation, and by considering how it would appear to me, when seen from that particular point of view. The second is the agent, the person whom I properly call myself, and of whose conduct, under the character of a spectator, I was endeavouring to form some opinion. The first is the judge; the second the person judged of. (TMS, iii, 1, § 6)

By means of sympathy we try to create a spectator position towards ourselves, we try to take up that view-at-a-distance which we perceive others take of us. This is a first sympathetic move. Next we try to imagine whether and to what extent such a spectator would be able to enter into our real position. This is a second sympathetic move. We then try to estimate the outcome of this second sympathetic move to see whether there will be agreement between our original motives and sentiments and those sympathetically created ones of the imagined spectator – that is, whether the imagined spectator approves or disapproves of our original sentiments and motives. Finally, we try to make this spectator approval or disapproval our own by a third sympathetic move consisting of a sympathy with the spectator. In this way we come to judge of our own behaviour by the same standard with which we judge of the behaviour of others, viz. whether it is proper or improper in the eyes of a spectator of our situation. All those moves are, I think, summarized in a single paragraph right at the beginning of Smith's treatment of the mutuality of sympathy, although his prose may not disclose it at first reading:

> We either approve or disapprove of our own conduct, according as we feel that, when we place ourselves in the situation of another man, and view it, as it were, with his eyes and from his station [first sympathetic move], we either can or cannot entirely enter into and sympathize with the sentiments and motives which influenced it [second sympathetic move and comparison]. We can never survey

our own sentiments and motives, we can never form any judgment concerning them, unless we remove ourselves, as it were, from our own natural station, and endeavour to view them as at a certain distance from us [first move]. But we can do this in no other way than by endeavouring to view them with the eyes of other people, or as other people are likely to view them...We endeavour to examine our own conduct as we imagine any other fair and impartial spectator would examine it [second move]. If, upon placing ourselves in his situation, we thoroughly enter into all the passions and motives which influenced it, we approve of it, by sympathy with the approbation of this supposed equitable judge. If otherwise, we enter into his disapprobation, and condemn it [third sympathetic move]. (TMS, iii, 1, § 2)

4 Common standards, ideal standards, and social adaptation

It is of the very greatest importance to understand exactly what role *others*, as spectators, play in the development and character of men's standards for moral self-evaluation. So far we have seen how they are a necessary condition for men's catching sight of themselves and their behaviour as objects of moral evaluation, and we have seen that this brings men to judge themselves by the same standard as they use for others, the standard of propriety. The question is, however, *what* propriety? Smith uses the whole first Part of *The Theory of Moral Sentiments* to explain propriety of action and the very first Section is 'Of the Sense of Propriety'. It is, therefore, natural to turn to that for an explanation:

In the suitableness or unsuitableness, in the proportion or disproportion, which the affection seems to bear to the cause or object which excites it, consists the propriety or impropriety, the decency or ungracefulness, of the consequent action. (TMS, i, i, 3, § 6)[26]

This may sound like an attempt at an absolute criterion of moral rightness. But one should not, of course, overlook the little 'seems': propriety is a principle to be used by men when as spectators they judge of each others' behaviour. And propriety-in-use clearly means the coincidence or agreement between the original sentiment of the agent and the sympathetic one of the spectator, with approval consequent upon the latter. And it is difficult to see how propriety could be anything but such propriety-in-use by particular spectators, for as Smith explains:

Every faculty in one man is the measure by which he judges of the like faculty in another. I judge of your sight by my sight, of your ear by my ear, of your reason by my reason, of your resentment by my resentment, of your love by my love. I neither have, nor can have, any other way of judging about them. (TMS, i, i, 3, § 10)

This sounds like a rather impossible subjectivism. But, of course, Smith's real feat is to show how men do have a common moral world with common standards. *How* do they get it? That is our problem, and the problem to which I alluded above by asking about the precise significance of the spectators. Now, if we stay in the first Part and the first Section, we will see that there already Smith goes some way towards what looks like an answer. He first points out how transitory and weak sympathetic feelings often are in comparison with their objects, the original feelings. He then goes on to say that this is normally anticipated and forestalled by the agent:

> The person principally concerned is sensible of this, and at the same time passionately desires a more complete sympathy. He longs for that relief which nothing can afford him but the entire concord of the affections of the spectators with his own...But he can only hope to obtain this by lowering his passion to that pitch, in which the spectators are capable of going along with him. He must flatten, if I may be allowed to say so, the sharpness of its natural tone, in order to reduce it to harmony and concord with the emotions of those who are about him. What they feel will, indeed, always be in some respects different from what he feels...; because the secret consciousness that the change of situations, from which the sympathetic sentiment arises, is but imaginary, not only lowers it in degree, but in some measure varies it in kind, and gives it a quite different modification. These two sentiments, however, may, it is evident, have such a correspondence with one another, as is sufficient for the harmony of society. Though they will never be unisons, they may be concords, and this is all that is wanted or required. (TMS, I, i, 4, § 7)[27]

This early passage is a prime example of how an adequate understanding presupposes knowledge of doctrines only stated later in the work. For quite clearly he is here using the idea of the mutuality of sympathy, of how sympathy is 'received', which I have presented already as it is developed in Part III. The 'lowering' of the passion on the part of the person sympathized with can only be understood in this way.

The reason for quoting the passage is that it ends by formulating a very important point rather clearly, namely that the operation of mutual sympathy unintendedly creates common social standards – standards which are at least sufficiently common to make social life possible. This again gives occasion for remarking various other points of very central importance in Smith. First of all, it shows that mutual sympathy is a mechanism for the selection of behaviour that is adequate to the situation, primarily the social situation, and that this is the efficient cause lurking beyond much of the teleological talk in Smith. This is possibly Smith's greatest contribution to social theory and it must be left for more extensive treatment at a later stage. Secondly, we are led to ask whether, according to Smith, the socially accepted and necessary is all there is to morality, or whether parts of morality can gain some independence of the commonly received, that is, whether moral ideals are possible. A theory to explain this must be able to account for how moral ideals develop out of social

morality, since the latter is the empirically given morality. It must therefore be a theory of how moral ideals can detach themselves from social
morality, how ideal morality can emerge from and become independent
of *de facto* morality.

It is exactly such a theory Smith is proposing. The standard by means
of which men judge of themselves is the same as that by which they judge
of others: propriety. And, as we remember, propriety is a question of the
aptness of a given action and its motive to its situation. This means that
although it is our appreciation of others' judgement of our behaviour,
through the mutual sympathy mechanism, that starts us judging ourselves,
this *leads* us to do so in terms of a standard *different from the opinion of
others*. We are started off by asking whether others would think our
behaviour proper, but this leads us to ask whether it is in fact proper. And
this latter question can only be answered if we take up the position of a
spectator of ourselves; not any concrete spectator, for he will have his own
particular interests and biases, just as we have ours. It must be the position
of 'a third person', an impartial spectator who is an ideal whom both
agents and actual spectators can approach. Instead of the propriety of
social morality, of the actual spectators, we are thus led to try and judge
ourselves in terms of an 'absolute' propriety for each given situation.

In this way it is *possible* for men to detach their morality, at least to
some extent, from the social circumstances which created it. And parallel
with this independence goes a desire to reach absolute propriety, for once
men feel that there is a distinction between that and what is thought to be
proper by society, they also realize that if there is any difference between
them, this must be due to misinformation on the part of the latter and that
only the former is genuine. There is here a healthy Socratic element in
Smith, as in Hume, to the effect that once the basic pattern of evaluation is
given the rest is to a large extent a matter of knowledge of the situation.

Just as a displacement can take place in the moral principle applied, so
it will be accompanied by a displacement in moral ideals. We are started
off in moral life trying to apply other men's ideas of propriety and aiming
at their approval and consequent praise; but we soon end up trying to
apply propriety as such, that is, the impartial spectator's idea of propriety,
and aiming at the approval and praise of the impartial spectator, aiming at
absolute approval and praiseworthiness.[28] This displacement is in no way
mysterious, for in scrutinizing our own behaviour and motives we must inevitably gain knowledge which is inaccessible to other men, and this makes
it possible for us to judge of and criticize other men's judgment of us. If we
thus come to the conclusion that we are either approved and praised or disapproved and blamed without deserving, or being 'worthy' of it, this
diminishes, or takes away, the pleasure/pain we receive from the judgment
of others. We do not consider their judgement morally correct any longer.[29]

In the same way, if we are not in fact praised or blamed but come to the conclusion that we deserve it, we put our own approval/disapproval in its place.[30]

When men in this way develop and internalize a morality which aspires to a certain independence, we can talk of the operation of their conscience, or of the impartial spectator in them: 'reason, principle, conscience, the inhabitant of the breast, the man within, the great judge and arbiter of our conduct'.[31] When men regulate their behaviour by this means we talk of their self-command, which is a kind of meta-virtue, since the other main virtues (prudence, justice, and benevolence) only gain their moral value when men are in command of themselves to perform them: 'Self-command is not only itself a great virtue, but from it all the other virtues seem to derive their principal lustre.'[32]

We have now seen how Smith's theory is able to explain the possibility of a morality which is independent, or at least partly independent, of social morality although it develops out of the latter with a displacement of actual spectators by the ideal of the impartial spectator. This distinction between 'high' morality and mere social opinion must, however, be handled with care, for although the former develops out of the latter, it will in its turn have a decisive influence on the latter. The subtleties of this relation are rather important to keep clear. First of all, we must notice that Smith insists that the seeking of social approval is not enough for the existence of society; a search for moral approval proper is necessary:

Nature, when she formed man for society, endowed him with an original desire to please, and an original aversion to offend his brethren. She taught him to feel pleasure in their favourable, and pain in their unfavourable regard. She rendered their approbation most flattering and most agreeable to him for its own sake; and their disapprobation most mortifying and most offensive. – But this desire of the approbation, and this aversion to the disapprobation of his brethren, would not alone have rendered him fit for the society for which he was made. Nature, accordingly, has endowed him, not only with a desire of being approved of, but with a desire of being what ought to be approved of; or of being what he himself approves of in other men. The first desire could only have made him wish to appear to be fit for society. The second was necessary in order to render him anxious to be really fit. (TMS, III, 2, §§ 6–7)

This may sound like little more than a traditional piece of homiletic natural theology, but in Smith it is always wise to think twice on such occasions. We shall leave the problem of teleological explanations till later and concentrate on the major question here: why is the search for social approval not enough for social life? Why is it necessary that men should seek higher moral approval? First of all we must remember that for Smith it is a simple matter of fact that men do seek such approval once society has started them in their moral life in the way we have already seen. But furthermore, we must remember that the seeking of social approval, of the approval of the actual spectators, is bound to lead to disagreement because we are differently related to our own behaviour in comparison with our spectators; we are naturally partial and we are often, in a sense, better informed. It is precisely this disagreement that induces us to look for a third and better standpoint from which to judge, and this search for a third standpoint is undertaken by agent and spectator alike. This is the point of Smith's comparison with the landscape seen through the little window and the landscape as well as the window seen from a third position equidistant from both.[33] It is in this sense we must understand that,

Before we can make any proper comparison of those opposite interests [our own and the spectator's], we must change our position. We must view them, neither from our own place nor yet from his, neither with our own eyes nor yet with his, but from the place and with the eyes of a third person, who has no particular connection with either, and who judges with impartiality between us. (TMS, III, 3, § 3)

In other words, the very seeking of social approval, of the approval of the actual spectators, has a strong tendency to become a search for another and higher judgement and approval which is *common to agent and spectator*. This search for a third standpoint of absolute impartiality may never, or very rarely, be completely successful, but the really important point, and the point which Smith tried to make in the previous quotation, is that it is the *search* itself which makes social life possible; it is the *search* for a common standpoint that is common, not necessarily the standpoint.[34] It is therefore this process of continuing search that really constitutes social morality.

But what does it mean that the moral life which keeps society together is such a process? It means that it is a continual weeding out of behaviour which is incompatible with social life. The operation of mutual sympathy in the search for a common, 'higher' standpoint is a mechanism for the adjustment of behaviour to the circumstances of society. Smith shows this by means of some striking examples from both the individual and the collective levels. Of the former, the most charming may be the case of how the child has its corners rubbed off:

when it is old enough to go to school, or to mix with its equals, it...naturally wishes to gain their favour, and to avoid their hatred or contempt...and it soon finds that it can do so in no other way than by moderating, not only its anger, but all its other passions, to the degree which its play fellows and companions are likely to be pleased with. It thus enters into the great school of self-command... (TMS, III, 3, § 22)[35]

The real spectator introduces the impartial spectator and the result is a lifelong adjustment of behaviour.[36] This idea of mutual sympathy as a selection procedure does, however, get a perhaps still better illustration when applied to the broader case of how a society adjusts to its situation. While his general description of this may sound like a rather vague form of functionalism, his application of the idea to particular types of societies makes it clear that he has more to offer by way of explanation. He contrasts 'barbarian' with 'civilized' societies, saying of the 'savage' that 'His circumstances not only habituate him to every sort of distress, but teach him to give way to none of the passions which that distress is apt to excite. He can expect from his countrymen no sympathy or indulgence for such weakness.'[37] By comparison,

A humane and polished people, who have more sensibility to the passions of others, can more readily enter into an animated and passionate behaviour, and can more easily pardon some little excess. The person principally concerned is sensible of this; and being assured of the equity of his judges, indulges himself in stronger expressions of passion... (TMS, v, 2, § 10)

More reasoning of the same kind allows Smith at length to draw his conclusion: 'In general the style of manners which takes place in any nation may commonly, upon the whole, be said to be that which is most suitable to its situation.'[38] We can now see that there is nothing strange in this conclusion, for Smith is very well able to specify the efficient cause for the general fittingness of behaviour to its situation. It is simply that behaviour which is not so fitted will tend to be weeded out by means of antipathy conveyed through the mutual sympathy mechanism, whereas behaviour which is fitting will tend to be reinforced by approval conveyed in the same way. This is of outstanding importance for it shows that however much teleological talk Smith allows himself, he can do so perfectly legitimately. He has an efficient cause which can explain the seeming purposefulness of human behaviour.

Again we find that Hume has anticipated this suggestion:

No quality of human nature is more remarkable, both in itself and in its consequences, than that propensity we have to sympathize with others, and to receive by communication their inclinations and sentiments, however different from, or contrary to our own. This is not only conspicuous in children, who implicitly embrace every opinion proposed to them; but also in men of the greatest judgment and understanding, who find it very difficult to follow their own reason or inclination, in opposition to that of their friends and daily companions. To this principle we ought to ascribe the great uniformity we may observe in the humours and turn of thinking of those of the same nation; and 'tis much more probable, that this resemblance arises from sympathy, than from any influence of the soil and climate. (T. 316–17)[39]

It is this kind of mutual sympathy which for both Hume and Smith provides the possibility of education. From the hand of nature all men are basically alike, but education can make them different for education

consists in exposure to a variety of situations from which new lines of
behaviour and thinking are picked up through mutual sympathy with
other participants in the educational process. Such education derived
from one's situation explains the difference between the philosopher and
the porter,[40] as well as the differences between the character of the Dutch,
the English, and the Scots in connection with commerce.[41]

We have so far allowed a certain amount of equivocation in our treatment of Smith's idea of the selection of behaviour through mutual sympathy. The point he is mainly trying to make in the chapter from which
we last quoted is that although the selection always takes place by means
of mutual sympathy, this may not lead to the implication of the impartial
spectator in certain limited areas of behaviour, because of the influence of
customs, habits, and fashions. In such limited areas the search for his
standpoint, that is, for 'natural' or absolute propriety, is not invariably
required for the very existence of society, and accordingly a certain straying away from this search can take place under the guidance of customs
and fashions without being weeded out. But this influence of custom and
fashion can only concern 'the propriety or impropriety of *particular*
usages' and not 'the *general* style of character and behaviour'. Smith
explains this by means of an especially horrifying example of a 'particular usage', the exposure of children in ancient Greece. This practice
had its origins in savage times when it was necessary and could be approved
of as proper; but it was continued into civilized times through the influence
of 'uninterrupted custom', reinforced by 'far fetched considerations of
public utility', although it must clearly be considered highly improper in
that situation if judged from an impartial viewpoint. When a thing like
this could happen under the influence of custom, one might think that
everything in human morality could be swayed by custom and fashion.
But this cannot be the case, according to Smith:

There is an obvious reason why custom should never pervert our sentiments with
regard to the general style and character of conduct and behaviour, in the same
degree as with regard to the propriety or unlawfulness of particular usages.
There never can be any such custom. No society could subsist a moment, in
which the *usual* strain of men's conduct and behaviour was of a piece with the
horrible practice I have just now mentioned [i.e. the exposure of children].
(TMS, v, 2, § 16)

In other words, if men did not in *general* search for 'the natural propriety
of action', instead of resting content with what is socially customary or
fashionable, then society would be in imminent danger of breaking down,
thus extinguishing such behaviour.

This discussion in Smith is, of course, designed to show how deviations
from the search for the standpoint of the impartial spectator can occur in
human life when we know that this search is a natural development for

man as a social being. Apart from the influence of custom and fashion, Smith discusses the influence of considerations of utility,[42] a discussion we will return to later, and he naturally deals with the influence of men's partiality and egoism. This latter is particularly important as it introduces the general rules of morality.[43]

5 General rules and moral value

Smith's contrast between 'particular usages' and 'the general style of conduct' in the discussion above of the selection of behaviour must not be confused with a discussion of general rules. Obviously, the kind of 'particular usages' he has in mind may very well be formulated in general rules. Nevertheless, there is an intimate connection between the selection of behaviour and the general rules: the result of the selection of behaviour is simply the general rules. Certain actions are repeatedly selected through sympathy as proper, others as improper, in the way we have had described above. By and by this recurrent pattern will stand out clearly and men can, so to speak, read it off as rules or guidelines for their behaviour:

We do not originally approve or condemn particular actions, because, upon examination, they appear to be agreeable or inconsistent with a certain general rule. The general rule, on the contrary, is formed by finding from experience that all actions of a certain kind, or circumstanced in a certain manner, are approved of. (TMS, III, 4, § 8)

The general rules of morality are thus the unintended outcome of a multitude of individual instances of natural moral evaluation, but once they are in existence they are quite capable of directing our moral evaluations. Then 'we frequently appeal to them as to the standards of judgment'. And since the general rules are mankind's attempts to sum up their approaches to the standpoint of the impartial spectator in various types of situations, men feel obliged by them because of their sympathy with the impartial spectator. This means that if they break the rules without an overriding moral reason, or a higher rule, they will feel that they are incurring the disapproval of the impartial spectator; and once this is internalized, a sense of duty has been created.[44] This theory of obligation and duty is obviously very similar to that of Hume, and while it is only vaguely outlined when Smith discusses general rules, it is worked out with great clarity in his treatment of contracts in the *Lectures on Jurisprudence*, as we shall see.[45]

All Smith's ideas of how a social morality is formed and of how an ideal morality develops out of it are given in purely descriptive terms. It is a *science* of morals. And yet I venture to suggest that it is of clear normative import as well. Like all good scientific laws, Smith's is universal. It covers himself as well as all other human beings and thus shows us how *he* understands moral ideas, how *he* evaluates. And just as with Hume, we must remember that in Smith's view men can never start morally from scratch: they are always living in a society and thus in a context of aims, values, and ideals. Moral evaluation is therefore only relevant in such a context. It is never a matter of goodness or badness, justice or injustice, *per se*; but of goodness or badness, etc., against the background of a number of other values. Each of these other values, aims, etc., may itself be questioned but never the whole system, for that would be equivalent to a state of nature. It would, in other words, be impossible.

It is in this light that I suggest we see Smith's idea of the impartial spectator. When we strive towards his standpoint we are in reality seeking the position which is most widely compatible with existing values, the position which fits the moral context. This is obviously not an absolute and final test. On the other hand it does not make moral judgements completely relative to the given system of morality for, as we have seen, the standpoint of the impartial spectator implies a universal rule and it is by seeking this that we can gain independence from the given social morality. So it would seem that when we judge of the moral value of an action we consider whether it is in accordance with a general rule and whether the type of action prescribed by this rule is generally compatible with existing values. Smith's strong stress on the primacy of the situational factors in the very structure of moral evaluations makes his account of the formation of the common moral ideals, the standpoints of the impartial spectator, more straightforward than Hume's. And also, Smith's theory of the mutuality of sympathy is considerably more detailed than anything in Hume. Despite these differences the basic approach is, however, the same. The decisive element in our understanding as well as in our exercise of moral evaluation is the social context or situation in which it takes place.

Smith's claim that human behaviour is judged on the basis of its situation, or in terms of propriety, makes moral judgement part of a general, contextualist view of human knowledge which we will discuss below.[46] And it is in this wide perspective that we must understand his treatment of the influence on our judgement of what follows upon any action judged of; for in his various discussions of this problem we can see it as a common general feature that there can only be such influence, if what follows upon the action is somehow put in relation to the situation in which the action took place. So the basic pattern of evaluation remains the same, situational propriety. Smith is particularly concerned with this problem when he discusses judgement in terms of merit/demerit in Part II of *The Theory of Moral Sentiments*, and when he presents his ideas on how utility influences 'the sentiment of approbation' in Part IV. But the theme also occurs in many other contexts throughout the book.

6 Merit and demerit

Smith introduces the problem of propriety versus merit in Part ɪ of *The Theory of Moral Sentiments*, when he points out that men in fact judge human behaviour and its motivation,

under two different aspects, or in two different relations; first, in relation to the cause which excites it...; secondly, in relation to the end which it proposes, or the effect which it tends to produce. – In the suitableness or unsuitableness, in the proportion or disproportion, which the affection [behind the action] seems to bear to the cause or object which excites it, consists the propriety or impropriety, the decency or ungracefulness, of the consequent action. – In the beneficial or hurtful nature of the effects which the affection aims at, or tends to produce, consists the merit or demerit of the action, the qualities by which it is entitled to reward, or is deserving of punishment. (TMS, ɪ, i, 3, §§ 5–7)

Smith then goes on to make the contrast between 'philosophers' and men 'in common life' which we noticed at the beginning of this chapter:

Philosophers have, of late years, considered chiefly the tendency of affections, and have given little attention to the relation which they stand in to the cause which excites them. In common life, however, when we judge of any person's conduct, and of the sentiments which directed it, we constantly consider them under both these aspects. (TMS, ɪ, i, 3, § 8)

The end of this quotation seems to suggest that the two principles of moral judgement are on a par and supplement each other, but this impression is deceptive, for when we turn to Smith's main treatment in Part ɪɪ 'Of Merit and Demerit', we will see that his whole point is that judgement in terms of propriety is the basic feature, whereas judgement in terms of merit is dependent upon this.

The foundation for judgements of merit and demerit is, naturally, two passions, gratitude and resentment, respectively. When an action meets with gratitude we say that there is some merit in it. If the reaction is one of resentment we say that the action has demerit. The first reaction naturally points towards reward, the second towards punishment, in a broad sense.[47] Smith takes care to point out that these two kinds of reaction are always tied up with the original action in the sense that the gratitude and reward, or resentment and punishment, are always given for, or because of, the action. This distinguishes gratitude and resentment from love and hatred which are likewise passions concerned with the happiness or misfortune of others, for the two latter passions need not be felt *because of* anything specifically done to the person who feels them.[48] This characteristic of gratitude and resentment leads directly to the heart of the matter. One can say that when a spectator tries to evaluate a judgement of merit or demerit, he is really concerned with two actions, on the one hand the original action, and on the other hand the action consisting of a

feeling of gratitude/resentment plus the consequent judgement of merit/
demerit and conferring of reward or punishment. This means that the
spectator can only judge the latter if he first judges the former; as the
latter is a reaction to the former, the former constitutes an essential part of
the *situation* in which the latter occurs. The propriety of reward or
punishment is naturally to be judged of in terms of the spectator's
sympathetically created, natural feelings of gratitude or resentment,[49] but
he can only reach this through an adequate picture of the situation, and
this involves a judgement of the propriety of the original action. And so, in
the words of the long heading to Chapter 3,

> where there is no approbation of the conduct of the person who confers the
> benefit, there is little sympathy with the gratitude of him who receives it:
> and..., on the contrary, where there is no disapprobation of the motives of the
> person who does the mischief, there is no sort of sympathy with the resentment
> of him who suffers it. (TMS, ii, i, 3)

The moral evaluation of one action is dependent upon the moral evaluation of another when the latter is part of the former's situational logic, but
both evaluations are conducted by means of sympathy and in terms of
propriety.[50] This leads Smith to the conclusion that 'the sense of merit
[and of demerit] seems to be a compounded sentiment'. It involves two
sympathetic moves, with two consequent moral sentiments of approval or
disapproval, one for the original action and one for the reaction, which
consists of gratitude or resentment – or as Smith says, 'a direct sympathy
with the sentiments of the agent, and an indirect sympathy with the
gratitude of those who receive the benefit of his actions', and in the
negative case of demerit, 'a direct antipathy to the sentiments of the agent,
and an indirect sympathy with the resentment of the sufferer'.[51] Smith's
distinction between direct and indirect sympathy here may seem curious.
As far as I can see, all there is to it is that in order to reach the indirect
sympathy and its attendant evaluation, one has to go through the direct
sympathy and its attendant evaluation.

We can conclude that Smith stays firmly within his theory of moral
evaluation in terms of propriety by this dissolution of judgements in terms
of merit/demerit into two propriety-judgements. But we can conclude
more than that. Smith's analysis shows that the moral evaluation of the
motives behind the original action is independent of whether or not the
action in fact results in invoking gratitude/resentment in those who are
affected by the action. When we judge we try to do so as independent
spectators, that is, in terms of our own sympathetically created feelings of
gratitude/resentment and not in terms of the actual feelings of gratitude/
resentment in others.

This is the standpoint an impartial spectator would ideally take, but it
is a standpoint from which both he and, to a much higher degree, any

actual spectator are only too easily deflected. Ideally the only important circumstance in the evaluation of the propriety or impropriety of a judgement about merit, is the propriety or impropriety of the motive behind the original action which called forth this judgement. But the action and its consequences will easily intrude themselves and can often more or less steal the show. 'And, as the consequences of actions are altogether under the empire of fortune, hence arises her influence upon the sentiments of mankind with regard to merit or demerit.'[52]

This distortion of men's sense of propriety through the influence of fortune can happen because the pleasure/pain which is created by the actual consequence of an action is spontaneously referred backwards to the motive or intention behind the action in the form of gratitude/ resentment. This happens to some extent even when the consequences cannot possibly have been intended. For although we now immediately correct ourselves when we feel resentment at, and maybe even 'punish', a stone over which we stumble, the history of law shows that men have not always undertaken such corrections of their spontaneous feelings with regard to inanimate things (let alone animals). Indeed, elements of this were still to be found in contemporary law, as Smith showed in his *Lectures on Jurisprudence*.[53]

When people's judgement can be so completely side-tracked by the 'actions' of inanimate things which cannot have any intentions behind them, it is hardly to be wondered at that this will be a feature of their judgement of their fellow men. Here both intentions and actual consequences do in fact function as causes exciting our judgement and if either of them is missing, the judgement is affected accordingly. Smith summarizes this effect in the following way:

The effect of this influence of fortune, is, first to diminish our sense of the merit or demerit of those actions which arose from the most laudable or blameable intentions, when they fail of producing their proposed effects: and, secondly, to increase our sense of the merit or demerit of actions, beyond what is due to the motives or affections from which they proceed, when they accidently give occasion either to extraordinary pleasure or pain. (TMS, ii, iii, 2, § 1)

This bias in all judgements of propriety is, naturally, communicated by means of mutual sympathy throughout any social group. Hence it is that although the ideal objects of our moral judgements are motives and intentions, the actual objects are often actions and their consequences.[54]

This is a most extraordinary combination of an ideal ethics of intentions with an actual ethics of consequences. Moreover, it serves Smith to good explanatory purpose, for it is precisely this combination which enables him to interpret morality as a guide to external action in a world of fortune and yet at the same time to see this morality as ultimately concerned with ideal and absolute propriety. It is important to notice that Smith particularly stresses the former in its negative aspect, in terms of transgressions of the negative virtue of justice. He is here providing the foundation for part of his theory of punishment:

Sentiments, designs, affections, though it is from these that according to cool reason human actions derive their whole merit or demerit, are placed by the great Judge of hearts beyond the limits of every human jurisdiction...That necessary rule of justice, therefore, that men in this life are liable to punishment for their actions only, not for their designs and intentions, is founded upon this salutary and useful irregularity in human sentiments concerning merit and demerit, which at first sight appears so absurd and unaccountable. (TMS, ii, iii, 3, § 2)[55]

But although this 'irregularity' provides useful guidance in the *forum externum* of social life, it by no means excludes a *forum internum* where the spectator tries to rid himself of all distortion in the search for a judgement based upon a standard of absolute propriety, the standard of the impartial spectator. The person whose merit or lack of demerit is being belied by the influence of fortune on his actions,

summons up his whole magnanimity and firmness of soul and strives to regard himself, not in the light in which he at present appears, but in that which he ought to appear, in which he would have appeared had his generous designs been crowned with success, and in which he would still appear, notwithstanding their miscarriage, if the sentiments of mankind were either altogether candid and equitable, or even perfectly consistent with themselves. (TMS, ii, iii, 3, § 6)

It should be noticed that this passage spells out what is behind one of Smith's frequently repeated, and somewhat strange sounding phrases: (a) what is, (b) what ought to be, (c) what upon a certain condition would be, the opinion of the spectator. The first gives the standpoint of the actual spectator; the second that of the impartial spectator; and the third indicates the way the former can approach the latter – through the sympathetic understanding of the situation and of human nature. It is this last point that makes Smith talk of consistency in the sentiments of mankind: hence the Socratic role of knowledge in morals. At the same time this formula sums up the ambitious dual intention that the theory should provide, on the one hand, the framework for explanations of social morality in a given society, and that it should be, on the other hand, a theory of universal and ideal morality. The great simplicity in the theory is that it uses the same explanatory principle for both, viz. selection through mutual sympathy. As we have seen, it is mutual sympathy between actual spectators, patients, and agents that establishes a social morality, but at the same time it inevitably establishes the search for the ideal spectator and his moral standards.

7 The role of utility

Smith's recognition that a regard to actions may disturb the actual spectator's appreciation of motives should of course not be taken as a concession to consequentialist theories of morality. Apart from all that has already been said above about the spectator approach, Part IV of *The Theory of Moral Sentiments* provides us with a direct criticism in this respect. This Part, which is entitled 'Of the Effect of Utility upon the Sentiment of Approbation', is one of the most intricate pieces of argument in the whole book. It is divided into two chapters; in the first Smith introduces the problem by showing what influence utility has on our evaluation of 'all the Products of Art' while in the second he transfers the discussion to moral evaluation. He starts off by a presentation of what he takes to be Hume's idea of utility, as a means to happiness, and of his idea of how utility pleases 'by perpetually suggesting', through the imagination, this pleasant end-result which the useful object of evaluation 'is fitted to promote', and he reminds us of how this becomes a common standard for evaluation through spectator sympathy.[56] By presenting Hume's views in this way Smith clearly shows that he did not think that Hume distinguished between the two meanings of utility which his dual use of the concept led us to suspect that he was getting at, namely means-utility and end-utility.[57] Furthermore, Smith himself does not clarify this distinction. For him the concept of utility encompasses both means and ends, but it should be noticed that the ends are never dealt with as anything of specific importance, let alone presented as of any particular content. This is a point of significance when we come to deal with the relationship between justice and utility below (pp. 87–9).

In a way it is puzzling that Smith does not achieve this clarification of the concept of utility for he plainly has, as it were, the means to do so. This is demonstrated throughout Part IV. His strategy is first to criticize Hume for not distinguishing between the influence of means and the influence of ends in our evaluations, and for operating with utility, in the sense of means-and-ends. All the same, he never connects these two points into a distinction between two senses of '*utility*'. He then devotes the bulk of Part IV to showing the importance of distinguishing between means and ends for the understanding of, first, aesthetic evaluations, then, moral evaluation. Taken in that order Smith's argument proceeds as follows.

Although Hume is quite right that we often conduct our evaluation of artefacts by reference to the value of the end they produce, it has generally been overlooked that very often the end itself is out of view and the evaluation proceeds entirely in terms of the means. That is to say, we judge a thing in terms of its goal-directedness without considering the goal, in terms of how well-contrived it is without taking into regard what it is contrived for:

> But that this fitness, this happy contrivance of any production of art, should often be more valued than the very end for which it was intended; and that the exact adjustment of the means for attaining any conveniency or pleasure should frequently be more regarded than that very conveniency or pleasure, in the attainment of which their whole merit would seem to consist, has not, so far as I know, been yet taken notice of by anybody. (TMS, IV, I, § 3)

Smith first illustrates this with three well-known and rather charming examples of an 'aesthetic' character; the man who absolutely must re-arrange the chairs, the man who cannot get his watch precise enough, and the 'many people [who] ruin themselves by laying out money on trinkets of frivolous utility'.[58] In all cases the general aim is lost sight of, and the system and order of the means is regarded as the main thing. This has been called 'value-displacement'.[59] In so far as this is taken as a literal description it may be rather unfortunate; it may very well be the case that no actual displacement occurs, if by this is meant a process of switching from a view of the goal to a view of the means. The goal may never actually have been clearly in the mind of any individual. This is shown by the following, much more important illustration. Smith simply argues that most of the striving for social betterment that goes on in society, and that begins as early as childhood and youth, is motivated by 'the same love of system, the same regard to the beauty of order, of art and contrivance', rather than by any clear view of what it is all supposed to lead to. This is his theory of vanity which is the focal point for some of the most important themes in Smith, including the idea of the mechanism that makes society a continuous process. We shall store these themes for later commentary and take only these important paragraphs as illustrating the structure of an important species of human evaluation.[60]

As if it was not enough for Smith to suggest to us the parallel between the rearrangement of chairs and social mobility in the broadest sense, his concluding paragraph allows us to see the parallel between 'frivolous trinkets' and the political institutions of society – as far, that is, as the mode of their evaluation is concerned. The latter are also often judged more with a view to whether they constitute a 'grand system' or not than whether they

> tend to promote the happiness of those who live under them. This is their sole use and end. From a certain spirit of system,[61] however, from a certain love of art and contrivance, we sometimes seem to value the means more than the end, and to be eager to promote the happiness of our fellow-creatures, rather from a view to perfect and improve a certain beautiful and orderly system than from any immediate sense or feeling of what they either suffer or enjoy. (TMS, IV, I, § 11)

This particular example provides a nice transition to the following chapter where Smith starts by making the point that, since various institutions in civil society serve to make up for deficiencies in human nature and since such institutions are evaluated according to how useful they are in creating happiness, it might be thought that the virtues which would make the institutions redundant, if such virtues were the rule among men, would be evaluated in the same way. In other words, Smith presents Hume's idea that human character and its motives are judged in terms of their tendency to be useful or harmful. Here follows Smith's second great qualification of Hume's theory in this context. The idea that moral judgements are made in terms of the tendency of the character judged of is, says Smith, a speculative philosophical construction and not a true reflection of how men in fact judge. In order to prosecute this criticism Smith invokes his own contextualist view of moral judgement to good purpose. When the philosopher looks upon human behaviour he does so from a general and abstract point of view. He relates characters and motives to their tendencies and evaluates and classifies them accordingly. This, however, inevitably leads him to neglect the situation, the context, in which the particular character functions in each individual case, and it is precisely in terms of this context that men in common life judge morally. Moral judgement is a particular judgement, not a general and typifying judgement. The general consideration of tendencies and effects is an afterthought which may come in later and gain some influence upon situational judgement, but the latter must remain the basic element.[62] It is thus Smith's contextualism that is the real background to his criticisms of Hume's 'Philosopher's mistake':

This beauty and deformity which characters appear to derive from their usefulness or inconveniency, are apt to strike in a peculiar manner those who consider, in an abstract and philosophical light, the actions and conduct of mankind. When a philosopher goes to examine why humanity is approved of or cruelty condemned, he does not always form to himself, in a very clear and distinct manner, the conception of any one particular action either of cruelty or of humanity, but is commonly contented with the vague and indeterminate idea which the general names of those qualities suggest to him. But it is in particular instances only that the propriety or impropriety, the merit or demerit, of actions is very obvious and discernible. It is only when particular examples are given that we perceive distinctly either the concord or disagreement between our own affections and those of the agent, or feel a social gratitude arise towards him in the one case, or a sympathetic resentment in the other. When we consider virtue and vice in an abstract and general manner, the qualities by which they excite these several sentiments seem in a great measure to disappear, and the sentiments themselves become less obvious and discernible. On the contrary, the happy effects of the one, and the fatal consequences of the other, seem then to rise up to the view, and, as it were, to stand out and distinguish themselves from all the other qualities of either. (TMS, IV, 2, § 2)

When we compare the argument of this very central passage with that of
the previous chapter, as outlined above, we can see the general idea in
Smith's treatment of utility. As far as the judgement of artificial objects is
concerned we normally go beyond the thing immediately judged of, and
are obliged to do so, in order to see what it is 'good for'. Hume is therefore right in saying that we judge such things in terms of their utility, if
this is taken to mean that we judge them according to their real or
imagined contribution to, or part in, some over-all system. But since we
may not have the faintest idea of, or interest in, what the system as a
whole is 'good for', there is no general standard by which we judge
artificial objects. In particular there is no reason to think that we always
evaluate such objects in terms of what they are 'good for' in creating
happiness. It is the over-all system, whatever its real or imagined nature,
and not any such universal value that is important. This is all very
different when we judge morally. We are here judging human character
and human motivation, but we can only judge these on the basis of their
expression in action. In contrast to objects, actions do, however, have an
extra element of concreteness, in that they are events which occur at a
particular time. In order to have an adequate understanding of them we
are therefore bound to judge them in their relationship to the immediate
background or situation in which they occur. It is only when we have done
this that any further relationships can be drawn in, and it is inevitable
that judgements – general or particular – about the 'utility' of actions,
about their underlying motive, or about the character of the agent, must
be secondary to judgements in terms of concrete situational propriety.[63]

Smith backs up this conclusion about moral judgement by two more
points. The first takes up seven lines, the second more than eleven pages,
but it would be foolhardy to judge their importance by their length. The
first reads as little more than a mere assertion:

first of all, it seems impossible that the approbation of virtue should be a sentiment of the same kind with that by which we approve of a convenient and well-
contrived building; or, that we should have no other reason for praising a man
than that for which we commend a chest of drawers. (TMS, IV, 2, § 4)

The 'convenient and well-contrived building' which appears here is a
reference to Hume's *Treatise*, p. 617, where 'a convenient house' also
appears and this little paragraph rebuts one of the central contentions of
Hume's theory. In the *Treatise*, p. 617, and, in greater detail, pp. 471–3,[64]
Hume tries to face up to the problem Smith mentions in the quotation
above:

if virtue and vice be determin'd by pleasure and pain, these qualities must, in
every case, arise from the sensations; and consequently any object, whether
animate or inanimate, rational or irrational, might become morally good or evil,
provided it can excite a satisfaction or uneasiness. (T. 471)

His answer is, briefly, that although there is a sufficient family resemblance between the various kinds of pleasure and pain 'to make them be expressed by the same abstract term',[65] the pleasure and pain attending moral judgement are, as a matter of empirical fact, distinct:

a convenient house, and a virtuous character, cause not the same feeling of approbation; even tho' the source of our approbation be the same, and flow from sympathy and an idea of their utility. There is something very inexplicable in this variation of our feelings; but 'tis what we have experience of with regard to all our passions and sentiments. (T. 617)

Smith did not find 'this variation of our feelings' so 'very inexplicable'. Although he would agree with Hume that both evaluations of artefacts and evaluations of moral matters are pleasant or painful,[66] he would claim that he could explain their differences by detailing the difference in their causes. The former is plainly the pleasure/pain of utility/disutility. The latter, the pleasure/pain of moral approval/disapproval, is obviously the pleasure/pain of agreement/disagreement between spectator and agent, and such agreement or disagreement is only to be found through a sympathetic inquiry into the situation of the person principally concerned, that is, through understanding of his background and context. When Hume, therefore, points out that, "'Tis only when a character is considered in general, without reference to our particular interest, that it causes such a [peculiar] feeling or sentiment, as denominates it morally good or evil',[67] Smith would quite agree, but he would at the same time point out that such a general and impartial point of view is reached through sympathetic understanding of another's situation and not through understanding of useful tendencies in the character concerned.[68] It is, I think, in this sense we must understand Smith's statement at the end of the second chapter of Part IV, 'that so far as the sentiment of approbation arises from the perception of this beauty of utility, it has no reference of any kind to the sentiments of others'.[69] It is not the useful tendency as such that interests us in, or refers us to, others; but when we, through social life, have in fact got an interest in others, by means of mutual sympathy, then utility can gain moral importance. This is what Smith can hide under the cloak of a mere assertion.

His second way of arguing against the idea that the useful tendency of characters and motives is the basis for moral evaluation is to show that the qualities of the human mind which are in fact useful either to the person himself or to his fellow men are rarely judged in terms of this as 'the first ground of...approbation'.[70] He does this by taking up a number of examples where those qualities (reason and self-command; humanity, justice, generosity, and public spirit) are approved of, not because of any useful tendency, and often in spite of harm to the persons themselves, but because they meet with the approval of the actual and/or the impartial spectator(s). The motive for moral behaviour is not utility but spectator approval and, if possible, the spectator praise and admiration which follow when we are able to surprise the spectator and make him wonder through an exertion above the normal and expected.[71]

Part IV constitutes a formidable piece of argument against utility as a source of moral evaluation, but Smith takes care not to overstate his case. He does not say that consideration of utility has no influence upon moral judgement. What he says is, 'that it is not the view of. . . utility or hurtful-ness which is either the first or principal source of our approbation and disapprobation'.[72] The question is, then, *how* does consideration of utility come to influence moral judgement, and thus behaviour? This is one of the most exciting questions one can ask in connection with Smith for it opens up a most extraordinary theoretical construction. Smith's immediate answer to our question is simply that the idea of utility is an 'after-thought'.[73] The useful tendency of a human character or action is some-thing we can recognize after the event and this recognition may thus strengthen our original judgement which was based upon propriety: 'utility, when we come to view it, bestows upon [moral actions] un-doubtedly a new beauty, and upon that account still further recommends them to our approbation'.[74] But this recognition of the utility of moral behaviour is not a common thing in men's moral judgements. It is a kind of abstraction because it goes beyond the context in which the action occurs and it is, therefore, more a matter for philosophical speculation: 'This beauty, however, is chiefly perceived by men of reflection and speculation, and is by no means the quality which first recommends such actions to the natural sentiments of the bulk of mankind.'[75] Such philo-sophical speculation will, however, be evoked not only by pure philo-sophical curiosity but also when moral judgements are challenged,[76] a theme we shall return to in connection with justice. Presumably regard to utility will come into men's moral outlook from both sources, functioning as a support for their ordinary moral judgement in terms of situational propriety. The reality of this influence is touched upon a number of times by Smith. Thus for example in his treatment of the broad classes of virtue he points out that,

In our approbation of all those virtues [of prudence, justice, and beneficence], our sense of their agreeable effects, of their utility, either to the person who exercises them or to some other persons, joins with our sense of their propriety, and constitutes always a considerable, frequently the greater, part of that appro-bation. – But in our approbation of the virtues of self-command, complacency with their effects sometimes constitutes no part, and frequently but a small part, of that approbation. (TMS, VI, Conclusion §§ 6–7)

Moreover when Smith criticizes Hutcheson's moral sense theory he points out that the following four sources of moral evaluation seem to be exhaustive, leaving no room for any special moral sense: (1) judgement of the propriety of the motives of the agent; (2) judgement of the propriety of the motives of the patient; and then two supporting sources: (3) the general rules formed out of, and afterwards to some extent regulating, judgements of propriety, and (4) regard to the useful tendency of motives and actions.[77]

Utility is a real source of moral judgement, although a secondary one. But in what sense secondary? Here the parallel with general rules is suggestive. Just as the general rules, as we noted earlier, arise out of individual actions which are judged morally in terms of situational propriety, so useful consequences tend to follow from such moral actions. In both cases this unforeseen product of moral behaviour and judgement is only recognized afterwards and it is only then that it comes to have an influence on moral judgement and behaviour.

Clearly Smith is here making the enormous presupposition that moral behaviour does in fact tend to have useful consequences in the world as we know it. This is, however, not merely a presupposition in Smith, it is an explicitly stated doctrine.[78] When men act in the morally proper way the outcome of such behaviour is, in general, of a useful tendency. Or, to put it bluntly, by and large in this world virtue pays: 'virtue is upon all ordinary occasions, even with regard to this life, real wisdom, and the surest and readiest means of obtaining both safety and advantage'.[79] We may take this as a rather extreme case of Enlightenment optimism or as one of the traditional teleological non-explanations of natural theology. We may also look closer at the text, for Smith goes on in the following manner:

Our success or disappointment in our undertakings must very much depend upon the good or bad opinion which is commonly entertained of us, and upon the general disposition of those we live with, either to assist or to oppose us. But the best, the surest, the easiest, and the readiest way of obtaining the advantageous and of avoiding the unfavourable judgments of others, is, undoubtedly, to render ourselves the proper objects of the former and not of the latter. (TMS, vii, ii, 2, § 13)

Men are bound to live in society and in most of their doings they are dependent upon the assistance of their fellow men, at least in the minimal sense that the latter do not obstruct their activity, and often in the sense of positive help. To have this condition fulfilled is one of the greatest advances towards success in one's actions. To obtain this it is, however, necessary to reach some conformity with one's fellows about the way in which one can go about one's business. Since such conformity is sought from all sides, it amounts to an adaptation which renders the behaviour of individuals as compatible as possible. This seeking of conformity in the outlook on behaviour is, as we know, reached by means of mutual sympathy and, as we also know, mutual sympathy has a tendency to gravitate towards a common, impartial standpoint, or at least to create the idea, and ideal, of such a standpoint. Obviously, the more this impartial standpoint is followed, the more compatible the behaviour of individuals will become; which is just another way of saying that the more people pursue their various aims in accordance with the impartial spectator's standards of virtuous propriety, the less resistance, and the more assistance, they will meet from their fellows, that is, the more useful they will be to themselves and to their fellow men. Optimism or not, Smith has an explanation to offer.

Smith is, however, not unduly optimistic. What he is saying is that unless men *in general* approached moral behaviour pretty closely, and unless this *in general* led to successful results, it would simply be impossible to understand how society, and thus mankind, could survive; but this does not, of course, prevent there being exceptions in individual instances and in particular kinds of behaviour.[80]

8 The role of religion

If one still finds Smith too optimistic and unrealistic because it is difficult to understand how disappointments in individual cases should not be enough to cause a more widespread breakdown of morality and thus of society, then one should remember two further features of his theory. First of all, the theory of the impartial spectator is a theory of how the reaction to such disappointments can be internalized. In cases where the virtue of a way of behaving is not understood and appreciated by the surrounding society, man has, at least to a certain extent, the ability to take up the standpoint of the impartial spectator which gives him the possibility of gaining the approval of the 'man within' independently of the judgement of the 'man without'. This approval can function as a compensation and consolation for lost opportunities in the social world.[81] Secondly, if this is not enough, man has 'an appeal to a still higher tribunal', to God.[82]

When Smith's theology is touched upon the sympathy of most commentators seems to become very weak indeed, but again I recommend caution and a close reading of what he has to say. Let us begin with a rather central formulation:

When we...despair of finding any force upon earth which can check the triumph of injustice, we naturally appeal to heaven, and hope that the great Author of our nature will himself execute hereafter, what all the principles which he has given us for the direction of our conduct prompt us to attempt even here; that he will complete the plan which he himself has thus taught us to begin; and will, in a life to come, render to every one according to the works which he has performed in this world. And thus we are led to the belief in a future state, not only by the weaknesses, by the hopes and fears of human nature, but by the noblest and best principles which belong to it, by the love of virtue, and by the abhorrence of vice and injustice. (TMS, iii, 5, § 10)

The first thing to note about religious belief is that it is a consequence of, a function of morality. Men believe in God and an after-life because they are led to it by their moral convictions. The former is a continuation and completion of the latter, and religion thus becomes a strong support of morality, 'religion enforces the natural sense of duty'.[83] This idea of religion as primarily a function and continuation of morality is so striking in Smith, that it seems reasonable to call his view moral theology, with due respect to Kant and no wish to make a comparison in the present context.

However, there is more to Smith's theology than that. When one goes through all the theological passages in *The Theory of Moral Sentiments*, it stands out as a striking feature in many, if not most, of them that he is really proposing a theory of human nature. Phrases like 'we naturally appeal', 'we are naturally led to believe', 'nature teaches us to hope', 'a hope and expectation deeply rooted in human nature', 'the natural principles of religion', etc. abundantly shows this to be his intention. We have already noted Smith's idea of religious belief as a continuation and completion of moral sentiments, and in the quotation given above we heard that men 'naturally...hope that the great Author of our nature... will complete the plan which he himself has...taught us to begin'. Elsewhere we hear that men can only give benevolence on the supposition that this contributes to, or is part of, a great universal system of happiness supervised by God.[84]

What Smith suggests is a completely naturalistic theory of religious belief which is part and parcel of his explanation of the moral sentiments and which is of importance for his general theory of human knowledge.[85] This naturalistic character of Smith's theory is confirmed by the very detached attitude of 'scientific' spectator which he takes throughout the *Lectures on Jurisprudence* when discussing the influence of religion on the formation of the law.[86] And it is of course illustrated by the subtle elements of a natural history of religion which he suggests in various contexts in *The Theory of Moral Sentiments*, such as this passage:

The justice of God..., we think, still requires, that he should hereafter avenge the injuries of the widow and fatherless, who are here so often insulted with impunity. In every religion, and in every superstition that the world has ever beheld, accordingly, there has been a Tartarus as well as an Elysium; a place provided for the punishment of the wicked, as well as one for the reward of the just. (TMS, ii, ii, 3, § 12)[87]

Although Smith can thus account for religious sentiments in terms of natural principles, it is always clear that religion in this form is very different from structured religious systems. The latter are speculation and philosophy, just as the consideration of utility is. Religious sentiments are at their most natural when they constitute the continuation of particular moral sentiments, but when they are made into a system they are a philosopher's construction. In line with this he insists that religion as such should not be concerned with action: it is a matter of consoling contemplation. 'Nature has not prescribed to us this sublime contemplation as the great business and occupation of our lives. She only points it out to us as the consolation of our misfortunes.'[88] It is connected with action only in that it is a factor strengthening our natural sentiments of morality, which is, of course, just another way of saying that man's life and morality constitute an independent sphere which is governed by its own natural principles:

> The administration of the great system of the universe,...the care of the universal happiness of all rational and sensible beings, is the business of God, and not of man. To man is allotted a much humbler department, but one much more suitable to the weakness of his powers, and to the narrowness of his comprehension – the care of his own happiness, of that of his family, his friends, his country...The most sublime speculation of the contemplative philosopher can scarce compensate the neglect of the smallest active duty. (TMS, VI, ii, 3, § 6)[89]

Religion is a more or less philosophical speculation which is superimposed upon men's natural sentiments of morality, more so for some men than for others. But to substitute the former for the latter, as monks try to do,[90] is contrary to nature and therefore ruled out for the bulk of mankind. In other words, men's religious beliefs are themselves selected according to natural principles:

> To compare...the futile mortifications of a monastery, to the ennobling hardships and hazards of war; to suppose that one day, or one hour, employed in the former should, in the eye of the great Judge of the world, have more merit than a whole life spent honourably in the latter, is surely contrary to all our moral sentiments; to all the principles by which nature has taught us to regulate our contempt or admiration. It is this spirit, however, which, while it has reserved the celestial regions for monks and friars, or for those whose conduct and conversation resembled those of monks and friars, has condemned to the infernal all the heroes, all the statesmen and lawgivers, all the poets and philosophers of former ages; all those who have invented, improved, or excelled in the arts which contribute to the subsistence, to the conveniency, or to the ornament of human life; all the great protectors, instructors, and benefactors of mankind; all those to whom our natural sense of praiseworthiness forces us to ascribe the highest merit and most exalted virtue. (TMS, III, 2, § 35)

Could anything be more like Hume's denouncement of 'the whole train of monkish virtues'? And could the reasoning behind it be any more similar to Hume's idea of 'artificial lives and manners'?[91]

Like Hume, Smith never makes clear his own personal attitude to the religious hypothesis. He limits himself to pointing out that men's teleological inferences about God and an afterlife are conducted along the same lines as the rest of human understanding but that it is purely speculative. He does not say that such speculation is invalid. From the tone of various of his passages one may get the feeling that he has brought Hume's criticism of such inferences thoroughly home to himself. His insistence upon the great gulf between the world of religion and the world of human action seems to indicate this. Indeed, one might say that Smith's insistence upon this gulf as far as the *praxis* of life is concerned brings men fully as close to a Kierkegaardian 'leap-of-faith' view of religion as does Hume's criticism of religion.[92] Whether either of them wanted to make the leap remains unknown.

The really important thing, however, is that it is irrelevant whether one wants to take the leap or not as far as moral theory and understanding are concerned. Nothing hinges on teleological explanations and thus on a guarantor of a teleological order. I think it is safe to say that wherever a piece of teleology turns up in Smith it is fairly clear where we have to look in order to find a 'real' explanation in terms of what we may broadly call efficient causes. We have already seen this done with large areas of human behaviour and we have been able to read off Smith's philosophical principles in this matter from his explanatory practice. We need not, however, rest content with this, for he does very clearly and forcefully formulate his views of explanation.

9 Teleology

In dealing with the problem of teleological explanations Smith starts off from the assumption that men do in fact perceive a goal-directed order in the universe in general and in the physical world in particular. Whether this is true is, of course, doubtful; it may well have been more true of eighteenth-century men than it is of twentieth-century men. Irrespective of this, it clearly serves the rhetorical purpose of throwing into relief his criticism of teleology as a mode of explanation. That people – or at least certain people, the philosophers – should discover a general order when they watch the plants and animals of the world is one thing; it is quite another to *explain* the operation of their various parts and thus the overall order. In order to arrive at explanations, 'we...distinguish the efficient from the final cause of their several motions and organizations'. And although we can see that things like digestion and blood-circulation are 'necessary for the great purposes of animal life', we still 'never endeavour to account for them from those purposes as from their efficient causes'. And just as we do not suppose that the blood circulates intentionally, so we do not imagine that the wheels of a watch have any particular desire to show the time.[93] In other words, in Smith's opinion the methodological discussion in his day had reached clarity about the distinction between the contemplation of order and the explanation of function as far as the physical world was concerned. But such clarity was far from reached in moral matters. Here the perception of order was still so dominant that the philosophical enquirer transferred it from his own speculation to the individuals he investigated, as if it were their principle of action:

When by natural principles we are led to advance those ends which a refined and enlightened reason would recommend to us, we are very apt to impute to that reason, as to their efficient cause, the sentiments and actions by which we advance those ends, and to imagine that to be the wisdom of man, which in reality is the wisdom of God. (TMS, II, ii, 3, § 5)

So far, this is essentially a negative doctrine. It is a denial that human reason is a power that can shape or construct the basic outlines of human life. Smith, however, is well aware of this, and one of his main objectives is to fulfil the positive task of pointing out the efficient causes which create order in human life. He starts from the foundation of man's existence, his mere physical survival, arguing that it is not left to 'the slow and uncertain determinations of our reason' to look after this. We are prompted to apply the necessary means for life and welfare by various 'original and immediate instincts. . . and without any consideration of their tendency to those beneficent ends which the great Director of nature intended to produce by them'![94] Smith's real feat as a philosopher, of course, is to point out that something exactly analogous applies to man's social life, and to have worked out a theory of the efficient cause which can, so to speak, take the place of (on the one hand) the instincts which direct our physical existence and (on the other) the kind of constructive rationality which only belongs to mankind in its philosophical mood. This is the theory of mutual sympathy as a selection mechanism of behaviour, which renders social life possible:

Though man. . .be naturally endowed with a desire for the welfare and preservation of society, yet the Author of nature has not entrusted to his reason to find out that a certain application of punishments is the proper means of attaining this end; but has endowed him with an immediate and instinctive approbation of that very application which is most proper to it. (TMS, II, i, 5, § 10)

All this amounts to a proper philosophy of unintended consequences: the idea that when men act for their own individual purposes, guided by the ordinary principles of human nature, something unforeseen and far beyond those purposes emerges, and this something will afterwards become recognizable as a kind of order. The basic idea for the theory Smith is spelling out came from Mandeville, but the idea of transferring it to the theory of justice he took from Hume.

Smith is so much clearer than Hume in this matter because of the precision with which he analysed the relative importance of the means-perspective and the end-perspective in our moral judgements of actions and characters. Once he got rid of Hume's troublesome concept of utility and replaced it with his own idea of situational propriety as the basic element in moral reasoning, he had a much clearer view of the role of reason in human action and hence in our explanation of human behaviour. Accordingly we never find the same difficult tensions in Smith's theory which we found in Hume's between the rationally created and the unintentionally occasioned. But then Smith never involves himself in a discussion of the distinction between natural and artificial which we hypothesized might be part of the explanation of Hume's difficulties. Whether Smith had any clear ideas of this or whether the logic of the discussion pressed him into an unintended clarity, we do not know.

10 Moral theory and human knowledge

Behind Smith's criticism of utility theories, and teleological theories generally, lies a distinction between two kinds of human knowledge which is of fundamental importance in his philosophy. With clarity bought at the expense of elegance, they might be called contextual knowledge and system knowledge respectively. The knowledge we have of human behaviour through the sympathy mechanism is of the former kind, as described at length above. It is the kind of concrete knowledge which arises from specific situations and which gives rise to common-sense ideas of behaviour wherever people live together.[95] It concerns the immediate circumstances of individual actions, and it almost automatically gives rise to an evaluation of the appropriateness, or propriety, of the action which was in fact taken. In contrast to this, system knowledge is the understanding of things, events, or persons in some sort of functional relationship to a greater 'whole' or system – or the understanding of all the elements in such a system. This takes a variety of forms ranging from the understanding of individual actions in terms of their tendency, or 'utility', to a view of all the elements of the universe as forming a teleological and perhaps divinely directed order. This form of knowledge is also closely allied to evaluation and, as we saw above, Smith in effect divides this into two forms, one applying 'means utility', the other 'end utility' as the standard. Of these, the former can be characterized as an appreciation of functional efficiency within a system, whereas the latter either is or implies an evaluation of the goal of the system as a whole, normally in terms of happiness.

System knowledge is thus always relational in the sense that its objects

are relations; and contextual knowledge is in *practice* always relational
because it always involves the evaluation of the relationship between
situation and action. This gives us the clue to Smith's ideas of how
knowledge grows. This happens when the established and expected relations are upset, or when suspicion arises that two hitherto unrelated
elements could be related. In such cases, 'We are at first surprised by the
unexpectedness of the new appearance, and when that momentary
emotion is over, we still wonder how it came to occur in that place.'[96] But
any person thus afflicted has a craving for the re-establishment of order so
that 'he can get rid of that Wonder, that uncertainty and anxious
curiosity' which has been created by the surprising event or thing.[97] It is
therefore the satisfaction of the imagination, 'and not any expectation of
advantage from its discoveries...which prompts mankind to the study of
Philosophy'.[98] There is, however, a very great difference between the two
kinds of knowledge. For while disorder in some sort of system always
creates great wonder and search for new knowledge, disorder at the level
of individual behaviour is not only small-scale, but has also a mechanism
for practical adjustment attached to it. Thus if a spectator is surprised
by improper behaviour in another person, his disapprobation – his different understanding of the situation – will normally through mutual
sympathy influence the future behaviour of that person. The issue is, in
other words, diffused at the practical level. This is, I suggest, the underlying reason for Smith's idea that moral 'philosophy' remained in the
form of proverbs and common-sense maxims for a long time, while natural
philosophy developed into systems.[99] There was simply not the same
pressure of curiosity to develop systems of morals, and when it was
attempted it was hampered by the fact that until very recently 'the
abstract science of human nature was but in its infancy', and 'the distinct
offices and powers of the different faculties of the human mind' had not
yet been 'carefully examined and distinguished from one another'.[100] And
this again was because we 'naturally [have] a greater curiosity to examine
the causes and relations of those things which pass without us, than of
those which pass within us, the latter naturally making very little impression'.[101] So while the natural philosophers developed more and more
intricate systems, the moral philosophers worked without any proper
foundation and tried to create system and precision where it could not be
got, namely in their treatment of the positive virtues, and overlooked it
where it could be got, namely in the negative virtues which form the basis
for natural jurisprudence.[102]

Smith takes the matter much further than this. He points out that the
same forces which – as suggested here – created less pressure for the
systematic treatment of morals, also led to much stricter demands on
systems in the moral than in the natural world. The basic requirement of

system knowledge is that of coherence; it must present whatever is its object as a coherent and orderly whole – as if it were a machine: 'Systems in many respects resemble machines... A system is an imaginary machine invented to connect together in the fancy those different movements and effects which are already in reality performed.'[103] This requirement of the integration of more and more phenomena into a more and more coherent system has been met by the physical sciences. Their history is an unending competition between different systems in exactly this respect. It was the 'superior degree of coherence, which it bestowed upon the celestial appearances' which led to the success of the Copernican system, although it left some empirical material unaccounted for and was, at the time, 'the most violent paradox in all philosophy'.[104] It was the same story with Kepler, Descartes, and – of course in supreme degree – with Newton.[105] The Newtonian principles are of such 'firmness and solidity' that

The most sceptical cannot avoid feeling this... And even we, while we have been endeavouring to represent all philosophical systems as mere inventions of the imagination, to connect together the otherwise disjointed and discordant phenomena of Nature, have insensibly been drawn in, to make use of language expressing the connecting principles of this one, as if they were the real chains which Nature makes use of to bind together her several operations. Can we wonder then, that it should have gained the general and complete approbation of mankind...[106]

This very Humean piece of teasing, double-edged scepticism underlines Smith's central point very well, namely that the physical sciences have been so persuasive as systems because the only strict requirement has been that they should satisfy the imagination with coherence and order. The moral sciences, by contrast, have had a much more difficult time gaining such acceptance. Their subject matter is the behaviour of ordinary human beings and no amount of coherence and machine-like orderliness will make up for any deficiency in the account of what people know about themselves and each other. In other words, a satisfactory system of morals must not only satisfy the requirement of coherence, but also be able to account for the contextual knowledge people have of themselves and others. It was in this respect that all moral philosophers had hitherto failed, in so far as they had tried to establish a system of morals. They had perceived some over-all order, real or imagined, in the moral world and had then accounted for the behaviour of individuals in terms of this system, as if such behaviour were aimed at producing order. This complaint applied even to the low-level order of 'utility' involved in Hume's moral theory. What Smith hoped to achieve with his theory of the selection of behaviour through mutual sympathy was an explanation of the behaviour of individuals through their own immediate contextual knowledge *and* an explanation of why this is formative of an order. This contrast between the natural and the moral sciences is spelled out in a long and very important section towards the end of *The Theory of Moral Sentiments*:

A system of natural philosophy may appear very plausible, and be for a long time very generally received in the world, and yet have no foundation in nature, nor any sort of resemblance to the truth...But it is otherwise with systems of moral philosophy, and an author who pretends to account for the origin of our moral sentiments, cannot deceive us so grossly, nor depart so very far from all resemblance to the truth. When a traveller gives an account of some distant country, he may impose upon our credulity the most groundless and absurd fictions as the most certain matters of fact. But when a person pretends to inform us of what passes in our neighbourhood, and of the affairs of the very parish which we live in, though here too, if we are so careless as not to examine things with our own eyes, he may deceive us in many respects, yet the greatest false-hoods which he imposes upon us must bear some resemblance to the truth, and must even have a considerable mixture of truth in them. An author who treats of natural philosophy, and pretends to assign the causes of the great phenomena of the universe, pretends to give an account of the affairs of a very distant country, concerning which he may tell us what he pleases, and as long as his narration keeps within the bounds of seeming possibility, he need not despair of gaining our belief. But when he proposes to explain the origin of our desires and affections, of our sentiments of approbation and disapprobation, he pretends to give an account, not only of the affairs of the very parish that we live in, but of our own domestic concerns. (TMS, vii, ii, 4, § 14)[107]

When moral systems which cannot account for the moral sentiments fall into the hands of men of affairs they create that 'spirit of system' which is so politically dangerous; for those who are imbued with it forget that 'in the great chess-board of human society, every single piece has a principle of motion of its own, altogether different from that which the legislature might chuse to impress upon it'.[108] Fortunately this principle of motion – as explained at great length in *The Wealth of Nations* – is sufficiently resilient to surmount 'a hundred impertinent obstructions with which the folly of human laws too often incumbers its operations'.[109] The principle in question is 'the natural effort of every individual to better his own condition' – which is, of course, completely dependent upon his knowledge of his own particular situation.[110] The big question is, however, what will make all these individual efforts compatible, and to answer that we shall have to investigate Smith's theory of justice.[111] For when it is properly done, moral philosophy is 'By far the most important of all the different branches of philosophy'.[112]

CHAPTER FOUR

Smith's theory of justice and politics

1 Positive and negative virtues

The two passages in which Smith explicitly criticizes teleological explanations, which we have dealt with at length (see pp. 77–9 above), occur in connection with his theory of justice and that is certainly no coincidence. Nowhere is his theory of the 'efficient cause' which selects behaviour clearer and of greater importance than in his account of how just behaviour is selected.

Justice was something of an enigma to both Hume and Smith. Although neither of them set out with the primary aim of formulating a theory of justice in their major philosophical work, both of them gave considerable space to such a theory and both of them kept referring to it in other contexts. The thing which struck them was that justice is so different from all other virtues. It seemed to be more precise and it could therefore be formulated in strict and general rules. Furthermore, men were always prone to enforce those rules. Now, what I suggest is that Smith had a highly original theory of why justice is so precise and, in close connection with this, why it is enforceable.

It may appear as a piece of the high-handed cynicism about man's lot in the world which he always criticizes in the Stoics, when Smith maintains that basically the bulk of mankind is in a position to be happy.[1] I will not deny that there may be an element of this in it, but this should not, as is common, obscure from us that he also puts forward an interesting theory about this matter. Surely the point he is making is that it is rather difficult to say much in general terms about what is needed to make mankind happy and the reason is that the difference between 'the happiness of the man who is in health, who is out of debt, and has a clear conscience' and 'the highest pitch of human prosperity' is 'but a trifle'. This trifling distance is traversed by men, not out of any basic needs, but under the guidance of vanity, a principle which is as variable in its contents, as it is permanent in its influence on mankind. In contrast to this narrow scope for happiness the possible depths of misery are 'immense and prodigious'.[2] This difference is also reflected in the fact that when we are surprised by happy events they immediately grip us and produce their strong effect on us, whereas when we are surprised by unhappy events, the effect, grief, 'comes slowly and gradually', as if we have a natural resistance towards it.[3] This fundamental asymmetry between happiness and misery is connected with the fact that 'Pain..., whether of mind or body, is a more pungent sensation than pleasure.'[4]

While this is noticed simply as a fact about human nature, it is interesting to see that in the *Lectures on Rhetoric and Belles Lettres* Smith ventures an extraordinary suggestion as to its possible explanation. It might be, he says, that we possess this reaction pattern because it has, what in modern terms would be called, the very highest survival value for us. Although we might survive well enough without any particular pleasure from the things and events which are to our advantage, 'it seems absolutely necessary that some considerable degree of uneasiness should attend what is hurtful, for without this we should soon, in all probability, be altogether destroyed'.[5]

Just as pain makes a greater impression than pleasure upon the subjects of these sensations, so there is a difference in the sympathetic communication of the two. That is more complicated, however. Sympathy with pleasure and joy is in itself pleasant, while sympathy with pain and sorrow is unpleasant, and we therefore have a natural tendency to like the former and dislike the latter.[6] On the other hand, sympathy with pleasure is something of an 'either/or' phenomenon: if we do not sympathize completely, it is not really sympathy. Sympathy with pleasure is a lively, but fickle kind of sympathy. Sympathy with pain and sorrow, on the contrary, is much more resilient; although it is often not so close to the original feeling in vivacity, it is always present in some degree: 'our sympathy with sorrow is...more universal, than that with joy'.[7] The fact that the difference between 'what may be called the natural state of our happiness' and 'the highest pitch of human prosperity' is 'but a trifle',[8] plus the fact that it is pleasant for a man in the former condition to go along with one in the latter condition, are the reasons why this kind of sympathy is more complete and the sympathetic feeling closer to the original. By contrast the fact that 'the distance is immense and prodigious' between the state of natural happiness and 'the lowest depth of misery' means that sympathy with the latter condition is much more strongly desired by a man in that condition:[9] 'we are still more anxious to communicate to our friends our disagreeable, than our agreeable passions;... we derive still more satisfaction from their sympathy with the former, than from that with the latter'.[10] So although sympathy with pain and sorrow is disagreeable, it is universally desired, and this means that it becomes a social necessity that an emotional compromise is established through mutual sympathy.[11]

The idea that pain and misery are more pungently felt than pleasure and happiness and that sympathy with the former is more distinct and universal is of the greatest importance for Smith.[12] It is with this contrast between what we might call the positive and the negative in morals that he opens his discussion of justice in *The Theory of Moral Sentiments*. Not only his argument but his very formulations are of such seminal importance for the rest of our discussion that we have to quote him at some length. His procedure is to compare beneficence and justice through a comparison of the *lack* of either, and a comparison of the reactions to this: 'the mere want of beneficence tends to do no real positive evil. It may . . . justly excite dislike and disapprobation: it cannot, however, provoke any resentment which mankind will go along with.' The man who does not show beneficence can at most be 'the object of hatred, a passion which is naturally excited by impropriety of sentiment and behaviour; not of resentment, a passion which is never properly called forth but by actions which tend to do real and positive hurt to some particular persons'. Accordingly, 'Beneficence is always free, it cannot be extorted by force, the mere want of it exposes to no punishment.'[13] So much for the positive side. But there is a negative correlate,

another virtue, of which the observance is not left to the freedom of our own wills, which may be extorted by force, and of which the violation exposes to resentment, and consequently to punishment. This virtue is justice: the violation of justice is injury: it does real and positive hurt to some particular persons, from motives which are naturally disapproved of. It is, therefore, the proper object of resentment, and of punishment, which is the natural consequence of resentment. (TMS, II, ii, I, § 5)

The whole distinction between the two virtues is thus drawn in terms of the reactions, first of the patient, afterwards of the spectator, to the lack of them, and the point is that the lack of justice 'does real and positive hurt' while the lack of beneficence does not. Hence the former meets with a much clearer and stronger response than the latter, with resentment rather than hatred.[14] This greater strength is shown in the fact that resentment is normally followed by action, i.e. punishment.

This is a natural pattern of reaction, which is approved of as proper by any impartial spectator. Not only is it approved of; often the sympathetic feeling is so strong as to lead to action as well, in the form of assistance to the injured in his pursuit of redress. Such an 'active' sympathy would obviously never gain any approval and support in the case of hatred at the lack of beneficence.[15] This spectator reaction is further communicated by mutual sympathy to all members of the social group and everyone contemplating an act of injustice will thus know it and fear it.

In this way Smith uses his idea of the moral primacy of the negative to draw a sharp distinction between all positive virtues, represented by beneficence, and justice. This 'remarkable distinction between justice and all the other social virtues' consists in this, that we feel ourselves to be under a stricter obligation to act according to justice, than agreeably to friendship, charity, or generosity; that the practice of these last-mentioned virtues seems to be left in some measure to our own choice, but that, somehow or other, we feel ourselves to be in a peculiar manner tied, bound, and obliged, to the observation of justice. (TMS, ii, ii, 1, § 5)

This distinction is also clearly seen if we turn our attention from the lack of the virtues to the reactions to the virtues themselves, for we shall then see that beneficence is naturally rewarded with gratitude while justice is judged to be nothing but proper:

There is, no doubt, a propriety in the practice of justice, and it merits, upon that account, all the approbation which is due to propriety. But as it does no real positive good, it is entitled to very little gratitude. Mere justice is, upon most occasions, but a negative virtue, and only hinders us from hurting our neighbour...We may often fulfil all the rules of justice by sitting still and doing nothing. (TMS, ii, ii, 1, § 9)

This contrast between the negative virtue of justice and all the positive virtues is pursued even further by Smith. He always insists that the fundamental rules of justice are absolutely precise, whereas the rules of the positive virtues are rather unclear and uncertain. 'The rules of justice are accurate in the highest degree, and admit of no exceptions or modifications but such as may be ascertained as accurately as the rules themselves, and which generally, indeed, flow from the very same principles with them.'[16] As far as the rules of all the other virtues are concerned, we go by their 'spirit', but with justice we follow the rules to the 'letter'. These rules are like the 'rules of grammar', the former like 'the rules which critics lay down for the attainment of what is sublime and elegant in composition. The one are precise, accurate, and indispensable. The other are loose, vague, and indeterminate.'[17]

Whence this great accuracy in the rules of justice? Smith never spells out his explanation, but in view of what we have already seen to be the foundation of justice the explanation seems rather obvious. The rules of justice are precise because they are derived from spectator reactions which are unusually 'universal' and 'distinct', namely the 'pungent' feeling of sympathetic resentment occasioned by 'real and positive hurt'. Smith's idea seems to be that clarity and accuracy are transferred in the following chain; the action (negative: hurting), the reaction (resentment and punishment), the spectator-reaction through sympathy (sympathetic resentment and assistance in punishing), and the general rule arising from spectator reactions.

The negative character of justice also implies that the general rules of this virtue arise somewhat differently from the rules of the other virtues. The latter arise from spectator approval of the practice of those virtues, but the rules of justice arise from spectator disapproval of injustice, of the non-performance of the virtue. If nobody had ever been unjust the rules of justice would never have been thought of, for they are but a specification of mere propriety.

2 Justice and utility

Smith's account of the foundation of justice in men's natural moral judgement provides one of the most important and interesting differences between him and Hume. Paradoxically, this may best be approached through their points of agreement. They agree that while all the positive virtues are an 'extra' which make society flourishing and happy, social life is quite possible without them,[18] but that there can be no society without justice:

Beneficence...is less essential to the existence of society than justice. Society may subsist, though not in the most comfortable state, without beneficence; but the prevalence of injustice must utterly destroy it...[Beneficence] is the ornament which embellishes, not the foundation which supports the building...Justice, on the contrary, is the main pillar that upholds the whole edifice. If it is removed, the great, the immense fabric of human society...must in a moment crumble into atoms. (TMS, ii, ii, 3, §§ 3–4)

This analogy inevitably recalls Hume's analogy in the *Enquiry*[19] between benevolence and a wall and justice and a vault; and it reminds us of how strongly Hume both in the *Enquiry* and in the *Treatise* stresses that justice in serving the public interest or utility, in the very special sense explained above (see pp. 39–41), is the minimum condition for any kind of social life in the present world.[20]

Equally for Smith, justice is the very minimum of a social framework, without which 'no social intercourse can take place among men'; and this extraordinary utility of justice has by some philosophers been taken as the very foundation of this virtue, 'the ground upon which we approved of the enforcement of the laws of justice'. For these people the basis of social life as such was an appreciation of its utility and this would lead to an 'abhorrence at whatever can tend to destroy it'. And since 'injustice necessarily tends to destroy it', 'every appearance of injustice...alarms [the individual] and he runs, if I may say so, to stop the progress of what, if allowed to go on, would quickly put an end to everything that is dear to him'.[21]

This account of the moral quality of justice in terms of its utility has certain virtues, according to Smith, for it explains the most important strengthening factor upon justice. This is important when people are to be punished for their crimes. Very often men will feel pity for the criminal about to suffer punishment and 'here, therefore, they have occasion to call to their assistance the consideration of the general interest of society'.

This is of importance for Smith's over-all theory of punishment, and our discussion of this below will throw further light on the relationship between utility and justice.[22] Smith also, however, makes his point in more general terms – and with a very interesting argument. He points out that when our fundamental rules of justice are met with destructive criticism and opposition, we will often defend them by referring to 'their necessity to the support of society', although it is really the 'intrinsic hatefulness' of such criticism which upsets us. Why is it that on such occasions we do not rely on our real reason? It is simply because the fact that people can put forward such criticism shows that the natural value-community between them and us has broken down: they have lost their sense of propriety, as we see it. Accordingly we try to refer to something else, and that will normally be the social necessity of justice and morality.[23]

But although there is such a role for utility considerations, they nevertheless do not form the foundation of justice. For, however obvious, such social utility is rarely thought of by the bulk of mankind. And yet people by and large abide by the laws of justice:

All men, even the most stupid and unthinking, abhor fraud, perfidy, and injustice, and delight to see them punished. But few men have reflected upon the necessity of justice to the existence of society, how obvious soever that necessity may appear to be. (TMS, II, ii, 3, § 9)

In other words, justice is a prime example of how philosophers have made use of an excessive rationalism, in the form of utility considerations, to interpret human morality. Smith accordingly invokes his criticism of this, which is that such considerations are foreign to the bulk of mankind. Indeed, he uses this discussion of the utility of justice as the occasion for formulating his general theory of efficient versus final causes in moral science which we have already dealt with above.

As far as justice and social utility are concerned, Smith also introduces a new and, as it seems to me, very valuable argument. He points out that it would be very odd if the application of justice were based upon a regard for the public, for the latter regard can only be made up of individual instances of regard for particular persons, since all moral judgement takes place through sympathy and sympathy can, of course, only be with concrete individuals.[24] In human morality there is, therefore, a clear primacy of the individual over any kind of social whole:

We are no more concerned for the destruction or loss of a single man, because this man is a member or part of society, and because we should be concerned for the destruction of society, than we are concerned for the loss of a single guinea, because this guinea is part of a thousand guineas, and because we should be concerned for the loss of the whole sum. In neither case does our regard for the individuals arise from our regard for the multitude; but in both cases our regard for the multitude is compounded and made up of the particular regards which we feel for the different individuals of which it is composed. (TMS, II, ii, 3, § 10)

The moral primacy of individuals for which Smith argues here is a basic feature of his moral philosophy, which is often reflected in his language.[25] But it is important to notice that the 'particular regards' involved in sympathy with resentment do not presuppose any special or personal relationship. Sympathy with resentment is so 'pungent', 'distinct', and 'universal' that no more is necessary 'than the general fellow-feeling which we have with every man, merely because he is our fellow-creature'.[26]

3 Political theory

We have now seen how justice gains its very special moral and social status because of its character as a negative virtue, founded on resentment at the lack of it. It is this theory which forms the basis for Smith's jurisprudence in its analytical, its critical, and its historical aspects, but in order to appreciate the significance of this application of the theory of justice it is necessary to look at the *political* implication of the distinction between the positive and the negative in morals.

We have already seen how the negative virtue of justice gains its special qualities of clarity and moral primacy from its close tie with the immediate contexts in which it is relevant. And we have seen that the basis for Smith's criticism of any utility-foundation for justice is that this is a speculative construction which ignores the particular context and endangers the separation of justice from the positive virtues. This gives us our lead: it is, I suggest, the combination of the distinction between the negative and the positive in morals with the distinction between the two kinds of knowledge which we traced above – contextual knowledge and system knowledge[27] – which determines the shape of Smith's *theory* of politics (as opposed to his policy proposals).

The importance of the contrast between the positive and the negative in human morality is brought out particularly clearly in the sections of *The Theory of Moral Sentiments* which seem to constitute Smith's comments on political ventures like the French revolution.[28] He there attacks those 'men of system' who try to create a complete happiness in society instead of trying to alleviate concrete misery. They 'seldom fail to hold out some plausible plan of reformation, which, they pretend, will not only remove the inconveniencies and relieve the distresses immediately complained of, but will prevent in all times coming any return of the like inconveniencies and distresses'.[29] The political approach of this type of person is to be contrasted with that of the person of real public spirit,

He will accommodate, as well as he can, his public arrangements to the confirmed habits and prejudices of the people, and will remedy, as well as he can, the inconveniences which may flow from the want of those regulations which the people are averse to submit to. When he cannot establish the right, he will not disdain to ameliorate the wrong. (TMS, vi, ii, 2, § 16)

This criticism of a morally utopian approach to politics and the suggestion of its replacement with a piecemeal approach of alleviating concrete evils is best understood as an extension of Smith's criticism of utilitarian interpretations of human morality. This form of utopianism seems to be nothing but a political exploitation of the latter.

That Smith wants to combine this use of the moral distinction between positive and negative with his two kinds of knowledge is made clear in the same context. The 'spirit of system' is an extreme intellectual arrogance[30] which leads the man who suffers from it to regard human society as a chess-board upon which he can arrange the individuals as he pleases. But as we saw at the end of the previous chapter, such a man forgets that 'in the great chess-board of human society, every single piece has a principle of motion of its own, altogether different from that which the legislature might chuse to impress upon it'.[31]

This contrast between the general system-knowledge available to rulers and the particular situational knowledge available to the individual citizen is frequently applied by Smith in *The Wealth of Nations* when he criticizes particular moves by actual men of system. And the care with which he formulates these points shows very clearly the connection with his general speculations about human knowledge. Thus when he discusses the advantages and disadvantages of a variable land-tax, he considers its likely effect on the improvement of land, and in this connection he contrasts not only the respective 'interests' of government and individual landlord, but also their different kinds of knowledge:

The attention of the sovereign can be at best but a very *general* and *vague* consideration of what is likely to contribute to the better cultivation of the greater part of his dominions. The attention of the landlord is a *particular* and *minute* consideration of what is likely to be the most advantageous application of every inch of ground upon his estate. (WN, v, ii, c. 18. My italics)

In other contexts, when commenting on various restrictions on the economic activities of individuals, he likewise points out the superior knowledge which individuals have of their 'local situations' and the implications of this for political measures.[32]

In so far as this line of argument derives from Smith's general consideration of knowledge, we would expect him to make a further and stronger point to back it up, namely that it is *impossible* that a ruler could have the kind of knowledge which the individual citizens have.[33] And he does indeed seem to suggest this. In a society where the sovereign does not presume to have such knowledge, he is completely discharged from a duty, in the attempting to perform which he must always be exposed to innumerable delusions, and for the proper performance of which no human wisdom or knowledge could ever be sufficient; the duty of superintending the industry of private people, and of directing it towards the employments most suitable to the interest of the society. (WN, iv, ix, 51)[34]

So far Smith's argument amounts to an outright rejection, for both moral and epistemological reasons, of utopian theories of how politics should and could be conducted. They are philosophers' constructions which are excessively speculative and take no account of the concrete situations in which individual men in fact evaluate and act. A piecemeal approach in politics which does not aim much higher than to remedy given evils will, by contrast, respect those individual situations to as high a degree as is possible, for it will only be guided by those elements in the situations which are most 'pungently' felt and which are most 'universally' and 'distinctly' sympathized with, namely pain and misery. Whereas for the rest the individuals' own lights provide safer guidance.

This is, however, only part of Smith's theory. From our earlier discussion of his ideas about the influence of utility upon evaluation, we know that he considered it a natural tendency in men to construct speculative systems and to evaluate individual things and events 'aesthetically' as parts of such systems – a tendency which is not least evident in connection with politics:

The perfection of police, the extension of trade and manufactures, are noble and magnificent objects. The contemplation of them pleases us, and we are interested in whatever can tend to advance them. They make part of the great system of government, and the wheels of the political machine seem to move with more harmony and ease by means of them. We take pleasure in beholding the perfection of so beautiful and grand a system, and we are uneasy till we remove any obstruction that can in the least disturb or encumber the regularity of its motions. (TMS, iv, 1, § 11)[35]

In this passage Smith strikes that perfect equipoise between irony and encomium which is so typical of him. On the one hand there is the indication of the satire on the man of system who 'is apt to be very wise in his own conceit', to which we now know the serious background. On the other hand there is genuine commendation. For while this speculative aestheticism in politics can lead some men to the unfortunate spirit of system, it can also lead to a genuine public spirit. 'Nothing tends so much to promote public spirit as the study of politics.' In fact, even the 'weakest and worst of [political disquisitions] are not altogether without their utility. They serve at least to animate the public passions of men, and rouse them to seek out the means of promoting the happiness of the society.'[36] General political theory can thus have a moral and educative function for the population at large. And it is important that this function

is looked after – especially in a commercial society with its wide division
of labour and its consequent extensive and graduated ladder of ranks. For
in such a society the sectional interests of the three great orders, the landlords, the labourers, and the business people, are always likely to be seen
by their members as distinct from the public interest.[37] And whereas there
is never any thought of spreading political wisdom by direct education,
Smith did believe that the provision of the most basic education for those
who are worst off in modern society would *lead* them to some political
insight. First of all it would tend to keep them out of 'the delusions of
enthusiasm and superstition' which would otherwsie be likely to satisfy
their need for over-all system and order. And secondly, it would enable
them to see the connections in the political system sufficiently well to be
on their guard against 'the interested complaints of faction and sedition'
which may disturb the established government. The political importance
of such education should be obvious: 'In free countries, where the safety
of government depends very much upon the favourable judgment which
the people may form of its conduct, it must surely be of the highest importance that they should not be disposed to judge rashly or capriciously
concerning it.'[38] The provision of basic education for those who at any
given time are worst off in modern society is therefore an essential task for
the public.[39]

While political speculations – 'if just, and reasonable, and practicable'[40]
– may serve to rouse the public spirit, and while this may have some effect
even amongst 'the lowest orders', their importance is by no means confined
to the citizenry. 'Some general, or even systematical, idea of the perfection
of policy and law, may no doubt be necessary for directing the views of
the statesman.'[41] It is the study of such ideas which constitute 'the science
of a legislator' – a somewhat shadowy character, whom we shall encounter
again below – for his 'deliberations ought to be governed by general
principles which are always the same'.[42]

We can now see that the intention behind Smith's criticism of excessive
rationalism, or utopianism, in politics is by no means the abdication of
reason. It is rather a very rational appreciation of its limits. For both
rulers and citizens the study of general principles has indispensable moral,
educative, and intellectual functions, and the utopian mistake is simply to
think that such principles are sacrosanct in action. For the statesman, or
anybody else, 'to insist upon establishing, and upon establishing all at once,
and in spite of all opposition, every thing which [his ideas] may seem to
require, must often be the highest degree of arrogance. It is to erect his
own judgment into the supreme standard of right and wrong.'[43] If general
political speculations become part of the actual political process, the result
is disaster – irrespective of whether the process is dominated by the crowds
of 'factions', or by 'sovereign princes'.[44]

This carefully balanced view of the role of general political speculations is remarkably similar to that which Hume put forward at the beginning of his 'Idea of a Perfect Commonwealth',[45] and like Hume Smith adopted it as the proper perspective on his own work.[46] Thus when he supported the idea of union with the American colonies – along the lines of the Anglo-Scottish union – in order to prevent their revolt, he stressed on the one hand its utopian character – it was 'perhaps altogether impossible'; but on the other hand such an idea might 'not, perhaps, be improper, in a speculative work of this kind', i.e. *The Wealth of Nations*. 'Such a specu-lation can at worst be regarded but as a new Utopia, less amusing cer-tainly, but not more useless and chimerical than the old one.'[47] And when he considered the same idea at greater length elsewhere, he pointed out that the real difficulty in its way did not derive from 'the nature of things, but from the prejudices and opinions of the people both on this and on the other side of the Atlantic'.[48] Opinions should be respected politically, but not necessarily intellectually – remembering that while the two are distinct they are not disconnected. But perhaps the most striking illustra-tion of this attitude is Smith's off-hand comment about that 'system of natural liberty' which in *The Wealth of Nations* he spent close on half a million words arguing for: 'To expect, indeed, that the freedom of trade should ever be entirely restored in Great Britain, is as absurd as to expect that an Oceana or Utopia should ever be established in it.'[49]

4 Politics and justice

Smith's attitude to utopian perfectionism is clearly reflected in his view of what ought to be the priorities of a sovereign: first, defence against foreign enemies; secondly, 'an exact administration of justice'; and thirdly, 'the duty of erecting and maintaining certain publick works and certain publick institutions, which it can never be for the interest of any individual, or small number of individuals, to erect and maintain'.[50] The principle behind the first governmental duty is obviously the simple one of maintaining a coherent society. The principle behind the second duty is the enforcement of the negative virtue of justice which is 'the main pillar that upholds the whole edifice' of society. The most basic principle behind the third area of duties is to supplement the market in those respects in which it may not fully or satisfactorily take care of certain functions which are thought important. But the principles which determine what those functions are may obviously vary. First of all there is room for straight-forward utilitarian considerations of convenience and prosperity, and for a concern with public order and decency:

The civil magistrate is entrusted with the power not only of preserving the public peace by restraining injustice, but of promoting the prosperity of the commonwealth, by establishing good discipline, and by discouraging every sort of vice and impropriety; he may prescribe rules, therefore, which not only prohibit mutual injuries among fellow-citizens, but command mutual good offices to a certain degree. (TMS, II, ii, I, § 8)

To find this degree requires more 'delicacy and reserve' than any other governmental duty. But to 'neglect it altogether exposes the commonwealth to many gross disorders and shocking enormities, and to push it too far is destructive of all liberty, security, and justice'.[51] Smith's illustration of this is the mutual obligation between parents and children, and when we discuss Smith's general treatment of domestic law below we shall find further room for governmental activity in this area, especially in relation to marriage law.[52]

Apart from this, the third area of governmental duty leads to a concern with basic human decency, especially in the provision of education for the poorest.[53] In a sense we are therefore dealing here with those 'acts of beneficence' which constitute 'the ornament which embellishes, not the foundation which supports the building' of society. But at the same time we should also remark that the duties of defence and administration of justice lend much of their urgency to various public institutions. Thus the establishments, such as customs and excise, which serve to protect trade in certain circumstances, have as their only rationale the concern for national defence.[54] It has also been very clearly shown to what extent Smith viewed the problem of defence as an educational one.[55] And we have just pointed out the close connection between education and political stability – and hence the possibility of a proper judicial system. The extent to which Smith's over-all idea of politics is centred around 'the minimum' of defence and justice, rather than any 'maxima' beyond this, is therefore even greater than may at first be apparent. This most basic perspective on the Smithian enterprise should not be disturbed by a misreading of his general statement that 'All constitutions of government...are valued only in proportion as they tend to promote the happiness of those who live under them.'[56] Smith is not here concerned with any utilitarian optimum, but with that condition of 'public utility' where each individual has the best possible chance of creating his own happiness. To turn Smith into a utilitarian of sorts on the strength of a statement like this is about as plausible as an attempt to stretch that label to cover Immanuel Kant, for the most significant part of the 'constitutions of government' which 'promote the happiness' of people is a system of justice which encompasses a strictly retributive theory of punishment, as we shall see.

The relationship between the three areas of governmental duties is given with Smith's order of priority. Defence overrules everything else. The well-known maxim that 'defence...is of much more importance than opulence' is not called in simply to justify the intervention of the Navigation Act in free trade.[57] It is a quite basic idea with Smith that without some power of defence there is no society. As we shall see when dealing with the historical aspects of his jurisprudence, it is the ability to conduct military campaigns which forms the first, rudimentary governmental function. Without that there cannot be the minimum of social cohesion which is a precondition for the development of some order in the execution of men's natural ideas of justice – much later to be supplemented by actual legislation.[58] And this is not just a matter of history: Smith takes exactly the same standpoint as Hume, that without sufficient strength to keep itself together, justice is pointless for a society:

Tho' the peace within doors be never so firmly established, yet if there be no security from injuries from without the property of individualls can not be secure. The danger to them on this head is no less to be feard than from those of their own society; and not only is the security of private persons in danger but the very being of the state. It is therefore requisite that an armed force should be maintained.[59]

However, if we assume that a society has strength to maintain itself as a unit, *then* it is true to say – as do the students' notes in the same context – that 'The first and chief design of every system of government is to maintain justice', and that 'Justice...is the foundation of civil government.'[60] The overriding character of justice in relation to other policies is only complicated by those cases where such policies are indispensable for the long-term maintenance of the system of justice or for defence. But that is best dealt with in the discussion of the system of law.

Smith's distinction between the governmental duties to administer justice and to maintain various public institutions is related to his distinction between 'laws of justice' and 'laws of police'.[61] Although he never spells out the exact meaning of the latter distinction, it is possible to work it out with reasonable clarity. It is striking that in three of the four places in the notes from the jurisprudence lectures where 'justice' and 'police' are distinguished, Smith uses the term 'regulations' for rules of the latter kind; and the phrase 'regulations of police' recurs a number of times in *The Wealth of Nations*.[62] Since we know that the contrasting laws of justice are general rules which are embodied in the standpoint of the impartial spectator and which consequently are abstract or 'anonymous', the implication of this terminology seems fairly obviously to be that the laws of police are regulations with specific or particular aims or objectives. This conclusion is confirmed when we are told that the object of such law is 'the regulation of the inferiour parts of government'.[63] The laws of police are administrative regulations which deal with 'the cheapness of commodities, public security, and cleanliness'. The last two are of no theoretical interest, while the first, which comprises 'Whatever regulations are made with respect to the trade, commerce, agriculture, manufactures of the country', became the subject of a large part of *The Wealth of Nations*.[64]

This simple division of the law is complicated by the fact that Smith lists 'Revenue and Arms' as separate objects of law,[65] although to us they would seem to be of the same administrative kind as the previous ones. Smith is not specific about his reasons for this division and it might be that he simply adopted traditional distinctions for educational purposes. Smith was, however, none too reverent towards traditional learning for its own sake, and it is not difficult to see that he could have good reason to treat revenue and arms as separate branches of law. Although the arrangement of the revenue system was an administrative matter, in Smith's eyes it raised very serious problems of justice because it involved forcible infringement of liberty, privacy, and property of individuals.[66] As far as the arrangement of the military is concerned, Smith's emphasis on the importance of defence would seem to warrant the treatment of this as a separate object of law: if this is not adequately attended to, all attention to the other objects of law may well be in vain. Regulations relating to the administration of such public institutions as law courts, parish schools for the poor, religious establishments, local authorities, etc., which Smith deals with from a revenue point of view in *The Wealth of Nations*,[67] are not specifically located in the legal system. But it would seem safe to think of them as part of, or closely related to, the regulations of 'police', and the same applies to regulations within domestic law, mentioned above.

Apart from justice, police, revenue, and arms, Smith does, like the natural law theoreticians, consider the laws of nations a separate branch of the legal system, to be treated by analogy with the laws relating to private justice.[68] These five constitute the whole of the legal system, and it is the general principles behind this system which are the subject of jurisprudence: 'Jurisprudence is the theory of the general principles of law and government. The four great objects of law are Justice, Police, Revenue, and Arms' – to which the laws of nations are added later.[69] It is of importance to notice that it is 'the theory of the *general principles*' that jurisprudence deals with, and not the five branches of law as such. If the latter had been Smith's intention, his whole jurisprudential project would have been seriously deficient for the following reason. He is emphatic that the discipline of jurisprudence which he presents is normative in character: 'Jurisprudence is that science which inquires into the general principles which ought to be the foundation of the laws of all nations.'[70] As far as the laws of justice are concerned, it can be shown that Smith provides a systematic normative foundation for them, and it is one of the objectives of the present study to show this. As far as the regulations of the military are concerned, the self-evident need for defence would seem to suffice. But 'police' and 'revenue' are not given any systematic and general normative basis *independent* of their relationship to justice.[71] Even if Smith on occasions talks in somewhat utilitarian terms about specific measures, he never presents a utilitarian *theory* to back this up, in the same way as he provides a complete theory of justice to back up his theory of the laws of justice. So part of the point of the 'general principles' is to show the centrality of the laws of justice and the dependence upon them of the other areas of law – in the way outlined above. If we understand Smith in this way, the avowed normative function of his jurisprudence becomes a possibility. Whether and in what sense it is realized depends on his use of the theory of justice.

This understanding of Smith's jurisprudence may find some further support when we consider his use of that legendary figure, the 'legislator'.[72] In a famous passage in *The Wealth of Nations* Smith contrasts the qualities of the real legislator with those of the ordinary politician – on the one hand, 'the science of a legislator, whose deliberations ought to be governed by general principles which are always the same', and on the other, 'the skill of that insidious and crafty animal, vulgarly called a statesman or politician'.[73] It is hardly too imaginative to suggest that the general principles of the legislator are those which are the subject of Smith's jurisprudence, and this is confirmed when we consider the role he plays in Smith's criticism of 'the men of system', which we discussed above. He is here clearly the man of public spirit who will strike the perfect Smithian balance between the enlightenment of 'Some general, and even systematical, idea of the perfection of policy and law', and the piecemeal action to alleviate concrete evils. 'When he cannot establish the right, he will not disdain to ameliorate the wrong; but like Solon, when he cannot establish the best system of laws, he will endeavour to establish the best that the people can bear.'[74] Understanding the general principles of law and government, he will *act* on the most general of all – the primacy of the negative, of justice. A person who can strike this balance will be rare, and the opportunities for his success even rarer, especially when it is most needed, in cases of civil disorder. But then Smith was not a believer in perfection, as we have seen, nor did he believe that the happiness and prosperity of mankind could be achieved by nothing less than perfection in its laws and institutions. As he remarked in a particular connection, 'If a nation could not prosper without the enjoyment of perfect liberty and perfect justice, there is not in the world a nation which could ever have prospered.'[75] What he did believe was that we can always do better, and consequently the philosopher should remember that the general principles upon which a legislator would act 'are the subject of a particular science, of all sciences by far the most important, but hitherto, perhaps, the least cultivated, that of natural jurisprudence'.[76]

Adam Smith's theory of politics might be thought an impoverishment of the subject, in favour of legal theory and positive economics, and certainly if one's standard is the wilder flight of utopian fantasies, he would be more than willing to plead guilty to the charge. But if less will do, Smith's ideas are of more interest than they have often been reputed to be. Outside the area of justice the richness of Smith's politics has been amply demonstrated.[77] That his jurisprudence might be a source of political enrichment in its own right is a possibility which will be discussed here, once we have gained some understanding of its general principles.

CHAPTER FIVE

Smith's analytical jurisprudence

1 The legal system

The view of justice as a negative virtue which we have traced in *The Theory of Moral Sentiments* is obviously that which has traditionally been called commutative justice. Smith is well aware that this is not the only meaning the word has taken in the philosophical tradition, and he is always careful to distinguish it sharply from distributive justice.[1] In the latter sense 'Justice consists in the proper exercise of all the social and beneficent Virtues' and it is therefore simply a collective label for all the positive virtues. It is, however, the negative virtue 'which can alone properly be called Justice',[2] and which is the basis for all law. Its negative character lends it precision so that it is formulated spontaneously in clear and universal rules, and the primacy of the negative gives it an urgency which with equal spontaneity leads men to attempt to enforce these rules. However, since men are hardly likely to have a clear view of justice in cases where their own interests are involved, 'civil society would become a scene of bloodshed and disorder, every man revenging himself at his own hand whenever he fancied he was injured',[3] unless the actual spectators in the social group intervened. As we shall see later, this spectator intervention is one of the original and one of the most important governmental functions, and it is the origin of all law:

The wisdom of every state or commonwealth endeavours, as well as it can, to employ the force of the society to restrain those who are subject to its authority, from hurting or disturbing the happiness of one another. The rules which it establishes for this purpose, constitute the civil and criminal law of each particular state or country. (TMS, vi, ii, intro., § 2)

The specific link between the general theory of moral sentiments and the jurisprudence is the concept of *rights*. This is hardly used at all in *The Theory of Moral Sentiments*,[4] but it is introduced in the *Lectures on Jurisprudence*. The concept of rights was of course central to the jurisprudential tradition, and Smith does to some extent follow writers like Pufendorf and Hutcheson in his definition of it. Thus he distinguishes between perfect and imperfect rights, of which the former are the object of commutative, the latter of distributive justice.[5] But this immediately makes it clear that the distinction is derived from that between negative and positive virtues and that 'right', like 'justice', is dependent upon the concept of 'injury': 'Justice is violated whenever one is deprived of what he had a right to and could justly demand from others, or rather, when we do him any injury or hurt without a cause.'[6] These concepts are connected repeatedly throughout the lectures. The object of natural jurisprudence is justice; and the rules of justice define our rights by laying down what actions constitute injuries against us. The concept of 'injury' is understood in pure spectator-terms: what the relevant, actual spectators – such as judges and juries – in a given society recognize as injury is in legal terms injury in that society at that time and is definitive of its rights and laws. And what the impartial spectator recognizes as injury is definitive of absolute rights and justice. This is never spelt out in so many words, but is simply taken for granted throughout, and it is indeed abundantly clear once we analyse Smith's concrete uses of the central concepts.

Smith's adaptation of the established categories of jurisprudence to his own theory goes well beyond this basic level. He is thus able to use a traditional division of the subjects of law which follows the division of rights. But this division is again determined by the various kinds of injury a person can suffer; and they fall into three broad classes: '1st, he may be injured as a man; 2dly, as a member of a family; and 3dly, as a citizen or member of a state.'[7] These three classes are exhaustive and exclusive,[8] and when they are subdivided they cover all the areas of law proper. The first class is divided into three, for as individuals we may be injured in our person (bodily harm or confinement), or in our reputation, or in our property. Family law is concerned with the injuries which can occur in relations between spouses, between parents and children, and between masters and servants. Finally, public law is concerned with the citizens' rights against the sovereign and the sovereign's rights against the citizens.[9] Before we analyse the principles behind these various areas of law we should, however, pay attention to yet another broad distinction which Smith adopts from the jurisprudential tradition and which cuts across the three categories of private law, domestic law, and public law. This is the distinction between natural and acquired (or adventitious) rights. To the former belong only the first two areas of private law, namely the rights pertaining to our personal integrity and to our reputation, whereas property law, family law, and public law are all concerned with the protection of acquired rights.[10] Smith never makes it absolutely clear what is the basis for this distinction, but the little he does say makes it possible to find an explanation – and a very interesting contrast with Hume.

The thing he stresses is that natural rights are quite evident in their content and need no lengthy analysis: what constitutes an injury to a man's person or reputation is immediately 'evident to reason'.[11] But acquired rights need much more explanation. This is simply because they are – acquired. They depend for their very existence, or their effective recognition, on some element of governmental authority in a society, and since the latter varies enormously from one epoch to another and from one country to another, so the rights must also vary, and consequently they can only be understood against the background of these circumstantial factors. It is in this sense that we have to understand Smith's statement in the introduction to LJ(B) that 'Property and civil government very much depend on one another. The preservation of property and the inequality of possession first formed it, and the state of property must always vary with the form of government.'[12] One can say that acquired rights must necessarily have a history and that they can only be explained in their historical context. As will become clear later, *one* of Smith's basic aims with his lectures – and undoubtedly with his planned book – was to provide such an explanation.

It should be noticed, however, that natural rights are not totally outside the vicissitudes of history. Thus Smith goes to some length to explain the social circumstances which made the exposition of children an acceptable part of ancient legal practice.[13] Similarly the historical significance of slavery preoccupied Smith both in his jurisprudence lectures and in *The Wealth of Nations* in a way which we shall have occasion to discuss below; and although it was mainly the family law aspects and their political importance which interested him, the idea that this institution infringed the most basic of natural rights was never far from the surface in Smith's attention to this, 'the vilest of all states'.[14]

It is features such as these which put one on guard against treating Smith's distinction between natural and acquired rights as an absolute distinction between 'historical' and 'non-historical' rights – and consequently against treating the original distinction itself as absolute. For obviously both classes of rights have the same foundation, namely the sympathetic resentment of the impartial spectator at the injuries against which the rights are a protection. This resentment, however, is proportional to the severity of the injury done, and accordingly we get rights and the corresponding rules of justice ordered into a scale of importance. The stronger the resentment of the impartial spectator, the more important are the rules of justice that arise from it:

The most sacred laws of justice...are the laws which guard the life and person of our neighbour; the next are those which guard his property and possessions; and last of all come those which guard what are called his personal rights, or what are due to him from the promises of others. (TMS, ii, ii, 2, § 2)[15]

Where on the scale the rights protected by family law come we are not told, but presumably they would be comparable to either property or contract. As far as public law is concerned, the measure of importance is so different – 'political' – that a comparison would make little sense. And as we shall see, it is this factor which has militated against the development of public law into a system on a par with the other branches of law.

It should now be fairly obvious that what Smith has in mind when he talks of natural rights as immediately 'evident to reason' is that the injury done in infringing them is so severe that nearly any spectator can reach the standpoint of the impartial spectator and react with the strongest sympathetic resentment, and thus maintain these rights. But in the case of infringements of acquired rights the injury may not be so immediately obvious and further explanation of the circumstances may be necessary.[16] Or, to exploit our earlier terminology, Smith operates not only with a moral primacy of the negative over the positive, but also with a moral and hence legal primacy of the more negative over the less negative!

We can conclude that Smith adopts the traditional distinction between natural and acquired rights as a mere heuristic device to draw attention to the significant differences in moral urgency and – more to the point for the plan of the lecture course – in the degree of historicality of the various rights which are protected by law. At the same time he has, of course, met the pedagogic necessity of acquainting his students with the existing literature. Altogether the whole episode is quite typical of Smith's pragmatic attitude to traditional learning.

Within the context of the present essay Smith's ambiguous attitude to the distinction between natural and acquired rights has a further significance: it inevitably recalls Hume's distinction between natural and artificial virtues and his treatment of justice as an artificial virtue; and first of all it reminds us that Hume's account of justice was mainly in terms of property (and allied 'acquired' rights),[17] whereas Smith's concept of justice, as we now see, covers natural as well as acquired rights. It was Hume's analysis of justice as 'artificial', in the very special sense discussed above,[18] which gave him some philosophical foundation for his novel evolutionary theory of law, and we have now seen this idea reflected in Smith's emphasis on the historical character of acquired rights. But it was the basis for the distinction between natural and artificial which made it difficult for Hume to incorporate the natural rights as part of his conception of justice. For whereas acquired rights, like property, were based on a sympathetic detour via 'public utility', and the virtue of respecting them was hence 'artificial', the natural rights, like safety of body, were based on a direct sympathy, and the virtue of respecting them was hence 'natural'. Smith's rejection of a 'utilitarian' or consequentialist account of rights and their accompanying virtues, and his adoption of a unitarian spectator account, gives him the best of both worlds: on the one hand he can keep natural rights well within his concept of justice and hence has a more complete tool for the analysis of law; on the other hand the natural primacy of the more negative over the less negative in the eyes of any spectator still makes it possible for him to retain some reasonably clear and useful distinction between the two groups of rights.

Since he considered natural rights to be so self-evident, it is hardly surprising that Smith gives no more than a brief outline of each of these rights. It may be more surprising – at least it surprised one reader – that he deals with them at great length *indirectly* in his theory of punishment. However, since I, like Smith, think that this is best discussed in the context of that theory,[19] I shall confine myself here to a few comments on his *direct* treatment of natural rights. They fall into two categories according to the injuries which can be done to an individual in his person and in his reputation. The former are subdivided into injuries to life and body, and injury to a person's liberty to move around and combine with other people in marriage, business, etc.[20] These are undoubtedly the most obvious rights of all. The account of the right not to be injured in one's reputation is interesting in two respects. First of all it is an excellent example of Smith's concrete application of the idea of the primacy of the negative in morals. Smith argues that injury to reputation occurs in two kinds of circumstances, namely when a person is 'degraded below the common sort of men' in ordinary moral reputation, or when a person is degraded below the common professional standards in his particular walk of life. It hardly needs to be argued that these common standards or levels are spectator-determined for a given society and period. But it is not recognized as injury if, on the 'positive' side of the common level, praise and commendation do not reach the expected pitch![21] The second point of interest in connection with this right is that it provides yet another illustration of the looseness of Smith's distinction between natural and acquired rights. For although he counts the right to protection of one's reputation as one of the natural rights, it should be fairly obvious that it is almost as changeable as many acquired rights, since it is determined by something as changeable as the standards of 'the common sort of men' and of professions.

Smith's main concern, however, is with all the acquired rights, and here it should be noticed that he follows different systematics in the two academic sessions from which we have reports on his lecture course. In LJ(B) he follows what he calls the method of the civil law and begins with public law, goes on with domestic law, and ends the Justice section of the lecture course[22] with private law – to which at the end of the whole course he adds a brief section on international law. But in LJ(A) Smith follows the same system as that of Francis Hutcheson, beginning with private law, going on to domestic law, and concluding with public law. The set of notes is incomplete in its coverage of the course and contains no record of the section on international law. The order followed in the very brief Anderson Notes is the same as that in LJ(A). Since the notes in LJ(B) in all likelihood cover Smith's course in his last year as a professor at Glasgow (the academic session 1763–4), the most obvious explanation for his change of system was his impending departure. We are, however, without any evidence about this and it seems impossible to find a clear explanation within the lecture notes themselves. In LJ(B) Smith declares that of the two systems 'that of the civil law seems upon the whole preferable', but he gives no reasons for this and he also makes it clear that he did not put much weight upon the choice between the two methods: 'There are several advantages peculiar to each of these two methods.'[23] Since nothing in the present argument depends on the order of the lecture course, I therefore feel free to follow the disposition in LJ(A) – simply because this is the fuller set of notes.

2 Real rights

The rights pertaining to a person's estate are divided into two basic groups, real rights and personal rights. Real rights are to particular things and can be upheld against any person whatsoever. 'Such are all possessions, houses, furniture', etc. Personal rights are rights against a particular other person. 'Such are all debts and contracts, the payment or performance of which can be demanded only from one person.'[24] The real rights are four in number, and the personal three, as shown in Fig. 1, which gives a complete survey of Smith's organization of the law.[25]

Property

The most important of the real rights is that to property, the principles of which Smith accounts for through a spectator analysis of the five ways it can be acquired, by occupation, by accession, by prescription, by succession, and by voluntary transfer.[26] Smith's intention to analyse these matters in terms of the spectator theory of *The Theory of Moral Sentiments* is signalled at the outset of his discussion of occupation, where he specifically refers his students to his outline of this 'system' earlier in the course.[27] And he follows this intention with great clarity.

Why is it, he asks, that the mere occupation or possession of something is commonly taken – everything else being equal, of course – to give the possessor a right to the thing to the exclusion of everyone else? Why is it considered an injury to that person if someone else disturbs him in his possession in any way – so much so that it is considered right and proper for him not only to protect his possessions against such injury, but to seek revenge or compensation for it? The reason is that any impartial spectator would participate sympathetically in these reactions, whereas he could not possibly go along with the infringement of possessions. The

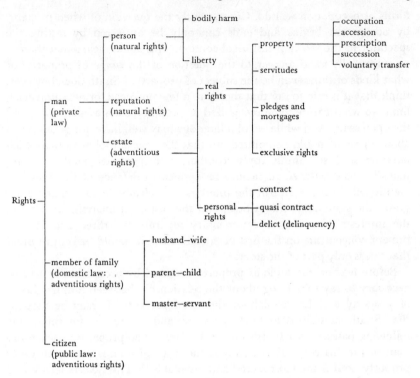

Fig. 1 Adam Smith's system of natural jurisprudence

background to this spectator sympathy is 'the reasonable expectation' which any possessor has of having the use and free disposition of his possession. It is obviously implicit in this view that it would be unreasonable if people could not in general form such expectations.[28] The common-sense significance of this unreasonableness has, I think, a philosophical background in Smith's speculations about human knowledge:[29] we may well take it to mean *incoherence,* for if such expectations were constantly frustrated they would render man's ideas of right and wrong actions totally incoherent. This suggestion only gains plausibility, however, as we see the recurrence of speculations about reasonableness and cognate ideas, and its full significance will only become clear in connection with the critical aspects of Smith's jurisprudence.

Which expectations are recognized as reasonable must depend upon who the impartial spectators are – or, rather, on the circumstances under which they try to be impartial. It is a historical question which must be answered differently for different periods and different countries. In some societies nothing but actual physical possession of a thing will be recognized as enough to sustain a claim to the thing; in others, much 'looser'

forms of occupation will do. Consequently the question of when property
by occupation begins and ends can only be answered by setting the
spectator in the relevant historical context. This again means that there is
no universally valid answer to the question of the *range* of property, or
what kinds of things can be the subject of property.[30] Smith does, however,
think that it is safe to say that there are a few universal, or near universal,
limits to what can become recognized as property, such as air, water, and
the open sea.[31] And while we of a later age may well have our doubts even
about these, it should be pointed out that the *critical* tool of justice which
later we shall see Smith apply to other, more contested kinds of 'commons'[32] could with equal facility be applied in defence of the ones just
mentioned. While Smith in the interests of a clearer lecture course integrates the systematic, the critical, and the historical analysis, we shall in
the interests of a clearer commentary separate the three and for the
present concentrate on the first perspective. But it should be kept in mind
that this is only part of the story.

Before leaving the topic of property acquired by occupation it may be
necessary to say something about the relationship between Smith's theory
of property and Locke's labour theory of property. It may be thought
that Smith subscribed to Locke's theory, and the reason for this is the
following passage in *The Wealth of Nations*: 'The property which every
man has in his own labour, as it is the original foundation of all other
property, so it is the most sacred and inviolable.'[33] This does indeed sound
very much like Locke – and very different from the spectator account of
property given in the jurisprudence lectures. The problem is just that it is
the *only* passage of this kind in Smith's work.[34] Furthermore, it is a passing
remark in the middle of Smith's critical discussion of existing apprentice-
ship laws.[35] It is therefore tempting simply to dismiss the passage. Nevertheless, if there is a conflict here it is between Smith's own published
word and the unpublished report of others on his word – albeit *two* reports,
which are mutually consistent and not only consistent with, but implied
by, Smith's published word elsewhere, in *The Theory of Moral Sentiments*.
But is there any conflict? I do not think so. First, it should be pointed out
that Smith is not talking about property *rights* – neither in the passage
quoted, nor anywhere in its context. The only thing which we might take
as an indication in this direction is the phrase 'original foundation'. But in
the absence of anything else of the same kind this may well be understood
simply as 'origin', in which case the sentence is simply saying that the
origin of property is the labour of individual men. Furthermore, the two
clauses beginning 'as' and 'so', respectively, seem to be parallels rather
than to constitute an argument in which the latter is a conclusion from
the former.[36] And if we look at the paragraph as a whole we shall see that
it is about freedom of activity, for the working man as for the employer –

a parallel which is nicely underlined by the use of the ambiguous 'patrimony' for the former's physical ability to work. Taken in this broad sense, Smith can obviously say that property has its origin in labour: if no one ever took to new forms of activity – such as keeping, rather than killing animals – new forms of property would never arise. But this is perfectly compatible with saying that the new activity will only be constitutive of a *right* if it becomes recognized by the relevant spectators as establishing a reasonable expectation. Indeed, it seems entirely plausible to argue that to bestow labour upon something would be one of the circumstances which would always tend to induce a spectator to sympathize with one's expectations of the use of the thing as reasonable. And there are two passages which confirm that this is exactly what Smith used Locke's labour idea for. The first is in the Anderson Notes where Smith is reported as saying that, 'To deprive a man of the beast or fish he has caught, or of the fruit he has gathered, is depriving him of what cost him *labour and so giving him pain*, and is contrary to the laws of the rudest society.'[37] The central thing is not the labour, but the pain which it heightens, and the pain is – as we know – the most obvious object of the spectator's sympathy. The other passage is a small mock-dialogue in the LJ(A) which occurs immediately after Smith has explained his spectator theory of property acquired by occupation and explained it with the example of picking an apple:

You may ask indeed, as this apple is as fit for your use as it is for mine, what title have I to detain it from you. You may go to the forest (says one to me) and pull another. You may go as well as I, replied I. And besides it is more reasonable that you should, as I have gone already and bestowed my time and pains in procuring the fruit. (LJ(A), i, 37)

The final sentence may remind readers of the labour theory,[38] but coming at the end of a very lucid exposition of the spectator theory of property and re-employing the term 'reasonable' for the third time within one page in the manuscript, it seems obvious to read it in the way suggested above: that 'time and pains' are amongst the important circumstances which would make one's expectations seem reasonable to an impartial spectator.

Accession

Property is also acquired by accession to things which somehow follow from or go with what one already owns, such as milk and offspring from domestic animals, crops on one's land or minerals underneath it, etc.[39] The account of this is again in terms of the spectator: it would appear to any spectator an 'impropriety' and an 'injustice'[40] not to allow the subject of accession to follow the thing from which it springs or with which it coheres.[41] The basis for this spectator judgement is a very nice combination of a standard Humean principle of association and Smith's idea of the

importance of coherence in human knowledge: we naturally tend to let
the minor and/or derivative follow the major and/or principal thing,[42]
and at the same time we have a natural wish to 'complete' things so that
they cohere in some sort of system: 'we are naturally inclined to compleat
or square ones property or any other right in the same manner as we
would incline to square his land estate; we do not incline to have corners
sticking into it'.[43] This 'aesthetic' completion of the law by spectators'
acceptance of our natural expectations as proper (or 'reasonable') is a
source of order very much like what modern jurisprudence refers to as
analogical reasoning. It is a form of argument which Smith employs in
various contexts. Thus it seems to be involved in his discussion of which
parts of the sea will be recognized as belonging to a country, namely bays,
firths, coastal waters, etc.;[44] it is the principle which must be understood
to decide when alluvial deposits come to belong to a private owner of
adjacent land and when to the country as a whole;[45] and in connection
with the law of succession we find it not only applied, but stated as a
general rule, that this stems 'From the inclination we naturally have to
square and compleat every thing, even when by this means we stretch the
originall constitution; and thus it is that all laws that found any new right
become in time of extensive interpretation.'[46] It is clearly implied in this
general statement that aesthetic completion of the law is not just a
principle of common-law reasoning, but also a principle of interpretation
of statute law. We shall later have occasion to notice another form of
analogical reasoning in connection with exclusive privileges.

Prescription

Like accession the principle of acquisition of property by prescription
presupposes the existence of property by occupation. It is the principle
that long *de facto* possession of a thing can lead to the recognition of a
property right to it, even though there is a previous owner who has never
relinquished his claim to the thing.[47] As soon as the forms of property have
developed beyond the most primitive stage (direct personal belongings)
this principle becomes necessary in order that there may be flexibility
without disorder in the property system: if the person who had long had
the use of something could not feel safe in his possession, 'property would
be always uncertain'.[48]

The explanation of this right to property is naturally in terms of

the same principles as that of occupation. For in the same manner as the spectator
can enter into the expectations of the 1st occupant that he will have the use of
the thing occupied, and think he is injured by those who would wrest it from
him; in the same manner, the right of prescription is derived from the opinion of
the spectator that the possessor of a long standing has a just expectation that he
may use what has been thus possessed, and that the former proprietor...has so

far lost all right to it, has no expectation of using it, as that it would appear injurious in him to deprive the present possessor. (LJ(A), i, 77)

It is interesting to compare this clear explanation with the very brief statement which corresponds to it in LJ(B), where Smith's point is simply summarized thus: 'Prescription is founded on the supposed attachment of the possessor to what he has long been possessed of, and the supposed detachment of affection in the old possessor to what has been long out of his possession.'[49] This illustrates very well the difficulty of appreciating the full detail of the integration of Smith's theory of moral sentiments and his philosophy of law as long as we had only the version of his juris-prudence lectures contained in LJ(B). The only indication of the spectator theory in the passage just quoted is the word 'supposed'! However, once the much fuller and more explicit application of spectator principles in LJ(A) has alerted us to it, we shall see that his language, as reported in both sets of notes, is completely pervaded by a number of standard expressions which indicate the spectator point of view.[50] These expressions include (apart from the usual spectator verbs 'enter into', 'go along with', etc.) 'be conceived', 'appear' (and 'apparent'), 'be considered', 'be looked upon', 'be supposed', and 'imagine'.[51] In addition, there are several looser, even more colloquial turns of phrase, the spectator meaning of which can only be seen from the context.

There is hardly any doubt that the application of this mode is a deliber-ate policy on Smith's part, not only because this would achieve his obvious wish to integrate jurisprudence as a genuine part of his over-all moral theory, but also because he thought that the best method of presentation, especially in human affairs, was that of 'indirect description', which means description of events through description of spectator reactions to them. This can be seen clearly in the *Lectures on Rhetoric and Belles Lettres* where he devotes much time to discussing the advantages of indirect description in history and poetry,[52] and puts forward the general rule

that no action...can be represented in such a manner as to be very interesting to those who had not been present at it, by a bare narration, where it is described directly, without taking notice of any of the effects it had on those who were either actors or spectators of the whole affair.[53]

This principle forms part of Smith's general situationist method which we shall discuss in connection with his view of history, and which springs out of his general view of knowledge as outlined above.[54]

Succession

Property is acquired through succession in either of two ways, by law or by testament.[55] Of these, testamentary succession was 'a considerable refinement in humanity' which only gained acceptance quite late. It is therefore impossible to account for succession by law in the usual way by reference to 'the supposed will of the deceased', which is the principle behind testamentary succession, for legal succession is known much earlier in history.[56] Instead Smith offers as the basic principle behind legal succession a most interesting application of his combined 'spectator-and-labour theory' of property, as I explained this theory above.[57] His idea is simply that all members of the family will have claims recognized for a share in the property of the deceased – who is naturally the male head of the family – because they have all contributed to the upkeep of the family in its acquisition of property:

All the members of the family came in for an equall share in [the property] at his death, as they had all contributed their assistance to the support of it. No distinction was made with regard to sex; sons and daughters equally give their assistance to the master...of the family, and for this reason were equall sharers in his possessions after his death. (LJ(A), i, 93)[58]

This principle applied in all its simplicity in primitive societies – hence the past tense in the quotation – but through history it has inevitably become entangled with the legal effects of changing sex-roles and, in connection with this, changing religious attitudes;[59] and as far as immoveables (land) are concerned, politics warped it beyond recognition with the introduction of primogeniture – a momentous development about which we shall hear a good deal more. But as far as moveables are concerned the basic principle still has a recognizable influence on modern law, despite the various historical changes.[60]

It should be noted that the spectator maintains a low profile in the descriptive account of succession by law as this has been reported in the two sets of notes. But, as if to make up for this, he has a leading role in the critical treatment of the topic, which we shall discuss in the next chapter. And so he has in the treatment of succession by testament. Testaments are puzzling, for to enforce them is simply to give legal recognition to the will of the dead. But 'What obligation is the community under to observe the directions [the dead person] made concerning his goods now when he can have no will, nor is supposed to have any knowledge of the matter'?[61] For Pufendorf the difficulty was so great that he 'whimsically accounts for this from the immortality of the soul'.[62] But irrespective of how much conventional religious phraseology Smith is prepared to accept on appropriate occasions, this is too much for him to consider seriously. Instead he harks back to his account of the basic principle of spectator sympathy which he expounded at the beginning of *The Theory of Moral Sentiments*. As we saw in an earlier chapter, he illustrated the situational dependence of this by means of a number of examples where the person sympathized with was in a position where he could not possibly have the sentiments which were the object of sympathy, and the crowning example was exactly that of sympathy with a recently dead person.[63] This is the basis for recognizing testaments: if we do not give such recognition, it is considered an injury to the dead person, whose 'interests' have a certain continued existence sympathetically in the spectators. 'The injury is conceived to be done to the dead person, as we enter into what would be his sentiments were he to live again.'[64]

Voluntary transfer

The fifth and final method of acquiring property with which Smith deals is that of the voluntary transference of a thing from one person to another, as in ordinary purchases. He only gives a brief, factual account[65] which adds nothing to our understanding of his basic principles and which calls for little comment, except to notice two points. First, Smith stresses the same two features of the law relating to voluntary transfer which Hume stressed in the *Treatise*, namely the necessity of a clear indication of the intention of the person transferring and the actual or symbolic delivery of the thing.[66] Secondly, the fact that *both* of these are required in order for a property right, which is a real right, to arise puts into relief what the former of them alone gives rise to, namely the personal rights from contracts.[67]

Servitudes, pledges, exclusive privileges

Apart from property the real rights are these three, which Smith deals with briefly and without much philosophical analysis.[68] Servitudes, which are 'burthens which one man has on the property of another', and pledges and mortgages, which are 'certain securities for the payment of debts', were originally instituted by contract and they were therefore personal rights. But in order to make them easily transferable, legislatures have changed them into real rights, and the history of this conversion is one of Smith's main concerns in these brief sections.

An exclusive privilege is the right a person has to exclude everyone else from something, but without being the actual owner of it. An heir is in such a position during the period between the death of the previous owner and his acceptance or refusal of the inheritance. There are two points to notice about Smith's discussion of this right. The first is the ease with which he engages in critical discussion of even relatively detailed matters of law. Thus he points out that if the exclusive privilege of an heir in the above-mentioned position is considered a real right, then all exclusive privileges have, by simple analogy, to be considered as real rights. He criticizes the Privy Council for mistaking an obvious case of breach of exclusive privilege for a breach of property. And he criticizes lawyers for frequently mistaking the exclusive privileges of mills and corporations for servitudes. The second point to notice is that he sharply distinguishes between those exclusive privileges which are 'founded on natural reason', and those which are 'intirely the creatures of the civil constitutions of states'.[69] The inheritance case belongs in the former category, monopolies in the latter.

3 Personal rights

A personal right is 'the right one has to demand the performance of some sort of service from an other'. Such rights arise from obligations under-taken, and must be three in kind, since there are three ways obligations can come about:

1st, from contract; or 2dly, from what the civilians call quasi contract, that is, the obligation one is under [to] restore to the owner whatever of his property has come into [one's] possession either voluntarily or otherwise; or 3dly, from some injury (or delict) he has done what is his [i.e. another's]. (LJ(A), ii, 42)[70]

Nothing more need be said about the law concerning quasi contract which, on Smith's account, fills a legal hiatus, so to speak, between property law and contract law. The spectator theory of contractual rights, however, is both interesting and important, not only because contracts in themselves are of great significance, but also because it is in this connection that Smith puts forward his theory of obligation.

Contracts are dependent upon promises and the question is therefore: what makes promises obligatory? Smith rejects the suggestion that this can be reduced to the obligation to tell the truth, the idea being that if a person does not perform what he previously promised then the statement of the promise was false.[71] Smith gives two arguments against this. First, 'all that veracity can extend to is either what is past or what is present', whereas 'with regard to what is future veracity can have no effect, as knowledge does not extend to it'.[72] This is a very dubious argument for the implication of it is that statements about the future cannot have any truth value. However, this assumes that we accept statements of the form, 'I promise to do something', as descriptions of future states of affairs, rather than as statements of present intention – and Smith is only doing so for the sake of the argument. His second argument is that the obligation to veracity is of less moral weight than the obligation to keep promises, since breach of the former constitutes a smaller injury than breach of the latter. Consequently the proposed reduction makes little sense, for in cases of conflict between the two obligations the one which is supposedly derivative must take precedence over the one from which it should be derived. This ingenious argument makes the assumption that the obliga-tion to honour promises is *always* morally the more important of the two, and this might be rather hard to prove. Smith also considers the sugges-tion that the obligation to perform a promise should 'proceed from the will of the person to be obliged', but rejects it on the grounds that promises made insincerely (without the will) may well be obligatory.[73] This argument is interesting because it leads into his own theory of obligation. Just as the obligation of promises does not spring from the will of the promisor, so it does not arise from the mere expression of his will. It only arises when the declaration of the promisor's will is such that the promisee can reasonably, i.e. by an impartial spectator, be said to depend upon the promise – or to have 'a reasonable ground of expectation'.[74] For only if this is the case can the promisee be said to suffer injury, with which the impartial spectator can go along if the promisor does not perform. 'It is the disappointment of the person we promise to which occasions the obligation to perform it.'[75] In other words, one is under obligation to perform that which the impartial spectator would resent the non-performance of, and one's feeling of obligation consists in internalizing this resentment so that one would resent oneself, so to speak, for not performing the thing promised. This is precisely the view of obligation which Smith briefly and somewhat vaguely suggested in connection with the obligation to follow the general rules of morality, and it is an explicit spectator version of the theory of obligation which we worked out for Hume.[76]

The theory brings out very clearly a basic feature of Smith's moral philosophy, namely that it is about the *relations*[77] between persons. It is not the 'isolated' quality or characteristic in a person, such as his will, which gives rise to moral problems. These only arise when some sort of connection is established with another person, such that there is a pattern of both action and reaction which an impartial spectator can evaluate sympathetically. This can only be the case, however, if there is some sort of public medium through which the relationship is established. In the case of property this medium is the thing in which property right is claimed, but in the case of promises, and hence contracts, the establishment of rights is dependent upon the abstract medium of language. Accordingly Smith stresses very strongly that contracts are only possible when language has reached a certain degree of clarity and certainty. But even then it is the case that 'Language at all times must be somewhat ambiguous',[78] and although something can be achieved by applying standard formulae for the conclusion of contracts, contractual rights will always seem more abstract and uncertain than other rights. People will therefore generally depend less upon such rights than upon other rights. This will naturally colour the spectator's attitude and the spectator sympathy with expectations arising from contracts and with the resentment at their disappointment will be significantly weaker than is the case with property. Consequently, contractual rights are the weakest in private law[79] and in fact they only have legal force when two conditions are met. Not only must the intention of the promisor be expressed so clearly that no impartial spectator can be in doubt about the content of the agreement; but, secondly, the things which are the subject of the agreement must also be considered of significant value. Unless the latter condition is met, no real injury is done if the contract is not fulfilled.[80] Both these conditions are only present comparatively late in the development of society, and it was in fact not until commerce was widespread that contract law became really significant. This is of the greatest historical importance,[81] but it is also of some importance for the understanding of Smith's analysis of the legal system. For as we shall see when discussing his theory of punishment, there is good reason to believe that he regarded at least parts of contract law as somewhat akin to the laws of 'police' which generally supplement the strict laws of justice in a commercial society. This ambiguous status of some contract laws is, I suggest, due to their tenuous spectator foundation.[82]

4 Delict, or theory of punishment

When any of our rights are infringed we are injured and this gives rise to a new right, the right to seek redress of the injury. This is a right *ex delicto*, 'from the delinquency of an other'.[83] And since the redress is sought from the person who did the injury, the theory of such rights constitutes the theory of punishment. The legal recognition that an action against a person is an injury is based upon the impartial spectator's sympathy with the resentment of that person, and the right to seek redress is therefore also based upon that spectator sympathy. It is, however, not only the right to seek punishment, but also the right to seek a particular degree of punishment which is dependent upon the approval of the impartial spectator:

in all cases the measure of the punishment to be inflicted on the delinquent is the concurrence of the impartial spectator with the resentment of the injured...a punishment appears equitable in the eyes of the rest of mankind when it is such that the spectator would concur with the offended person in exacting it. (LJ(A), ii, 89–90)[84]

What the spectator can go along with is 'the natural measure of punishment', and that is 'a reasonable retaliation'.[85] Smith's idea can perhaps be further clarified by considering his somewhat different formulation of it in an early manuscript. There he maintains that while the infringement of rights is a clear matter which can be contained in precise rules, this is not the case with the proper degree of resentment and punishment due for such injury. The proper degree of punishment only becomes precise by the fact that 'Improper punishment, punishment which is either not due at all or which exceeds the demerit of the Crime, is an injury to the Criminal, may and ought to be opposed by force, and if inflicted, exposes the person who inflicts it to punishment in his turn.'[86]

This explanation of the proper degree of punishment never recurs in Smith's later, published writings, and it has been suggested that this was because in the interval he had developed the full spectator theory according to which the proper degree of punishment is that with which the impartial spectator can go along.[87] This can hardly be the full story. First, the difference between the manuscript explanation and the full spectator explanation is more in the formulation than in the substance. For in determining what constitutes 'improper punishment', the main consideration, or determining situational factor, would obviously be our perception of the original action (the crime, or alleged crime). All that the full spectator theory adds is a clear specification of this. The point of the manuscript formulation is that the degree of punishment will be imprecise if the act of punishing is not subjected to the same test as all other actions (including the original injury). This amounts to saying that resentment and punishment will remain imprecise if and when there is no impartial spectator to undertake such a test. This idea Smith never dropped. First of all he kept maintaining that in itself 'Resentment is on the whole a very indiscriminating principle',[88] which has to be kept in check by spectator reactions. And secondly, his whole history of the development of private law is the record of mankind's Herculean task in providing such a check on people's excessive resentment and craving for the punishment of their fellows. This attempt only met with some success once governments became strong enough to put real force behind the impartial spectators, who in the process had become judges.

What then became of the idea, in the manuscript, that improper punishment in itself is a *punishable* injury? While the formulation is never repeated, the idea is certainly used. Thus in the early periods of social development, when punishment tends to be a matter of direct revenge, one of the sources of instability is exactly that excessive punishment is considered an injury in itself. Later, when government has gained strength to administer justice more strictly, it is no longer the injured party but the sovereign who punishes.[89] Consequently, improper or excessive punishment becomes a matter between the party who is punished and the sovereign, and that takes the matter out of private law and into public law. This would, of course, not prevent Smith from talking of improper punishment as injury and injustice, and he is quite willing to accuse sovereigns of injury and injustice to their subjects, at least in general terms. But he cannot characterize this as *punishable*, for the idea of punishment of the sovereign would conflict with his theory of sovereignty, as we shall see later.[90] Although an impartial spectator could agree that a sovereign had committed an injustice, how could he go along with punishment of the sovereign as proper when this would constitute a threat to the continued existence of sovereignty? In short, as far as early society is concerned, Smith could and did use the idea that 'Improper punishment ... is an injury... and... exposes the person who inflicts it to punishment in his turn'; as far as developed society is concerned, he could not use it consistently, and that seems a good reason for not doing so.

Although the principle that improper punishment is itself punishable was thought inconsistent with the strong sovereignty required in developed societies, Smith obviously thought that the principle had had a very significant *influence* on such societies. For it would seem to be exactly this principle that lies behind the appeal procedures which are institutional-ized in societies with as regular an administration of justice as Britain. Although the sovereign power cannot be punishable, it can in its judicial branch be divided into various layers, through which proper punishment may successively be sought. In the same way the principle could be said to lie behind provisions like Habeas Corpus and bail: these are attempts to avoid improper 'punishment' before a trial has begun. And in these two somewhat special cases the improper 'punishment' is in fact punished – by heavy penalties on the judge concerned![91]

These connections between various strands of Smith's thought are in-evitably somewhat speculative. They do, however, seem fairly obvious and they suggest why Smith may have avoided further use of the 'punishable punishment' principle in purely abstract spectator terms. It would be very difficult to keep these terms completely abstract when they refer to such a socially and politically suggestive relationship as 'punishable punishment'. There are areas of morality which are so basic and universal in their humanity that the impartial spectator need know little or nothing about the individuals involved in them in order to determine his sympathies, and punishment is certainly one of them.[92] But the idea that punishment itself could be punishable is not quite so simple; here the spectator will need to know more about the individuals involved than just their humanity – such as their social and political circumstances. A spectator cannot be impartial pure and simple; he has to be impartial in relationship to somebody. While this person may be anybody, he must be individuated, and that may well require substantial knowledge of his situation. Smith's growing realization of these *complexities* in the spectator theory may, I suggest, have led him to avoid repetition of the principle in the manuscript.[93]

By whatever avenues Smith arrived at his theory of punishment and its measure, the theory itself is clear enough. In modern terms it would prob-ably be described as retributive, and that is justified in as far as it is obviously the injury which gives occasion to the punishment. But it is a description which is apt to obscure the fact that it is not the injury which somehow *in itself* justifies the punishment. Although the connection between crime and punishment is 'natural' in the sense that it is provided by the impartial spectator, who embodies certain universal decision procedures, it is all the same changeable over time because the situation in which the spectator takes his decisions is subject to historical change. Irrespective of what label we might want to put on Smith's theory of punishment, however, it is explicitly anti-utilitarian – in all senses of that term. This is simply a consequence of his general criticism of utility accounts of justice,[94] but he reinforces his standpoint by some further reflections on punishment. If some sort of utility were the proper measure of punishment, then we could take it that our criminal law had hardly ever been visited by the impartial spectator, for it would be very different from what it actually is. This is shown quite clearly if we look at cases where the law does use utility, rather than spectator sympathy with resentment, as the standard for punishment. In such cases the legally imposed measure of punishment can be so much at variance with that which the society, as impartial spectators of the crime in question, will go along with that it becomes impossible to impose it.

Thus some years ago the British nation took a fancy...that the wealth and strength of the nation depended entirely on the flourishing of their woolen trade, and that this could not prosper if the exportation of wool was permitted. To prevent this it was enacted that the exportation of wool should be punished with death. This exportation was no crime at all, in naturall equity, and was very far from deserving so high a punishment in the eyes of the people; they therefore found that while this was the punishment they could get neither jury nor informers. (LJ(A), ii, 91–2)[95]

In other cases where *some* aspects of the original action may be naturally criminal, the resistance to the legally enforced punishment may be much less and may even be more in spirit than in action. This is the case, for example, when the sentinel in an army is executed for falling asleep while on guard. Such a punishment is derived entirely from 'the consideration of the publick good', but 'tho' the punishment be just and the injury that might have ensued be very great, yet mankind can never enter into this punishment as if he had been a thief or a robber'.[96]

The conclusion must be that if utility had been the standard by which punishment was imposed by the actual spectators in a society, then the whole of our criminal law would have been significantly different from what it is. And if utility had been the standard of the impartial spectator, then all human ideas of punishment and justice, and their embodiment in laws, would be perverted. But although considerations of utility do not provide a justification for punishment, it is perfectly understandable that people[97] should have thought so. For punishment based upon spectator sympathy with the resentment of the injured person does in fact *lead to* the kind of useful results which have been taken as its justification, namely the correction of the offender, the deterrence of both him and others for the future, and – presumably only in certain cases – 'compensation for the injury'.[98] As usual in Smith, we must distinguish between the reasons that justify and motives that lead, and the order of things that ensues – a lesson he took from Hume, and took more thoroughly to heart than the master. Utility considerations can, however, have a direct and positive influence by strengthening our resolve to punish in cases which are controversial or where we are excessively influenced by pity for the offender.[99]

Since the rights from delict (the rights to inflict punishment) arise from the infringements of other rights, the system of the former rights runs wholly in parallel with that of the latter, as shown in Fig. 2, with the following exceptions.[100] Since Smith deals with punishment as part of private law, he does not include here punishments relating to domestic and

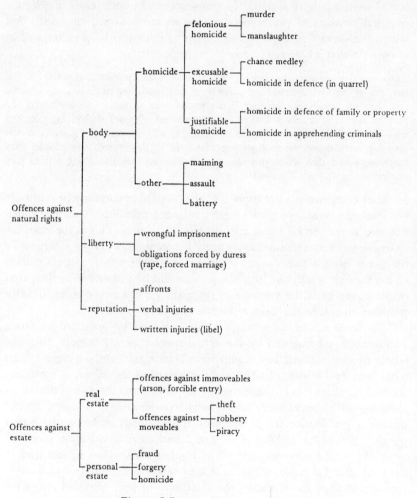

Fig. 2. Offences within private law

public law. Apart from the requirements of the taxonomy of the law, he may well have had further reasons for this. As far as domestic law is concerned, 'laws of justice' are here strongly interwoven with 'laws of police', and since punishment for transgression of the latter can be rather different in its principles from that of the former,[101] he may well have found it difficult to deal clearly with it in his general theory of punishment. And as far as public law is concerned, this is so irregular as a branch of law, because of its immediate political significance, that it is difficult to apply the general theory of punishment to it.[102] Finally, there is no provision in the system for punishment of infringements of the rights of delict themselves. This would amount, however, to punishment of improper punishment which – as we saw above – is a matter of public law in any developed society (in so far as it is a matter at all).

While the over-all system of punishment is determined by the relationship to the system of rights contained in private law, the most detailed subdivisions derive from Smith's adaptation of the traditional legal distinction between 'willfull injury' and 'culpable negligence', of which the latter again has three degrees (in Smith's version), 'culpa lata', 'culpa levis', and 'culpa levissima'.[103] The most severe punishment is imposed for wilful injury, and it is scaled down until we reach the minimum for cases of the slightest negligence. This scale is particularly fine-tuned to cases of bodily injury, partly because of their fundamental importance, and partly because the levels of intentionality here are both many and very complicated, owing to the many possible interrelations between offender and offended. This is well brought out in Smith's many examples in the lectures.[104] It is typical of Smith's method of instruction that he first introduces his students to these traditional distinctions, but then refers them to the spectator explanation of them and uses that in his own exposition.[105] Punishment of wilful injury is the standard case and needs no further explanation; there is here both actual harm and a matching motive to resent. But punishment for injury which arises out of negligence is in need of explanation, since the motive to do harm is here either 'deficient' or even entirely lacking. This explanation was given in *The Theory of Moral Sentiments* – the main principles of which Smith had lectured on before he began the jurisprudence course – where he showed how men to a certain extent judge morally in terms of the motive typical for an action, even in cases where the motive was not, and maybe could not have been, present.[106] This accounts not only for punishment in cases of negligence, but also for the many provisions in the history of law for 'punishment' of animals and even inanimate things, and hence for the derivative institution of deodand (which was only abolished in England in the nineteenth century).[107] Whenever injury is done, there is room for resentment and hence a tendency to punish. This stress on the significance of actual behaviour for the imposition of punishment also accounts for the opposite kind of situations. Where there is an injurious intent but no action actually following from it, the punishment is either strongly reduced or non-existent, because the resentment of the would-be sufferers and spectators is weak or does not occur at all.[108]

A very interesting feature of Smith's treatment of punishment is the prominence he gives to the punishment of crimes against *natural* rights.[109] When he dealt with these rights themselves at the beginning of the lecture course he had very little to say about them beyond the elementary spectator explanation; but via the theory of punishment in the area, they are given as much legal detail and sophistication as was given to the rights of 'estate' in direct discussion. This is a very practical illustration of the primacy of 'the negative' in Smith's moral philosophy, and it makes much more plausible his claim that the natural rights are the most basic of all. At the same time it also shows the basic structure of his moral philosophy – and indeed of his philosophy generally. Things have to be dealt with relationally, in their coherence with other things, and as far as moral matters are concerned this means that there must be some relationship between two or more persons which a spectator can evaluate sympathetically. With property rights this is automatically the case because they are about 'public', tangible things to which anyone *could* have a right and where the right of someone in particular therefore entails the relationship of excluding others.[110] And this public character is only slowly and gradually assumed by more abstract things, like contracts.[111] But with natural rights there is no such public medium; they are not in themselves about anything concrete. In a sense they do not exist at all until some injury to a person in his body, liberty, or reputation has taken place and a concrete relationship between an offender and an offended thereby put in front of spectators for judgement. Or to put it negatively, natural rights are not properties or qualities in individuals.

Smith's theory of punishment is part of his spectator theory of law and as such it naturally relates only to those laws which have a spectator basis, namely laws of justice. But as we have seen, there are other kinds of laws, laws of defence, 'police', revenue, and international relations.[112] The question therefore arises: upon what principles are crimes against such laws punished? The answer has to be pieced together, for Smith never gave a completely systematic account of these principles. His general idea is, however, clear enough. The rationale of the laws of defence is the most basic 'utility' imaginable, the survival of society as a coherent unit, and it is therefore to be presumed that offences against these laws should be punished to serve the same purpose. The laws of 'police' can be instituted to serve a multiplicity of purposes such as supporting and 'servicing' an effective market, lending indirect support to the defence of the country, providing education for the poor, etc.; the punishment of offences against them should therefore rationally be directed to serve the same purposes. Similar arguments could be expected to apply to revenue laws and laws of nations. This is exactly how Smith argues:

> Upon some occasions...we both punish and approve of punishment, merely from a view to the general interest of society, which we imagine, cannot otherwise be secured. Of this kind are all the punishments inflicted for breaches of what is called either civil police, or military discipline. Such crimes do not immediately or directly hurt any particular person; but their remote consequences, it is supposed, do produce, or might produce, either a considerable inconveniency, or a great disorder in the society. (TMS, II, ii, 3, § 11)[113]

The best-known example of this is the case of the sentinel who under military law is sentenced to death for falling asleep while on guard. 'This is intirely founded on the consideration of the publick good', for here 'the preservation of an individual is inconsistent with the safety of a multitude'.[114] Punishment in the area of 'police' is illustrated with the one-time death penalty for the exportation of wool in Britain; the security of 'the wealth and strength of the nation' was part of the legislature's over-all purpose in enacting laws to prevent such export.[115] Similarly, the provisions for punishment in cases of smuggling seem to be nothing but part of the general revenue system, which is aimed at defraying the sovereign's expenses.[116] Finally, under the laws of nations, why is it that the innocent subjects of, say, the king of France become the legitimate targets of 'punishment' from the king of England just because the former has somehow damaged the interests of the latter? This 'must be [founded] upon necessity':

> Whenever it suits the *conveniency* of a public enemy...the goods of the peaceable citizens are seized both at land and at sea; their lands are laid waste, their houses are burnt, and they themselves, if they presume to make any resistance, are murdered and led into captivity; and all this in the most perfect conformity to what are called the laws of nations. (TMS, III, 3, § 42)[117]

However, it is not naturally any crime to fall asleep: 'The natural atrocity of the crime seems to be so little.'[118] The exportation of wool is 'no crime at all, in naturall equity'.[119] It is no natural crime to import tobacco, but the revenue laws of many countries make 'that a crime which nature never meant to be so'.[120] Nor, finally, is it naturally any crime to be a Frenchman, but the laws of international war make the subjects accomplices of their sovereign. In all these instances we have examples of the fact that 'When the sovereign commands what is merely indifferent, and what, antecedent to his orders, might have been omitted without any blame, it becomes not only blameable but punishable to disobey him.'[121] In many cases the punishments which are thus justified by the over-all utility of the laws which they are meant to protect will be *inconsistent* with natural justice and punishment. This gives rise to the question of which principle takes priority, natural justice or public utility. Smith never gives a direct answer to this question, but it is quite obvious that the system of punishment must follow the area of law to which it is related. This means that the provisions of the military laws take precedence over everything,[122] and accordingly we see that he hesitantly agrees with the strict measure in the sentinel case: 'This severity may, upon many occasions, appear necessary.'[123] As far as the laws of 'police' and revenue are concerned, it is well known that Smith was extremely critical of the necessity of a large part of them, and his judgement on the accompanying punishments follows suit:

The severity of many of the laws which have been enacted for the security of the revenue is very justly complained of, as imposing heavy penalties upon actions which antecedent to the statutes that declared them to be crimes, had always been understood to be innocent. But the cruellest of our revenue laws, I will venture to affirm, are mild and gentle, in comparison of some of those which the clamour of our merchants and manufacturers has extorted from the legislature, for the support of their own absurd and oppressive monopolies. Like the laws of Draco, these laws may be said to be all written in blood. (WN, IV, viii, 17)[124]

This does not apply, of course, to all laws of 'police' and revenue. There are, as we have already seen, a number of necessary tasks for such laws,[125] and presumably Smith would attach reasonable provisions for punishment to them. The point is, however, that unless it can be shown that such laws are of the greatest importance in supporting the defence system of the country[126] or are in some other way essential to the continued viability of society,[127] the requirements of natural justice must take precedence.

Apart from this there are a number of areas in the law which seem to be based upon a mixture of considerations, including both fundamental public utility and other forms of utility. The most obvious example is the legal enforcement of the most basic education. This is justified with reference to both political and social stability and to defence, but at the same time Smith also invokes a simple humanitarian concern.[128] If we put *all* the emphasis on the latter aspect, and if we accept that enforced basic education constitutes an infringement of the liberty of the child and/or parent, then we are here as close as we will ever come to a case where Smith allows utility, other than that connected with ultimate social, political, and military survival, to override natural justice. But then, perhaps, it deserves notice that even this 'utility' is rather negatively defined: Smith is not concerned with any positive standard of education, but only with preventing men from becoming 'mutilated and deformed' in 'the proper use of the intellectual faculties'.[129] We do not know what sort of punishment Smith would attach to this particular area of law; it is hard to imagine that it would generally be very heavy.

In a few places, in connection with the sentinel case, Smith neglects his usual terminology and says that punishments justified by military necessity are 'just and proper'. This is hardly a sign that he is being inconsistent in his doctrines, but rather that he is using 'justice' in a wider and looser meaning.[130] He is clearly doing so in the parallel case from international law, when he says that the justification of the 'punishment' of the subjects of a foreign sovereign in a war 'can by no means be founded upon justice and equity *properly so called*; it must be upon necessity, which indeed in this case is a part of justice'.[131]

Finally, for the sake of completeness, a peculiar detail in Smith's theory of punishment should be accounted for. In connection with the punishment of offences against rights of 'estate', Smith makes it clear that the utility principle of deterrence will have to be invoked in order to strengthen the natural spectator punishment for such crimes. 'For wherever the temptation and the opportunity are increased, the punishment must also be increased.'[132] This is particularly the case with some forms of fraud and forgery, but can of course have place in other cases where the system of justice might otherwise be endangered.[133] This is interesting, for the kinds of fraud and forgery Smith has in mind are offences against contractual rights, and since these rights are the ones which have the weakest or most uncertain foundation in spectator principles, because of their 'abstractness',[134] the same must be the case with the punishment of offences against them. Hence the need for supplementary principles. This confirms our impression that while all contract law has a spectator basis, some parts of it are so abstract that they need reinforcement from considerations of public utility – which makes them in some respects akin to laws of 'police'. This is even more obvious from the fact that, in cases of breach of contract, courts have in time gone beyond their spectator basis. 'It is indeed the natural idea of a court to redress injuries', but now courts force 'the person to a performance of the agreement'.[135] This was originally introduced into the law under the influence of the church which treated contracts as matters of conscience, but it was taken over by the civil law, and in England by the Court of Chancery. This subservience of the principles of punishment to political purpose clearly shows the in-between status of much of contract law.

5 Domestic law

Smith's treatment of domestic law might perhaps provide a convenient starting point for someone attempting a psychoanalytic interpretation of his work, or it might be of use to someone interested in women's history – perhaps the two tasks could be combined. It is, however, of limited significance when dealing with his natural jurisprudence. This branch of law had always been so intimately connected with religious and political problems that laws of 'police' here virtually dominated over laws of justice, and a general introduction to the law, such as Smith's lectures were meant for, accordingly had to be much more concerned with factual history than with general principles. But even then it is of interest to see how clearly domestic law can be located in Smith's system of natural jurisprudence.

The rights which are protected by domestic law arise out of the relationships between husband and wife, parents and children, and masters and servants.[136] In all cases, therefore, they consist in the claims which one of the parties can have upon the other, and the main question we have to consider is which of these claims are recognized by an impartial spectator and which are created by the laws of 'police'.

Husband and wife

The most important rights here consist of the various claims to the exclusiveness of the relationship, which are those concerning fidelity, number of other spouses (read: wives), and divorce. The reports on Smith's treatment of fidelity are rather brief, but he is obviously employing his standard way of arguing. First he rejects a utility account, namely that fidelity is enforced in order to prevent illegitimate offspring; then he substitutes his spectator explanation, to the effect that it is the spectator's sympathy with the hurt feelings of the injured party which establishes the rightful claim.[137] Throughout history the actual spectators with any power have, however, commonly been men and the laws concerning adultery have therefore normally been tilted grossly in their favour, making infidelity an offence in women but hardly or not at all in men. But under the influence of the Christian clergy the sexes 'were put alltogether on an equall footing in allmost all respects'. The clergy had to be celibate and therefore 'were much more impartiall judges',[138] who could see that the injury was equal for both sexes. This gives Smith occasion to display the capacity of his spectator theory to cope even with details: although the injury from infidelity is very nearly the same for man and for woman, it is not quite the same. In contemporary society the man was regarded as the superior in the family and there was accordingly a greater injury to his honour than to that of the wife in cases of adultery. Consequently the wife was still 'punished' with 'the greatest ignominy'.[139]

Smith's position concerning polygamy is very clear. A woman's right to be the only wife is nothing but an invention of 'police'; naturally there is no injury done her if she 'consents to be one of five or twenty or more wives'.[140] But there are a large number of utility considerations which lead civilized societies to forbid polygamy, ranging from purely paternalistic concerns for the moral well-being of everyone inside and outside the polygamous family, through worries about declining population, to the interesting military and political consideration, that in a polygamous society there will be no hereditary nobility and consequently no natural leaders against external violence from abroad or internal violence from a monarch.[141]

The argument about divorce runs parallel to that about polygamy. Naturally there is no injustice done if one party terminates the marriage relationship, provided this was part of the marriage contract.[142] But this use of natural justice is also considered 'very inconsistent with a well regulated police',[143] for a number of reasons which all centre on the likelihood of public 'disorders'. In earlier periods of social development such disorders were only avoided because the stronger party in marriage arranged both adultery and divorce laws to suit himself: only the husband had the right to divorce. The good 'police' of modern, civilized society avoids both the inequity and violence of the latter practice and the disorders consequent upon the former. 'The method of marriage now in use avoids all those inconveniencies, as the union is here indissoluble.'[144]

Finally, in connection with marriage law, we should take notice of Smith's account of the principles behind prohibited degrees.[145] These are of interest because they exemplify the full scale of Smithian principles of analysis in the law: first, the spectator approval which takes place in any known society and seems to be bound up with the viability of social life; secondly, the spectator approval which takes place in some societies, depending upon various circumstances; and thirdly – moving from justice to 'police' – considerations of utility. In the first category falls the prohibition of marriage between mother and son. This can never be approved of because it goes counter to all the mother–son relations naturally approved of and because it brings two natural principles of social authority into contradiction, namely that of parent and child and that of husband and wife.[146] Spectator disapproval of marriage between father and daughter is of nearly the same universal strength; but there is not the same strong contradiction as in the previous case, and therefore we find some barbarous societies allowing such marriages.[147] Concerning marriage between brothers and sisters Smith is unclear. In one place he declares that this is 'prohibited with great reason and according to naturall [law]';[148] but elsewhere he says that it 'seems to have been prohibited chiefly from political views'.[149] The details of his examples seem very much to favour the latter view.[150] Marriages between uncles and nieces and aunts and nephews have generally been prohibited for natural reasons analogous to those applicable to father–daughter and mother–son.[151] Finally, 'It is to be observed that the rules of affinity are rather rules of police than of nature, for it is not contrary to nature that a man should marry his wife's sister.' And Smith's lack of dogmatism is never better displayed than in his discussion of the expediency of various arrangements in this respect.[152]

Parent and child

In so far as the rights of children against their parents and of parents against their children have a legal backing on top of their strong social sanction, this is an invention of 'police'. We are here in the area where the 'civil magistrate...may prescribe rules...which not only prohibit mutual injuries among fellow-citizens, but command mutual good offices to a certain degree'[153] – which means the legal enforcement of the most basic forms of 'confined benevolence', as Hume called it. In concrete terms this means that 'the father is bound to provide for and aliment his children', and that the 'children are in like manner bound to maintain their parents if they should happen to become destitute and unable to maintain themselves'. The former duty has in fact become so entrenched in both morality and law that at least gross neglect of it is considered on a par with serious injury, and punished accordingly.[154] Apart from that, a man has both as husband and as father a certain *de facto* power, but the only part of this which modern law wants to recognize is the right to apply 'a moderate correction'.[155]

Master and servant

Apart from the measures mentioned above and a few others, mainly to do with property, the relationships between spouses and between parents and children are no more the business of the law in modern civilized society than any other relationships between individuals; they are only regulated negatively, by the laws of justice. The achievement of much the same situation with the relationship between masters and servants is one of the fruits of civilization. For even the 'greatest dependents among us', the menial servants, 'have almost the same priviledges with their master, liberty, wages, etca.'[156] But the law does recognize some few special rights in the relationship. 'The master has a right to correct his servant moderately'; if the servant should chance to be killed during such correction, the existence of this right is a mitigating circumstance. The master–servant relationship is also considered a mitigating factor in cases where either the master or the servant, in defending one another, should happen to kill a third party. And a servant is recognized as the master's agent in various forms of business.[157] In his very brief treatment of these matters Smith does not indicate which of these are laws of justice and which are laws of 'police', but it seems that at least the second sort of provision could easily be accounted for by spectator principles. His concern in this part of the lecture course, however, is even more historical than in other parts, for the relationship between masters and servants has for most of mankind's history been so dominated by force and violence that hardly any rights were recognized in it at all, and the law was a mere weapon for an oppressive 'police'. His story, therefore, is largely the history of slavery and its gradual dissolution in a few places in the West.[158]

6 Public law

The right not to be injured 'as a member of a state' is the subject of public law, which falls into two branches, one dealing with the rights of the sovereign against the citizens, and one dealing with the rights of the citizens against the sovereign.[159] The form of injuries which a sovereign can suffer from the subjects depends upon the nature of sovereignty in the state in question. For the purposes of his general discussion of this, Smith operates with the two ideal types of monarchical and republican government,[160] and argues that in the former any action against the particular ruler constitutes an injury (treason). But in a republic it is 'whatever affects the dignity of the people as a body' that counts as treason, and that primarily means any attack on 'the liberties of the people'.[161] Smith maintains that this makes treason 'much more easily distinguished' in a republic than in a monarchy,[162] and his point is, I suggest, that treason in a republic is against an *office* which is clearly defined by law;[163] but in a monarchy it is against a particular person and his *activity* – which is something much more indistinct. He also expresses his point by means of the classic idea of tyrannicide. In a monarchy tyrannicide is the highest form of treason; in a republic it is the main weapon against treason, for here the worst form of that crime is the misuse or the usurpation of office.

When the sovereign exercises the judicial power to administer private or domestic law he judges sympathetically as a spectator of the injuries done to other people. But with injuries against himself as sovereign – especially treason – he is looking after his own rights and, 'as he judges in his own cause, he is very apt to be more violent and sanguinary in his punishments than the impartial spectator can approve of'.[164] This accounts for the fact that the laws of treason commonly punish the mere attempt at crime as severely as the committed crime.[165]

The sovereign's right to protection against the most basic forms of treason obviously has a firm foundation in general spectator principles.[166] Such crimes include attempts on the sovereign's person, levying of war and conspiring against the sovereign, and killing of high public officers when in office.[167] But in England there are a number of other actions which are only considered treasonable because of political expediency of one kind or another. And they accordingly come in for Smith's critical consideration, as we shall see.[168]

The second branch of public law is concerned with the rights of citizens against their sovereign, or the duties of sovereigns towards their subjects.[169] This is an extremely unclear area in the law simply because the respective rights and duties are so unclear.[170] In private law and in the first branch of public law there are long-established precedents, based on clear principles and administered by specifically appointed officers. But it is not so in this branch of public law, nor *can* it be – at least not to the same extent as in the other parts of the law. The problem is that nobody has ever been – nobody, at least, has ever been recognized as – an impartial spectator in disputes about what the sovereign could and could not do to the subjects, and consequently there is no clearly established idea of what constitutes injury in this relationship. Consequently, 'All disputes of this sort have been decided by force and violence', and it has been the successful party only which has been in a position to judge. 'Sometimes the decision has been right and sometimes wrong, but they can never be of such weight as the decisions of a cooll and impartial court.'[171] The reason for this is not just that the sovereign power is the accused party in such disputes. Smith is emphatic that it is genuinely difficult to ascertain what is right and what is wrong in these matters, and he is led to this conclusion by his ideas about the nature of sovereignty and the necessity of strong government.

In the absence of clear principles and established law, 'one who is to consider this matter must set out anew and upon his own bottom', and Smith suggests that the best bottom is an understanding of the principles behind the absolute *power* which the sovereign in developed societies in fact has. The sovereign power has grown over time to become absolute in three respects: an executive, or federative, power to manage society in international relations, and especially war; a judicial power to administer justice; and a legislative power to regulate the judicial.[172] This power which has been concentrated in the sovereign can be accounted for by means of two basic principles, which Smith calls 'authority' and 'utility'.[173] Recognition of power in terms of authority is due to the natural deference which men feel towards people they consider their superiors. The basis for this deference is that such 'superiors' naturally attract the sympathetic attention of other men.[174] And the qualities which cause them to be considered superiors fall into four groups; first, 'superiority of personal qualifications'; secondly, 'the superiority of age'; thirdly, 'the superiority of fortune'; and fourthly, 'the superiority of birth'.[175] The principle of authority gives rise to a habitual obedience very much like the obedience a son shows his father, and it is the principle which forms the backbone of Toryism in British politics.[176] On the principle of utility, people support the sovereign power because they appreciate the necessity of it for 'the security and independency of each individuall'.[177] In Britain such people tend to side with the Whigs.[178] The principle of authority is generally associated with a monarchical form of government, while utility prevails in republics, but both principles are to be found in any government –

although not in the same form. The principle of authority is dependent upon the sympathy mechanism, and it is therefore naturally directed towards particular persons. This, however, is inconsistent with republican ideas, according to which power springs from the whole people, and the principle is therefore actively discouraged in republican states. Nevertheless it has influence because people pay their respect to *offices*.[179] This detail gives an interesting background to Smith's general appreciation of the importance of institutions. In the light of our previous discussions of Smith's ideas of utility, it is also interesting to notice that in settled societies with a certain tradition behind their institutional set-up, 'the principle of authority is the foundation of that of utility or common interest'. It is here the traditional authority of institutions which *makes* them useful.[180]

Smith's suggestion is that sovereign power as it in fact exists can be accounted for by these two principles of authority and utility, either singly or in combination – the latter being particularly clearly illustrated in the British 'mixed' form of government. This exercise in political realism undoubtedly has the same polemical purpose as Hume's parallel arguments: to counter the unrealistic legalism of the contract theory of government which had been so fashionable in political thinking since Locke. And in accordance with this objective we find Smith giving his students an excellent résumé of Hume's well-known criticism of the contract and consent ideas of Locke.[181] The main burden of Smith's criticism is not just that it is in fact unrealistic to found citizens' rights against their sovereign on a contract or on tacit consent, but also, I suggest, that this is *necessarily* so: the situations in which a sovereign has to operate are so changeable and complex that it makes little sense to imagine him under a general duty to respect a set of wide-ranging rights, which are supposed to be backed by a fundamental right of resistance in the citizens.[182] Smith's emphasis on political realism, combined with his criticism of excessive legalism, also serves as a dramatic background which will throw into relief what *can* be said in clear moral terms (i.e. negative terms) about citizens' rights against the sovereign. For 'there are some things which it is unlawfull for the sovereign to attempt and entitle the subjects to make resistance'.[183] Thus 'All agree that lunacy, nonnage [i.e. minority], or ideotism entirely destroy the authority of a prince.' While this is a danger only in monarchies, all forms of government can succumb to 'perverseness, absurdity, and unreasonableness' of such a degree that it will 'entitle the subjects to resistance in the eyes of every unprejudiced person'. In such extreme cases the 'unprejudiced person' will recognize that both 'authority' and 'utility' have broken down.[184]

The problem is, however, that this clarity in moral terms is not institutionalized in law which is administered by a particular authority:

tho the sovereign may be resisted, it cant be said that there is any regular authority for so doing. The property, life, and liberty of the subject are in some measure in his power; nor is it or can it be ascertained what abuses justify resistance. No laws, no judges, have or can ascertain this matter, nor formed any precedents whereby we may judge. (LJ(A), v, 138)

Here Smith is not only talking of what is not the case, but also of what *cannot* be the case. The reason for this is his theory of sovereignty, which consists of two lines of argument. First, Smith argues with a completely Hobbesian logic of power that sovereignty by its very nature has to be absolute:

For if what we called the summa potestas was liable to be called to account by any man, any body of the people or the whole people, this person or body would be the summa potestas, and if this again was under the authority of another, this would be the summa potestas. So that we must always end in some body who have a body liable to no controul from a regular power. (LJ(A), v, 140)[185]

This seemed to Smith so obvious that he allows himself to restate it in terms of a joke on Locke's mixture of politics and religion in his idea of an 'appeal to Heaven' as a limitation on sovereignty: 'God is the only judge of sovereigns, and we cannot say how he will determine'![186] When Smith talks of sovereignty as absolute he thus means that it is the ultimate power. This only applies, however, to the sovereign power as a whole, and there is no necessity that all this power should be united in the same hands. This is his second line of argument. Sovereignty, although absolute, may be divided so that different agents take care of the different branches of power which make up sovereignty, and those are the executive, the judicial, and the legislative powers.[187] If this is done, then a semblance of regular law may apply to the sovereign, for it may regulate the relationship between the various branches of sovereignty. If one branch trespasses on the area entrusted to one of the others, this will constitute an infringement of the right of the latter, which can therefore 'with all justice and equity'[188] defend its right, even by force:

When the sovereign power is divided amongst different hands, tho it is impossible to say how far the whole sovereign power conjoind may go, it is easy to ascertain when any of those amongst whom it is divided go beyond their lawfull bounds; for this is the case whenever any one of them attempts to exercise the power which belongs to another... The very definition of a perfect right opposed to the offices of humanity, etc., which are by some called imperfect rights, is one which we may compell others to perform to us by violence. – If therefore the severall parts of the government have a perfect right to their severall provinces, it must be supposed that they are intitled to defend themselves in them by force. (LJ(A), v, 141–2)[189]

Given the impossibility of an institutionalized impartial spectator of the conduct of the sovereign, the regulation of the relationship between the three branches of power must undoubtedly remain a mere semblance of law. There is no indication that Smith thought of the citizenry as would-be impartial spectators of the three branches of sovereignty, and this could anyway in his eyes have no institutional force. His point is the much more modest one that a clear division of power makes it possible for all the actual (and partial) spectators to form a clearer, a *more* impartial judgement about right and wrong in the exercise of power, than they otherwise would. In other words, the division of power is an institutional device which will tend to make people's opinion of the sovereign power more enlightened, because it will be concentrated on a *negative* question about transgression of rights, and such questions can be answered with a high degree of precision.[190]

For Smith, as for Hume, opinion is the basis for government,[191] and he undoubtedly saw the educational effect of the division of power as one way in which this basis could become more informed and hence more secure, because less exposed to the alternative forms which opinion could take, such as 'enthusiasm', 'ambition', 'fear', etc.[192] This could not, of course, come about unless the population at large had that minimum of education which made them 'more disposed to examine, and more capable of seeing through, the interested complaints of faction and sedition'.[193] And Smith's science of politics is clearly designed to promote the same educational aim[194] by demonstrating the inherent complexity of sovereignty. It is not possible, without destroying it, to limit sovereignty directly by subjecting it to strict rules. Hence it is impossible to give the same direct and clear information about it, which can be given about the regular branches of the law. But it *may* be possible to let the sovereign power limit itself by dividing it internally, without this leading to its destruction. But the success of the arrangement depends very much upon a general understanding of this division as internal, and not as an external limitation. This is the point of Smith's criticism of the attempts to formulate general rights of resistance as if they could be the subject of regular law.

He is sceptical towards Whiggism because its principles of consent and right of resistance mistake the indirect for the direct method of limiting sovereign power, and he obviously thought that his science might help to correct this misunderstanding. At bottom, the issue involves a sharp distinction between *extent* of government and *strength* of government, and Smith's message is that the former should not be limited by limiting the latter. The central thesis in his history of law and government is that wide individual liberty is not even a possibility without strong government. It becomes a possibility if a society has strong government, and it becomes a reality if the absolute sovereignty of that government is exercised within certain limits without being weakened.

The question arises whether a full division of sovereignty into three powers is the only way to achieve the indirect limitation necessary for individual liberty. Smith never answers this question directly, but it is quite obvious that it is not an either–or question. The most essential requirement is the independence of the judicial power from the executive:

When the judicial is united to the executive power, it is scarce possible that justice should not frequently be sacrificed to, what is vulgarly called, politics... upon the impartial administration of justice depends the liberty of every individual, the sense which he has of his own security. (WN, v, i, b. 25)

The achievement of this, however, is not just a British, but a *modern* and, in varying degrees, a West European phenomenon:

The separation of the province of distributing justice between man and man from that of conducting affairs and leading armies, is the great advantage which modern times have over ancient, and the foundation of that greater security which we now enjoy, both with regard to liberty, property, and life. (LRBL, 170)[195]

Even absolute monarchies like France can, at least to a certain extent, keep justice and politics separate and thus secure individual liberty.[196] Since, however, a completely regular administration of justice is only achieved when the judges' independence of the executive is counterbalanced by their dependence upon rules of law laid down by a legislative power,[197] a tripartite sovereign is necessary to achieve 'perfect security to liberty and property'.

Before leaving Smith's theory of sovereignty, it may be useful to place it in a broader perspective. If one views it in the light of conventional associations in political theory, it has an air of paradox about it. It is a theory of the absoluteness of sovereignty, and yet it is not continued into the command theory of law as it was by Hobbes, by Bentham and Austin, and by many others since. On the contrary, Smith very strongly criticized this theory of law, as we shall see.[198] At the same time Smith did not see sovereignty as a matter of Burkean precedents and conventions. Precedents and conventions were certainly important in forming the opinions which under the principle of authority supported government. But authority was not the only opinion-forming principle in a modern commercial society, particularly not when that society lived with a divided government, as it did in Britain. The principle of utility, in cases like this, was a significant factor in forming the opinion people held of the government, and hence affecting the way they influenced the government. And utility in this connection meant first of all the government's ability to secure justice – which was certainly not simply a matter of precedent, but of natural justice. Smith's theory of absolute sovereignty did not allow room for any form of constitutionalism – either for the 'Ancient Constitution', consent, and right of resistance celebrated in Whig lore, or for any premonitions of a written constitution.[199] And yet it embodies the idea of limiting the extent of sovereignty by institutional means.

All the complexities of Smith's theory of sovereignty should make it plain why he considered 'the duties of the sovereign towards his subjects and the crimes he may be guilty of against them...a question which I can not pretend to answer with such precision' as the other duties and rights within the law.[200] But at the same time they should also make it clear why the law is by no means irrelevant to it.

7 Laws of nations

International law is as uncertain as the branch of public law which we have just discussed, and for the same reason, 'for where there is no supreme legislative power nor judge to settle differences, we may always expect uncertainty and irregularity'.[201] In fact 'neutral nations are the only indifferent and impartial spectators. But they are placed at so great a distance that they are almost quite out of sight.'[202] Although the prospects for a regular administration of justice on the international scene are so dismal because of the prevalence of 'the mean principle of national prejudice',[203] the basic outline of an international system of justice is clear enough. In peacetime the laws of nations are mainly a matter of the rights of aliens in a sovereign's territory, and that calls for no comment here.[204] It is in time of war that the big questions arise, for it is then that nations pre-eminently behave as individual units against each other. From the legal point of view two problems are particularly important; first, when can a nation be said to be injured and treated unjustly; and secondly, what is the proper measure of resentment and redress for injury which one nation can seek from another?[205] The former is the question of what justifies war, and although it may be extremely difficult to find an answer to it in concrete situations, the answer is in principle clear. 'In general whatever is the foundation of a proper law suit before a court of justice may be a just occasion of war.' This means that if one nation infringes the rights to life, liberty, property, etc., of the subjects of another nation, and if no redress can be obtained, then 'there is a foundation for war'.[206] While Smith thus opens his discussion of the laws of nations by applying the analogy between nations and individual persons in much the same manner as Grotius had done, it immediately becomes clear that this is the only place where the analogy brings some clarity. Indeed, the point Smith makes in his discussion of the second problem is that it is nearly impossible to evaluate corporate action in the same way as individual action. He does not deny that the proper measure of resentment and 'punishment' between two nations is clear in principle. 'In general, when an injury is clearly and distinctly done or when it is plainly intended, and satisfaction refused, resentment is necessary and just.'[207] The problem is, however, that nations consist of individuals; it is individual persons who do injury, and it is only individuals who can be the object of resentment. But in war we resent and 'punish' another nation collectively, although normally the great majority of our enemies are perfectly innocent. This may be very *necessary* – and in that broad sense 'just'[208] – but if we consider it properly it is 'quite contrary to the rules of justice observed with regard to our own subjects. We would rather chuse that 10 guilty persons should escape than that one innocent person should suffer.'[209] We can *explain* this by reference to the distance between the individuals in each nation, which suspends the proper function of the sympathy mechanism and hence all discrimination between people's actions; and we can see how as a consequence 'our resentment rises against the whole nation instead of the government'.[210] But to try to *justify* this is impossible, and it is obvious that the laws of nations in this respect are 'laid down with very little regard to the plainest and most obvious rules of justice'.[211]

What Smith is saying about the status of the laws of nations, then, is that we can say with *some* degree of clarity and certainty when injustice is being done and when resentment and redress are due in international relations. But the ordinary measure of what degree of resentment and what amount of redress are proper cannot be applied corporately, and this question is therefore wholly a matter of necessity, which means a matter of defence and allied policies. Here more than elsewhere it is true that 'The partial spectator is at hand: the impartial one at a great distance.'[212] This together with the lack of international jurisdiction makes foreign affairs in general and the conduct of war in particular wide open to the same interested influences which are so apt to warp domestic justice. And Smith has a very realistic appreciation of the extent to which actions in the international scene are taken for domestic reasons.[213]

CHAPTER SIX

Smith's critical jurisprudence

1 Introduction

The predominant mode in both *The Theory of Moral Sentiments* and in the *Lectures on Jurisprudence* is descriptive. We are told what people consider morally right and what the law recognizes as injustice, not what *is* right or unjust. This has led one commentator to the conclusion that 'it is possible to interpret Adam Smith as making no ethical statements at all, that is, solely as a moral psychologist engaged in analysing and explaining acts of approval and disapproval'.[1] Another commentator agrees that 'this is the correct interpretation of the *Moral Sentiments* (provided that the term "psychologist" is not taken to exclude a sociological approach)'.[2] According to this view of Smith as the scientist of morals it was never part of his intentions to be the moralist who tells men what is right and wrong. In so far as he brings in his own evaluations at all it is at a contemplative level, where he, with the few philosophers, legislators and scientists who have the ability, tries to take a God's-eye view of mankind in its moral aspect – which means in its social life. From this elevated vantage point he will judge everything in terms of its utility, admiring the way God has brought about a universal order which secures the basic happiness of man. On weekdays this order provides the scientist with his explanatory tasks, on Sundays it stands as the object of the contemplative utilitarian's admiration. Whenever the latter perceives that the order leaves something to be desired in order to promote the happiness of man, the former will be in a position to rectify it. 'Utility is...very much *the* meta-principle for Smith.'[3]

Smith's concept of utility cannot be taken in any Benthamite sense of uniform happiness,[4] but even without that this is an interesting interpretation. It suggests the idea that in so far as Smith had any evaluative intention at all it stood outside his main concern, which was scientific explanation. And it further gives the idea that if Smith's standard of evaluation is not utilitarian, then it is that 'aesthetic' pleasure which accompanies system-knowledge.[5] Now, there is no doubt that on a purely intellectual level Smith evaluated 'aesthetically' in this way and would measure his own system of morals by this standard. The problem is that this perspective tends to obscure the direct normative significance of the

135

content of the system in the world of action. As I argued when we first stopped to consider this basic problem,[6] the description of the impartial spectator is a description of the criteria which mankind must use in deciding whether an action or character is morally valuable or not. The argument could be said to have this in common with transcendental forms of argument, that it spells out the principles which are implicitly the necessary conditions for moral judgements; and the existence and function of at least some forms of moral judgement are matters of empirical fact. If we read Smith in this way his science of morals does assume a genuine normative significance. For although the impartial spectator does not supply us with positive moral rules, the spectator principles do show us how moral judgements can be critically discussed and tested. Those moral judgements which do not comply with the principles embodied in the impartial spectator can, at least for the time being, be discarded. Smith's theory is not a set of basic moral doctrines, nor a prescription for how to construct such a set. On the contrary, it presupposes the existence of a moral life; but it specifies the principles for discussion within that life. By supplying such principles Smith's science of morals becomes more than a science; it becomes a critical tool. This aspect of Smith's science is of great significance – not least for a full understanding of that branch of it called jurisprudence.

In order to explain this I shall first survey the spectator principles with special regard to the law; I shall then show how these principles are applied in concrete legal criticism; and finally I shall discuss the full programme for a critical jurisprudence which Smith outlined but never carried out.

2 Legal reasoning

What gives unity to Smith's theory is the spectator approach. The previous chapter has shown at length how the system of law is analysed from a spectator point of view, and, as one would expect, the language of Smith's jurisprudence lectures is permeated by expressions from the spectator theory. Thus, instead of hearing how things were at a given time, we are told how they were *conceived* or *looked upon*. Actions have a *seeming* or *apparent propriety* or *impropriety*, and people can or cannot *go along with* them or *enter into* their motives. However, it is not just the actual spectator, but also the impartial spectator who is present in Smith's discussion of law. Apart from the direct evidence of the impartial spectator's activity, his presence is also reflected in the language used. Thus we hear about norms and values being *natural* or *unnatural, arising from nature* or being *contrary to nature*. Furthermore, the natural is connected with the rational, so that *nature and reason dictate*; there are *laws of natural reason*; and rules can be more or less *agreeable to reason*, to take but a few examples. It is interesting that in his lectures Smith was so willing to talk of reason and the reasonable in the principles of the law, for it gives a strong indication of how narrow was his dispute with rationalism in ethics. He obviously subscribed to an emotivist theory of the origin of all evaluation, but the spectator approach means that the main emphasis is upon the processes which give evaluation its concrete forms. The core of this is the sympathy mechanism, and the procedures adopted for 'correcting' sympathy so that it becomes the sympathy of the impartial spectator may perhaps be denominated practical reasoning. The law can then be looked upon as an area where evaluation is given a particularly important form, and legal reasoning can be seen as practical reasoning of special importance. This perspective on Smith gains further interest when we remember the intimate connection between the character of an impartial spectator and the character of a judge – a connection so close that it would be interesting to speculate about the influence which Smith's study of law may have had upon the formation and development of his idea of the impartial spectator. There is no sharp distinction between moral and legal terminology. The spectator is an 'impartial judge', and 'the magistrate. . . acts in the character of an impartial spectator'.[7] This makes it even more obvious than it might otherwise have been to see the principles of practical reasoning employed by the impartial spectator as at the same time principles of legal reasoning.

The most obvious of these principles is naturally the principle of impartiality, which really amounts to a principle of universality. What the impartial spectator approves of is what everyone is able to go along with, if they are properly informed. It is, in other words, what is possible as a general rule. And for reasons which have already been explained, such rules are formed particularly easily in cases concerned with the negative virtue of justice. The implication of this idea of universality is that the rule of justice must be applicable to all whose circumstances are similar in relevant respects. This affects both case law and statute law. As far as the former is concerned, 'It is evident that, in quoting precedents, the more directly they agree with the case in hand in all its circumstances, it will be so much the better.'[8] And statutes are 'those general rules which the sovereign lays down to direct the conduct of his subjects'; they are 'regulations which shall bind themselves, their posterity, and even persons who are unwilling'![9] Closely connected with the requirement of universality are two others which we might call consistency and coherence. One of the elementary requirements for an impartial spectator's judgement must be that it is not contradicting any of the other judgements he would make, and another is that the behaviour to which it leads and the rest of the behaviour following from the spectator judgements must cohere – they must make a sensible pattern of behaviour. Very often these two principles will, of course, come to the same thing, since incoherent behaviour will tend to follow from inconsistent judgements. Thus once a society has acknowledged private property in animals, it will make little sense not to acknowledge that this gives a similar right to the offspring, milk, etc., from such animals. But not only will this appear an arbitrary way to behave; the spectator recognition of property-right to what one has, in some sense, in one's power will be inconsistent since both the animal and its offspring or milk are in one's power. This is the basis for property by accession, which becomes more and more intricate as it is used in different contexts, and particularly as property becomes extended to more and more areas, especially land. This coincidence of the two requirements seems generally to take place within the law proper, but the requirement of coherence can play a more independent role in determining the vaguer relationship between the law and common morality, traditions, etc. Thus while it might not involve any formal contradiction if the law did not recognize testaments as a valid way of succeeding to property, it would make little sense once 'humanity' has become so refined that there is a general respect in society for the will of the newly dead.[10]

When these formal principles are added to the substantial one of the primacy of the negative, we have the criteria which are relevant for a discussion of law.[11] The principles as outlined here are in fact nothing but abstractions from Smith's concrete discussions, and both their full meaning and their significance only become clear when they are put back into their context. This context must naturally be the state of a particular branch of the law in a given country and at a particular point in its development, and this is a matter for the history of the law. Just as the judgement of the impartial spectator in general cannot be understood except in a particular context, so legal criticism can only be understood in a particular historical context. There is therefore a close and necessary connection between the critical and the historical aspects of Smith's jurisprudence, and since the latter provides the history of how the various parts of the system of law were developed by actual spectators, we see how the analytical or systematic aspect is tied in with the two others. When we look at the lectures as reported in the students' notes it is, however, the historical and analytical approach which predominates. They were not meant to be an agenda for systematic law-reform – how could they be? – but an introduction to the basic principles of the law as it is. Nevertheless, throughout the lectures there are a number of examples of how Smith would use the test of natural justice to criticize existing law. And of course his criticism in *The Wealth of Nations* of various forms of legislation in the economic sphere had a similar jurisprudential side, quite apart from their economic and social aspects. As far as the lecture notes are concerned, we must also remember that these are more a catalogue of opinions than of arguments – as is natural – and that to some extent it is a matter of good luck when Smith's actual reasoning is recorded. But even allowing for that, we can see the reforming intent in Smith's theory in several different areas of the law.

3 Legal criticism

The Wealth of Nations was an inquiry into 'Nature and Causes', and in so far as human actions were amongst the 'Causes' they were evaluated for their causal efficiency. Throughout the work, however, a strong juris-prudential background is abundantly evident, according to which it is possible to evaluate human action in terms of natural justice. This composite structure of the critical side of Smith's argument is clearly represented by his strictures on various limitations imposed upon manufacturers and farmers: 'Both laws were evident violations of natural liberty, and therefore unjust; and they were both too as impolitick as they were unjust.'[12] At the same time this passage indicates the main target of Smith's juris-prudential criticism in *The Wealth of Nations*, namely infringements of one of the most basic rights within private law, that of individual liberty. This is no less the liberty of ordinary folk to work at what they want to and where they want to, than it is the freedom of the merchant and manufacturer to do business as they want to. This is why he condemns oppressive apprenticeship laws; they are not only harmful but also 'a manifest encroachment upon the just liberty both of the workman, and of those who might be disposed to employ him'.[13] It is in the same spirit that he criticizes the laws of settlement: 'To remove a man who has committed no misdemeanour from the parish where he chuses to reside, is an evident violation of natural liberty and justice.'[14] Much the same applies to the restrictions on 'artificers' who want to practise their trade overseas: 'It is unnecessary...to observe, how contrary such regulations are to the boasted liberty of the subject, of which we affect to be so very jealous; but which, in this case, is so plainly sacrificed to the futile interests of our merchants and manufacturers.'[15] Smith's parallel criticism of all the laws 'which the clamour of our merchants and manufacturers has extorted from the legislature, for the support of their own absurd and oppressive monopolies', is too well-known to need much commentary: 'Like the laws of Draco, these laws may be said to be all written in blood.'[16] And the reason is plain: 'To hurt in any degree the interest of any one order of citizens, for no other purpose but to promote that of some other, is evidently contrary to that justice and equality of treatment which the sovereign owes to all the different orders of his subjects.'[17]

It is peculiarly difficult, from the point of view taken here, to deal adequately with the other big issue in the natural rights area of private

law, that of slavery. It is again a matter of infringement of personal
liberty, and Smith's condemnatory attitude is never in doubt. He refers to
slavery as 'the vilest of all states', in which people are sold 'like so many
herds of cattle, to the highest bidder in the market' – a fate no less cruel
than complete extirpation.[18] Equally, he talks in universal terms of 'the
unfortunate law of slavery', and declares that, 'It is evident that the state
of slavery must be very unhappy to the slave himself. This I need hardly
prove, tho some writers have called it in question.'[19] But the problem is
that we have no record of a direct criticism in terms of natural justice,
despite the clarity of Smith's standpoint. Instead he devotes all his attention to explaining how this vile practice came to be so prevalent in the
history of mankind – and to arguing against the economy of it. This
assumed cynicism has a very significant point. Smith's argument in
essence is that although slavery is so obviously poor economy,[20] it is nevertheless the case that 'The love of domination and authority over others,
which I am afraid is naturall to mankind' makes it well nigh impossible
that human society can ever be without slavery.[21] In fact it was only a set
of historical coincidences which led to the abolition of slavery in a 'corner
of Europe'.[22] If we disregard this for the moment, the best a slave can
hope for is to live in an absolute monarchy, for although such a government is not strong enough to abolish slavery, it is generally strong enough
'to intermeddle even in the management of the private property of individuals', and 'common humanity naturally disposes' many a monarch to
do so in the case of slaves, thus easing their lot. But it is very different in
republican governments, because there 'The persons who make all the
laws...are persons who have slaves themselves.' It is therefore extremely
difficult or impossible to get any intervention on behalf of the slaves – let
alone get slavery abolished.[23] This is probably the most dramatic illustration of Smith's sharp distinction (following Hume's) between political
liberty, meaning popular participation in politics, and personal liberty,
meaning the protection of individual freedom by laws of justice. If a
politically free society has slaves, it is this very freedom which leads to the
most severe suppression of the personal liberty of the slaves; whereas it is
the lack of such political freedom which can lead an arbitrarily governed
society to maintain at least a minimum of the natural rights of slaves. And
this is a lesson which Smith's contemporaries could learn not only from
history, but from the contrast between the state of their very own sugar
colonies and those of the absolute monarchy of France.[24]

The interest of the argument goes further than this, however, for it
clearly demonstrates that there is no automatic harmony between even
the most basic rights of men. Slavery constitutes such a problem because
of the conflict between one man's right to personal liberty and another
man's property right. We can now see that the former takes priority, and

hence that the latter is no right at all when the two conflict, that is when property-right is claimed in persons. But many generations have to be schooled in humane respect for the individual before we reach a state of impartiality in which we always recognize injury in this respect as more severe than injury to property. And it requires first of all the very greatest strength in a government before it can act on such impartial views and impose a just priority between the two rights.[25] The connection between the strength of government and the possibility of justice is a theme to which we shall return, but it is useful to link this theme here with Smith's discussion of slavery because it coheres with some further points in that discussion.

Smith's argument about the continuation of slavery in politically free societies as a consequence of the influence which slave owners have on government is strikingly similar to his arguments about the danger of the influence of vested interests on government in a commercial society such as Britain, to the detriment of the lower ranks. This similarity becomes a parallel when Smith goes on to argue that the condition of slaves can only be tolerable if the condition of their owners is better by no more than a narrow margin; otherwise all social communication through the sympathy mechanism breaks down.[26] This is also the argument which lies behind Smith's wish for a graduated ladder of ranks in commercial society.[27] But whereas the closeness of the social ties in a society with slavery can only be maintained if the society stays poor and 'barbarous', this can be achieved in a society of freemen if the gaps between each of the various ranks are kept narrow, even if the difference between the lowest and the highest ranks is very considerable. But the condition for this is that 'interests' are kept at bay and mobility between the ranks secured – and that burden falls upon a strong maintenance of justice. The point of Smith's apparent cynicism in dealing with slavery, therefore, is to put it in this wider perspective of the protection of poor people in any society: given the interested influences on governments, this was a problem of such immensity that a direct argument from the natural right to personal liberty was likely to be much less effective than an indirect argument from the viability of the general system of justice.

Smith's discussion of the big issues concerning the natural right to personal liberty demonstrates the depth of critical concern in his jurisprudence. The critical comments he makes about various parts of the law pertaining to 'estate rights' show us the type of spectator reasoning which lies behind that concern. In many ways the best example is Smith's discussion of the state of the law concerning all those things which 'must continue common by the rules of equity' even when property has been 'extended to allmost every subject', such as 'wild beasts' and 'the fish of the sea and rivers'.[28] 'The tyranny of the feudal government and the

inclination men have to extort all they can from their inferiours...
brought property in some measure into these subjects', and this has since
been continued by various statutes from time to time.[29] But, says Smith,
since *everyone* could hunt such animals without any *injury* being done,
'There can be no reason in equity given for this constitution.'[30] Furthermore, such statutes make nonsense of our property laws, for the ordinary
criteria for property do not apply to such animals: 'they are not in our
power, nor can they be considered as belonging to an estate as they are
often changing their place, but ought to be common to all'.[31] So whatever
reason might be given for these restrictions on 'the lower sort of people',
'the real reason is...the delight the great take in hunting and the great
inclination they have to screw all they can out of their hands [i.e. those of
the poor]'.[32] Similar reasoning is then extended to the Franchises of Waifs
and of Treasure Trove, and it is used to support the freedom of the sea.[33]

Moving on to property acquired by succession, we find that Smith's
criticism of the laws pertaining to the succession to land is on a very
similar basis. The enforcement of primogeniture and entail began in feudal
times and had to a large extent remained part of the fabric of the law ever
since. Both in the lectures and in *The Wealth of Nations* he goes to some
length to show what were 'the circumstances, which first gave occasion to
them, and which could alone render them reasonable'.[34] But whatever the
political necessity at one time, there is never any doubt that these arrangements were and are 'contrary to nature, to reason, and to justice'.[35] As far
as primogeniture is concerned, it rested on principles completely inconsistent with those of an impartial spectator, for 'the natural law of succession divides [land], like [moveables], among *all* the children of the family'.[36]
And as far as entails are concerned:

in the present state of Europe, when small as well as great estates derive their
security from the laws of their country, nothing can be more completely absurd.
They are founded upon the most absurd of all suppositions, the supposition that
every successive generation of men have not an equal right to the earth, and to
all that it possesses. (WN, III, ii, 6)[37]

This Lockean statement about property-rights to the earth rests, I think,
on most un-Lockean arguments. The principle of entail is simply inconsistent with the ordinary basis for our property law. Property law is based
upon spectator approval refined over generations into the laws of occupation, accession, and prescription; but the spectator works only amongst the
living, so that the earth belongs to each generation of men 'altogether as
well as it was their predecessors in their day'.[38] The only way in which
the spectator goes beyond the living is when a person is newly dead and his
memory is still fresh. Then,

we enter as it were into his dead body, and conceive what our living souls would feel if they were joined with his body, and how much we would be distressed to see our last injunctions not performed. Such sentiments naturally enclined men to extend property a little farther than a man's lifetime. (LJ(B), 165)[39]

This piety for the dead is the foundation for testamentary succession, and it is by analogical extension of this that entail arises.[40] This extension was to a large extent due to the influence of the Christian belief in the continued existence of the soul of the deceased.[41] But it is clearly a *false* analogy which renders the principle of entail inconsistent with the law of testamentary succession, which was based on spectator sympathy with the will of the newly dead. Such sympathy cannot naturally be supposed to be concerned with anybody but 'those who are alive at the same time with him'.[42] To go beyond that is to introduce a wholly arbitrary element into the law which makes nonsense of the principles which can otherwise guide our behaviour in this area.

Finally, from the real rights area of the law, I should like to point to the way in which Smith deals with exclusive privileges. He first points out how 'Some of them are founded upon natural reason', and gives a clear spectator account of these. But he then goes on to say that 'The greatest part...of exclusive priviledges are the creatures of the civil constitutions of the country.'[43] The basis for these can only be public utility, and 'Some indeed are harmless enough', such as time-limited patents and copyrights. 'But there are few so harmless. All monopolies in particular are extremely detrimental.'[44] In other words, their supposed rationale is non-existent, and since they have no foundation in 'natural reason' they ought to be condemned.

Smith criticizes the laws concerning punishment both as they pertain to laws of justice and to laws of police. From the former area three examples are particularly clearly stated, namely those of affronts (right to reputation), theft (property-right), and the expiration of various crimes. The law relating to the punishment of affronts had already at an early stage fallen behind the general development of society. It was still only prescribing minor pecuniary fines for such crimes, but this was totally inadequate in 'those countries where the laws of honour are received', because there affronts are resented as very great injuries. If the law does not recognize the full significance of honour as a factor in people's situation, it has little chance of reaching an impartial standpoint for 'It is intirely from this new notion of honour that the injury of such affronts has arose.' 'The small punishment therefore which is incurred by these affronts according to our law...is to be accounted a deficientia juris' and it has led to the grisly practice of duelling. 'For when the law do not give satisfaction somewhat adequate to the injury, men will think themselves intitled to take it at their own hand.'[45]

The criticism of the punishment for theft is completely straightforward:

The punishment which is commonly inflicted on theft is certainly not at all proportionable to the crime. It is greatly too severe, and such as the resentment of the injured person would not require. (LJ(A), ii, 149)

Theft appears naturally not to merit a very high punishment; it is a despicable crime and such as raises our contempt rather than any high resentment. – It is however punished capitally in most countries of Europe. (LJ(A), ii, 147–8)[46]

Most crimes are allowed to expire after a certain time if they have not been prosecuted, and Smith is very emphatic that this is as it should be. In fact he stresses this so much that his discussion reads like a call for a general review of this part of the law.[47] Smith gives two arguments for a fairly tight prescription of crimes, one from consistency and one from the nature of resentment which forms the basis for punishment. The former argument is that 'In the same manner as debts, so the punishment due for the commission of crimes, whether it be due to the public or to individualls, ought reasonably to prescribe in a time considerably shorter than that of a mans life time.'[48] In the preceding pages, Smith has explained prescription in connection with debts and other contractual obligations and has strongly indicated that the usual forty years may be too long.[49] But whatever it may be, punishment for crimes should expire as well, obviously because the principle of punishment is the same. Smith's second argument is that 'the resentment of the injured person or his relations...must wear away by time; one who had been guilty of a great injury against me would not raise my resentment 20 years after near so much as at the time the deed was committed, or even in a much shorter time. On this principle it is plain therefore that the punishment of crimes should not extend for a very long time.'[50] While Smith does not state his argument fully, his point is obviously that once we are outside the reach of resentment, we are outside the natural measure of punishment, namely the resentment which an impartial spectator can go along with. But when the natural principles for punishment break down, the way is open for arbitrariness. It is perhaps remarkable that Smith applies this reasoning equally to private crime and to treason.[51]

Smith's criticism of the punishment of transgressions of various laws of police has already been explained at length and all the significant cases have been quoted in our discussion of the general principles of punishment above.[52] As we saw, the general idea is that the measure of punishment is determined by the necessity of the laws to which the punishment is tied. If there is a conflict between the punishment actually imposed and the requirements of natural justice, the latter ought to take precedence unless the law which is being protected by the punishment is so important for the existence of the society that it is in itself more important than the laws of justice.

The critical potential of Smith's jurisprudence within domestic law is clear as far as the laws concerning divorce and polygamy are concerned. For he stresses that while he subscribes to the ban on these practices, this is purely a matter of necessary 'police',[53] and if we look at them with the eyes of natural justice we shall see that

> there is not any reall injustice either in voluntary divorce or in polygamy in those countries where they are allowed by the laws of the country[54]...For with regard to voluntary divorce, there can not be said to be any injustice done to the person who is turned away in this manner...In the same manner where polygamy is allowed...there can be no injustice in taking a wife in that manner. [When she knows the conditions], there can not be said to be any injury done her. (LJ(A), iii, 24–5)[55]

In other words, it would not be against the principles of natural justice to introduce voluntary divorce[56] and polygamy into the law. I shall not speculate how radical Smith's students may have considered this theoretical possibility – despite his many utility arguments against its desirability. Let us note instead that he took the matter one step further by arguing that if the natural circumstances were different and the number of women in a society was much higher than that of men then 'it would be altogether proper that polygamy should take place'.[57] It is interesting to think what Smith's conclusion might have been if the *social* circumstances, and hence the consequences, were different from what he thought.

There is one more point which shows Smith's flexibility in these matters. Having produced all the arguments from social necessity which confirm the traditional, strict view of divorce, which he obviously wants to believe in despite the verdict of natural justice, he ends the discussion on a note of hesitation: 'The knot indeed may perhaps be too straitly tied in some cases. It has been very justly thought proper that the infidelity (of the wife at least) should give occasion to a divorce. That injury is such that there can be no harmony or agreement, but continuall distrust and animosity amongst the parties.'[58] While one would dearly like to know what the brackets and the 'at least' in the student's notes reflect from Smith's actual argument in the lecture, the general question mark over the prohibition on divorce is clear; and it becomes quite striking when we see how Smith extends his argument by means of the principle of consistency: 'Now for the same account all injuries which excite the same resentment and hatred, and which render the union equally uncomfortable, ought to produce a divorce as well as the others.'[59]

In the branch of public law dealing with the rights of sovereigns Smith finds unjust a number of the statutes relating to treason. Thus 'counterfeiting of the king's coin...should not properly be treason, because it is no attempt on the essence of government'. This is simply a case of partial and incorrect judgement of the injury involved, which is 'no more than forgery', and fortunately it 'is usually punished as such' in modern times.[60] Apart from that, Smith criticizes a number of statutes which make activities treasonable which are not naturally so, but which once were so because of the political situation of Britain. The first is the whole cluster of anti-Catholic laws enacted in the late sixteenth century. A large number of activities 'were made treasonable as being against the subsistence of the government and encouraging a religion which tended to overturn it by every possible means'. But although these laws are no longer enforced, 'it were proper that they were repealed, as very harmless men may be in danger from accidents of no consequence and meet with great trouble, especially if he has by any form or means offended the government'.[61] In other words, all emergency being past, these laws could be a dangerous weapon with which government could arbitrarily prosecute behaviour which is not naturally unjust. Exactly the same holds for the laws which made it treason to dispute the right of king and Parliament to alter the succession to the Crown, and to maintain the right of the Stuart family after the Revolution settlement. For although such laws were necessary in the early years after the Revolution, the government is now completely established, 'and these laws can serve little other purpose than to involve innocent or harmless people in trouble'.[62]

The other branch of public law which is concerned with the rights of subjects against their sovereign is so unsettled that we can hardly expect much jurisprudential criticism in this field. Nevertheless it deserves notice that Smith sets his fairly standard Whig criticism of the actions of James II clearly within the framework of his theory of divided sovereignty: the king's behaviour was unjust because it infringed the real right which Parliament had in its part of the sovereign power. 'Thus K. James, on account of his encroachments on the body politic, was with all justice in the world opposed and rejected.'[63]

International relations are on the whole regulated by the political considerations of national interests and needs, rather than by laws of justice, and accordingly Smith's critical concern is more with political prudence than with natural justice.[64] The thing he particularly stressed was that strong defence and free trade are – with one or two specific exceptions – not in conflict, but go hand in hand as worthy objects of government policy. His arguments for this are well-known from *The Wealth of Nations*, but it may not be out of place to quote a particularly dignified expression of his opinion from *The Theory of Moral Sentiments*:

France and England may each of them have some reason to dread the increase of the naval and military power of the other; but for either of them to envy the internal happiness and prosperity of the other, the cultivation of its lands, the advancement of its manufactures, the increase of its commerce, the security and number of its ports and harbours, its proficiency in all the liberal arts and sciences, is surely beneath the dignity of two such great nations. These are all real improvements of the world we live in. Mankind are benefited, human nature is ennobled by them. (TMS, vi, ii, 2, § 3)

But although the nature of international law is such that Smith has to keep his criticism predominantly in the political mode, this is not completely so. There are some basic things which can be said clearly about justice in the international scene, and Smith does not neglect to do so. He repeatedly and in no uncertain terms condemns the injustice of the European subjection of less developed people around the world:

Folly and injustice seem to have been the principles which presided over and directed the first project of establishing those colonies; the folly of hunting after gold and silver mines, and the injustice of coveting the possession of a country whose harmless natives, far from having ever injured the people of Europe, had received the first adventurers with every mark of kindness and hospitality.[65]

Equally Columbus's colonial scheme is condemned for its injustice and its 'pious' Christian missionary purpose brushed aside as a cover-up.[66] And Smith's talent for meaningful word-play does not fail him when he sums up one aspect of the colonization of America: 'The savage injustice of the Europeans rendered an event, which ought to have been beneficial to all, ruinous and destructive to several of those unfortunate countries.'[67]

It is an interesting perspective on Smith's assessment of the relationship between Britain and the North American colonies that he is willing to judge the mother-country's severe restrictions on the colonists' trade and manufacture in terms of the laws of nations – terms which it is informative to compare with his statement about the relationship between England and France, quoted above: 'To prohibit a great people...from making all that they can of every part of their own produce, or from employing their stock and industry in the way that they judge most advantageous to themselves, is a manifest violation of the most sacred rights of mankind.'[68] On the other side of that coin it does perhaps deserve notice that in Smith's opinion, 'It is not contrary to justice that both Ireland and America should contribute towards the discharge of the publick debt of Great Britain', as long as this was contracted, to a great extent, in order to defend these two countries![69]

4 The critical programme

This discussion of concrete legal criticism in Smith's work is hardly complete,[70] but it is complete enough to show the critical capability which he thought his jurisprudence had. And this critical intent was not just a matter of occasional practice, but of a systematic programme.

Smith's legal criticism obviously presupposes that the negative and precise virtue of justice is 'natural' in the sense that it is *somehow* outside the grip of social change. But we know that justice consists in the verdict of the impartial spectator on what is properly considered injury in concrete situations, and, in close connection with this, his verdict on the proper degree of resentment and punishment in the case. This would seem, however, to make the impartial spectator dependent upon the situation in which he judges: he cannot be purely and simply impartial – he must be impartial in relation to actual and particular people and circumstances. This raises the question of whether his verdict in itself is not dependent upon, or relative to, the situation? In which case, what becomes of the idea of *natural* justice?

We can understand how Smith avoided the horns of this dilemma in the following way. Some parts of the impartial spectator's verdict are universal – and in that sense 'natural' – while others are dependent upon the situation in which he judges. Thus, his impartiality and what it implies of universality, consistency, and coherence, are everywhere the same; and equally the primacy of the negative is a natural principle. Furthermore, some situations involving injury are so basic to human life that the spectator's verdicts will always be recognizably similar. That is why Smith is willing to adopt the traditional distinction between natural and acquired rights: some rights are so basic that they can be taken as universal or natural.[71] For the rest, the kind of situational dependency Smith had in mind can perhaps be shown in the following way. It would make little sense for an impartial spectator to recognize trespass as injury in a society which had no idea of property in land; but clearly the principles upon which he recognizes theft of animals as injury amongst a society of nomads and those upon which he recognizes trespass as an injury amongst a farming community are the same.

If we do not find room for the natural and universal in Smith's theory of justice, his whole project for a natural jurisprudence becomes unintelligible, as does the devastating criticism of positivistic command theories of law which clears the way for his programme.[72] Just like Hume, Smith chooses Hobbes as the specific target for this criticism because he there found a clear identification of social life with life directed or organized by civil government, and hence an identification of moral standards and positive law. As Smith read him, Hobbes was saying that 'The laws of the civil magistrate...ought to be regarded as the sole ultimate standards of what was just and unjust, of what was right and wrong.'[73] This, however, presupposes that there are no moral distinctions between right and wrong, just and unjust, 'antecedent to all law or positive institution', and this cannot be true:

Law, it was justly observed by Dr. Cudworth, could not be the original source of those distinctions, since, upon the supposition of such a law, it must either be right to obey it, and wrong to disobey it, or indifferent whether we obeyed it or disobeyed it. That law which it was indifferent whether we obeyed or disobeyed, could not, it was evident, be the source of those distinctions; neither could that which it was right to obey and wrong to disobey, since even this still supposed the antecedent notions or ideas of right and wrong, and that obedience to the law was conformable to the idea of right, and disobedience to that of wrong. (TMS, vii, iii, 2, § 4)

Although Smith can take over this fundamental criticism of legal positivism from Cudworth, he has to part with him, of course, on the question of *how* men can have those ideas of what is naturally right or wrong independent of civil society. For Cudworth this was possible by means of universal human reason,

and this conclusion...was more easily received at a time when the abstract science of human nature was but in its infancy, and before the distinct offices and powers of the different faculties of the human mind had been carefully examined and distinguished from one another. (TMS, vii, iii, 2, § 5)[74]

Smith, however, has had the benefit of this development of the 'abstract science of human nature', and consequently he has been able to do better than Cudworth with his theory of the moral sentiments, of their communication through mutual sympathy, and of their formation of the ideal morality of the impartial spectator.

There is, then, a natural justice independent of civil society, for 'Among equals each individual is naturally, and antecedent to the institution of civil government, regarded as having a right both to defend himself from injuries, and to exact a certain degree of punishment for those which have been done to him.'[75] This 'natural law' is not only independent of civil society and its positive law; it constitutes the ideal foundation for positive law, the very principles upon which positive law ought to be formed, and that is the reason why natural jurisprudence is such an important discipline:

The wisdom of every state or commonwealth endeavours, as well as it can, to employ the force of the society to restrain those who are subject to its authority from hurting or disturbing the happiness of one another. The rules which it establishes for this purpose constitute the civil and criminal law of each particular state or country. The principles upon which those rules either are or ought to be founded, are the subject of a particular science, of all sciences by far the most important, but hitherto, perhaps, the least cultivated – that of natural jurisprudence. (TMS, vi, ii, intro., § 2)

Natural justice is, therefore, an ideal standard which is to be searched for, not only in the case of individual actions, but also in the total legal code of any given civil society: 'Every system of positive law may be regarded as a more or less imperfect attempt towards a system of natural jurisprudence, or towards an enumeration of the particular rules of justice.'[76] Such a system 'of what might properly be called natural jurisprudence' would be truly universal for it would be 'a theory of the general principles which ought to run through, and be the foundation of, the laws of all nations'.[77] This universality is, of course, one of the principles embodied in the impartial spectator, and it reigns supreme in the virtue of justice because of its negative, and hence precise, character.

An obvious implication is that such a system of natural law would be a weapon for criticism of positive law which falls too short of its standards, for

In no country do the decisions of positive law coincide exactly, in every case, with the rules which the natural sense of justice would dictate. Systems of positive law, therefore, though they deserve the greatest authority, as the records of the sentiments of mankind in different ages and nations, yet can never be regarded as accurate systems of the rules of natural justice. (TMS, vii, iv, § 36)[78]

In view of all this it seems somewhat difficult to understand the suggestion that 'When...[Smith] contrasts laws that are in accordance with nature with those that depart from this "norm" he simply means that the latter do not accord with the consensus of moral opinions in that type of society.'[79] Whole systems of law deviate from natural justice, and there is no reason to think that even 'the consensus of moral opinions' should not be capable of doing so on occasion. To identify natural justice with the consensus is to overlook, not only Smith's outline of a new doctrine of 'natural law', as quoted above, but also most of what he has had to say about the ideal, impartial spectator. Although the *origin* of a man's understanding of the spectator's standpoint is the 'consensus', this does not affect its validity.

Smith points out that 'it was very late in the world before any such general system was thought of, or before the philosophy of law was treated of by itself, and without regard to the particular institutions of any one nation'.[80] He maintains that the attempts which have been made are all rather incomplete and imperfect, the best of these, that of Grotius, included.[81] This, of course, is in spite of the fact that the moral reasoning of men with regard to justice has at all times in the history of man had an implicit, and in individual cases maybe explicit, reference to natural justice. It is the standard they fall short of and the ideal that in particular cases they aspire to. Natural justice has thus been with men since the beginning of time and has been developed through men's reactions in particular contexts. But exactly because the laws of natural justice are rules which emerge unintentionally from such reactions in particular situations, the formulation of the laws and their organization into a system will always trail behind. The formation of such a system is a philosopher's task and Smith thought of himself as such a philosopher: 'I shall, in another discourse, endeavour to give an account of the general principles of law and government...'[82]

This was Smith's promise in the first edition of *The Theory of Moral*

Sentiments; he had promised it even earlier, and he repeated the promise in the very last year of his life.[83] What he had managed to execute of 'this great work' was burnt before he died, and we are left to rely on the general plan outlined at the end of *The Theory of Moral Sentiments* and the partial realization of it in the lectures from which we have the students' notes and in *The Wealth of Nations*. Of the last two sources, the book is mainly focused on 'police, revenue, and arms', rather than on the hard core of jurisprudence, which concerns natural justice, while the lectures are meant as a general introduction to the principles which form law as it is and has been. It is only the brief, programmatic statements in *The Theory of Moral Sentiments*, which have been quoted and discussed here, that give the full flavour of what should have been, and show the real significance of the exercises in concrete legal criticism which we traced on pp. 139–47. And it is only if we presuppose something as systematic in character and weighty in critical content as this theory of natural justice that Smith's allocation of roles to laws of justice *vis-à-vis* all the other areas of law yields any meaning.[84] It is this natural jurisprudence which provides the general principles from which all other principles in the discipline of jurisprudence derive their function, and it is therefore the backbone of the science of a legislator.

5 The object of criticism

The fact that we have only a general programme in addition to incidental performances makes interpretation precarious, not only because of the insufficient information about content, but also because of the misleading impression one easily gets of the character of Smith's enterprise. Smith saw it as a philosopher's task to formulate a system of jurisprudence; but this must not be taken to mean that it was to be a philosopher's *construction*. The principles of natural justice are the principles of the impartial spectator and the philosopher's task is to understand how these principles can work in various kinds of situations, and on this basis formulate what should be the rules of law in its various branches. For it is, indeed, 'the end of jurisprudence to prescribe rules for the decisions of judges and arbiters'.[85] Such understanding, however, is best gained through a study of the attempts which mankind have in fact made to find the standpoint of the impartial spectator. And of these attempts those of 'judges and arbiters' are not only the earliest, but also those which in the long run are least exposed to the influence of considerations other than those of natural justice. Law which is made by some authority other than a judge of concrete cases is liable to be guided by political and religious objectives, whereas judge-made law based on precedent has a better chance of approaching the principles of natural justice. Smith therefore has a very definite preference for case law over statute law in general, and for English law over French and Scots law in particular – at least as far as the *study* of law is concerned. For in contrast to French and Scots law,

The English law was...formed into a system before the discovery of Justinians Pandects; and its courts established, and their method of proceedings pretty much fixed, before the other courts in Europe were instituted, or the civil or cannon law came to be of any great weight. It is for this reason that it borrows less from those laws than the law of any other nation in Europe; and is for that reason more deserving of the attention of a speculative man than any other, as being more formed on the naturall sentiments of mankind. (LJ(A), ii, 74–5)[86]

It is, however, not only in the study but also in the court that case law is preferable. It is simply much more exact and directly applicable than statute law. This is because it is formed in concrete cases of injury, whereas statute law is thought out in the abstract:

Common Law...is found to be much more equitable than that which is founded on Statute only, for the same reason as what is founded on practice and experience must be better adapted to particular cases than that which is derived from theory only. (LRBL, 169)[87]

This is a direct consequence of Smith's distinction between contextual knowledge and system knowledge. The decisions out of which case law arises are prime examples of the former, statute law to a greater or smaller degree of the latter. The precision of case law is, of course, further strengthened by the fact that in it the negative, injustice, is inevitably the matter for consideration – that is what a court case is about. This is by no means necessary in the making of statute law.

These ideas are closely connected with the further consideration that while common law is old law, statute law and its attendant institutions are only too easily renewed, and 'New courts and new laws are...great evills ...It takes time and repeated practise to ascertain the precise meaning of a law or to have precedents enough to determine the practise of a court. Its proceedings will be altogether loose and innacurate.'[88] Consequently, 'In no other country of Europe is the law so accurate as in England because it has not been of so long standing.'[89] The precision of case law means that although it is an unplanned growth, it will over time form itself into a system: 'This attention, to practice and precedent, necessarily formed the Roman law into that regular and orderly system in which it has been delivered down to us; and the like attention has had the like effects upon the laws of every other country where such attention has taken place.'[90]

Smith's high regard for old law has nothing to do with the obligatory character of law. It is not old age but the approval of the impartial spectator which makes law morally valid. In complex matters, however, it takes time to find the standpoint of the impartial spectator, and it is therefore wise to look where the search has been going on systematically for a long time. Also, Smith's preference for case law and warnings about the dangers inherent in statute law must of course not be taken to mean that the latter can be dispensed with. Like every exercise of power, that of the judiciary is best when it is checked by some other power, namely by the legislature. However, because of their general and abstract character, 'Written and formall laws are a very great refinement of government, and such as we never meet with but in the latest periods of it.'[91] Furthermore, such laws have the character of general regulations for all members of a society, and they therefore presuppose the kind of strong government which only develops relatively late in history.[92] But when a system of law has already grown out of the activity of judges, then the supplementation of this system by statute law can function as a check on the authority of the judges, and can become accepted as such:

Laws are...posterior to the establishment of judges. At the first establishment of judges there are no laws; every one trusts to the naturall feeling of justice he has in his own breast and expects to find in others. Were laws to be established in the beginnings of society prior to the judges, they would then be a restraint upon liberty, but when established after them they extent[93] and secure it, as they do not ascertain or restrain the actions of private persons so much as the power and conduct of the judge over the people. (LJ(A), v, 110–11)[94]

Smith's view is a finely balanced one. Case law cannot fulfil all the needs of a complex society, and to rely solely on it would give judges too much power. But on the other hand, it tends to be much more precise and closer to the basic principles of natural justice than statute law, and it is therefore much more important for a formulation of the system of natural jurisprudence. The abstract character of statute law and the fact that it is systematically created law leave it wide open to influence from concerns other than those of natural justice. But on the other hand it is indispensable as a control on the judiciary and as a supplement to common law. Under these circumstances it is not surprising that Smith sees both kinds of law as very worthy objects of criticism by his system of natural jurisprudence; the guiding ideal for both case law and statute law should be natural justice.[95] This is already clear from all that he had to say about the relationship between natural justice and positive law, as quoted and discussed above.[96] And it is stated concisely in the early manuscript:

The Rules by which the magistrate...actually regulates all his decisions... *whether established upon express Statute, upon accidental custom or upon their own evident equity* constitute the civil and criminal Jurisprudence...The Rules by which it is most suitable to the natural principles of Justice...that such decisions should be regulated, constitute what is called Natural Jurisprudence.[97]

CHAPTER SEVEN

Smith's historical jurisprudence

1 Introduction

We have in the previous chapters discussed the analytic and critical aspects of Smith's jurisprudence. One of the most unusual features of his planned discourse, however, is that it should deal not only with 'the general principles of law and government' but also with 'the different revolutions they have undergone in the different ages and periods of society'.[1] While this historical dimension may seem strange to modern eyes, the history of law has two rather obvious functions within the framework of Smith's argument. First, as we saw on pp. 151–2, we only gain an understanding of how the principles of the impartial spectator work in practice by studying how men have tried, and maybe failed, to use them. And secondly, the history of law explains the present state of the law which is the object of critical evaluation from the standpoint of natural justice. This evaluation consists in 'negative' tests for injustice within a given system of law, and it is therefore of obvious importance to understand how this system arrived at its present composition. It is particularly important to see whether the necessity which led to the introduction of the various laws of police was genuine and whether it continues to be of vital importance to the country. If the answer is negative, then the laws in question fall within the ambit of natural justice, and if they are in conflict with its principles, they are condemned. This form of argument is used repeatedly in both the *Lectures on Jurisprudence* and in *The Wealth of Nations*. These are the only two functions history can have within Smith's system of jurisprudence, and it should be stressed that there is no room for the sort of traditionalism according to which antiquity in itself bestows validity upon law.

We have already seen from various points of view how law is integrated with the rest of mankind's activities, and its history must accordingly be treated as part of history generally. In reviewing this broad treatment which Smith gives the subject, we should remember that he firmly subscribes to the old idea that history can teach us through its examples – not so much directly through descriptions of human deeds and misdeeds, as indirectly through its descriptions of situations so that we can evaluate sympathetically what would be the proper action to take in that *kind* of situation.² This is of importance for our understanding of why Smith casts his net so wide in order to write the history of law; and it is of importance not least for our understanding of his view of the historical process itself – and hence for our understanding of what the science of a legislator might be good for, apart from the divertissement of contemplative utilitarians.

Smith presents an abundance of historical material, but the intention here is only to discuss the major factors of jurisprudential importance as well as to present enough material to make it possible to appreciate Smith's view of history.

2 Primitive society

In Smith's view, law had its basis in practices, not in ideas. In tracing its history, therefore, he would not in the first instance look towards intellectual traditions, like Greco-Roman philosophy or the Christian religion. He would look at types of social life. He chose as a heuristic device four broad 'ideal–typical' stages of social development: 'ist, the Age of Hunters; 2dly, the Age of Shepherds; 3dly, the Age of Agriculture; and 4thly, the Age of Commerce.'³

Hunting, fishing and gathering can only support a limited number of people in a given area, and primitive society therefore is first of all small and scattered, a society of villages with little and tenuous communication and only the occasional loose association in time of war.⁴ Secondly, it is a poor society: it has only the most rudimentary division of labour; consequently, its collective pool of skills, its 'technology', is extremely limited, and it can have no production which allows of accumulation.⁵ Thirdly, it is a weak society which is an easy prey for more developed societies, as is shown by the history of European colonization. It is weak because it is small and scattered and has no technology,⁶ and because it has no organized form of government.⁷ The weakness of government is the fourth fundamental feature of primitive society, and it is owing to the circumstances that none of the factors which tend to concentrate power are present in this form of society. The only things which will distinguish one man above others in such a society are his age and his personal eminence in the skills which are relevant to the life of the tribe, and although old age particularly is of importance, both are of limited influence since they will both die with the individual concerned.⁸ Authority cannot go beyond this because the other two sources of it, superior wealth and noble birth, are unknown phenomena in primitive society.⁹ The concept of property is tied to the essential activities of the society, hunting and warfare, and it therefore stretches no further than a person's immediate possessions.¹⁰ Nor is there any pressure to extend the idea of what one person could lay special claim to, since there is no division of labour which would make possible the exploitation of animals or land and the accumulation of stock. And since distinction by birth is derivative from that by wealth, there will be no hereditary nobility, but all will be more or less equal.[11] Corresponding to the weak foundation of governmental authority is the weak demand for it – they are two sides of the same coin. With property only extending to the most obvious personal possessions, there will be little possibility of conflict in this area and only scant jurisdiction will be called for.[12] Other areas of conflict will be settled by simple family jurisdiction.[13] The exercise of governmental authority will therefore only be occasional and intermittent.[14] When authority is used, it will commonly be under some guidance from the person who has established a role of natural leadership in war, but basically the form of government is 'democratical' in both war and peace – in both its 'executive' and its 'judicial' functions – in as far as the general equality means that all have to be heard.[15] Under these circumstances no legislative power is called for, nor would 'government' be strong enough to supply it.[16] All it can do is to try to act as arbitrator in disputes which are so serious that they threaten the continued existence of the society, which means disagreement arising from cowardice ('treason'),[17] and from serious bodily injury to – especially murder of – members of other families. The latter, however, does not lead to proper criminal jurisdiction, for all that primitive government can hope to do is to re-establish public peace through reconciliation – much like modern 'civil law'.[18] All in all, the law is therefore very weakly established. There are no proper courts to administer whatever law is recognized, but the whole people – or a large body of it – intervenes as arbitrator.[19] There is no formal law; of the natural rights only the most basic receive any attention, but not enough to establish a proper criminal law; in the area of estate rights, only the simplest ideas of possession are recognized, and property by accession, succession, or through contract is unknown.[20] Domestic law was unknown in all primitive societies simply because government was too weak to intermeddle in the private affairs of families, and all regulation was therefore left to the absolute supremacy of the husband, father, and master.[21] And since among hunters 'there can be very little government of any sort', it is scarcely relevant to speak of public law.

In one form or another this kind of society is the base-line from which other societies develop. It is 'the lowest and rudest state of society, such as we find it among the native tribes of North America', and nearly such as Julius Caesar found in Britain.[22] Unfortunately Smith is never entirely clear concerning the forces which dissolve this form of society and provide a transition to the shepherd stage. In some cases he seems to be saying that it is human needs which lead to the ingenuity requisite for their satisfaction; in others it seems that it is ingenuity which leads to a situation where more needs can in fact be satisfied. But whether it is population pressure which first gives people the idea of keeping animals rather than killing them, or whether it is the new fashion of keeping animals which makes it possible for more people to survive, the fact is that it happens.[23] And this transition from hunting to the keeping of herds 'is of all others the greatest in the progression of society, for by it the notion of property is extended beyond possession, to which it is in the former state confined'.[24] Suitably for a step of such momentous importance, it is a long-drawn-out process. As Smith accounts for it in the *Lectures on Jurisprudence*, it is the story of how the possibility of strong government slowly emerges hand in hand with the need for it.[25] And at the end of the process so many institutional factors have developed in mankind's situation that we can no longer explain the further social evolution by reference to the simple needs of survival.

3 Shepherd society

When some people get the idea of keeping live animals, what was previously 'common', or open to anyone's claim, is no longer so. This dramatically increases the possibility of conflicts in a society, and these can only be settled when the whole of the social group intervenes.[26] In this way the new property-right will become *generally* recognized in society. This role of the whole social group as spectator–judges is repeatedly stressed by Smith and is important for our understanding of how the recognition of the new property-right is psychologically possible. His somewhat schematic presentation of a hunting society of great equality which is replaced by a shepherd society of great inequality only makes full sense when we allow for this mechanism of stepwise acceptance by society as a whole of several property in animals which were previously common. And the popular assembly continues, in one form or another, to have this kind of importance right through the development of shepherd society. But in the shelter of the general recognition of private property in animals, greater and greater inequality of wealth will grow up, some people having the good luck to get numerous herds, others none at all. This will make the poorer dependent upon the richer people, and the latter will therefore carry much more weight in the popular assembly.[27] It is this set of complex interrelations, rather than the mere accumulation of stock, which is the driving force in the development of shepherd society. While the inequality of fortune is driven to an extreme, the sway of the rich over the assembly of the people steadily increases so that the rich man and the chief will always be one and the same. This is further secured by the fact that it is not only the poor who are dependent upon the rich, but also the

rich upon the poor. In a society of this nature there is simply no other outlet for a man's riches than to spend it on retaining an appropriate number
of dependents. Wealth will therefore become entrenched in one or a few
families and both wealth and influence will become hereditary, thus
adding nobility of birth to the factors creating subordination.[28] 'Birth and
fortune are evidently the two circumstances which principally set one man
above another. They are the two great sources of *personal* distinction';[29]
and they are the natural objects of that deference which reinforces the
whole system. But alongside these tendencies to concentrate power in particular persons (or families) there are also other factors leading to the
organization of central governmental authority. Compared with earlier
society, shepherd societies are much bigger and they have a much more
complicated property structure. This means that the exercise of judicial
power will increase dramatically in both volume and difficulty. Similarly,
such a society will be abler and more willing to act as a unit against other
societies, and the executive power will therefore expand correspondingly.
So while the final decision remains with the people as a whole, particularly
in matters of war and peace,[30] a chosen assembly will by and by be instituted to take care of such business and it is in this assembly that the
chieftain will exert his superior influence.[31] The over-all effects are a
steady strengthening of governmental power and the beginnings of
specialization in the judicial power. The government will be able to intermeddle more in people's private disputes and in more serious cases it may
even be possible for it to go further than mere arbitration, seeking to
impose punishment for offences.[32] These are, however, only faint beginnings; but in cases involving the community as a whole – particularly
concerning warfare – the government would at an early stage become
absolute.[33]

The most significant development of the law in this period is obviously
the extension of the concept of property to include animals, and Smith
takes great care to explain how the original requirement of actual possession was gradually relaxed to much looser forms of 'power' over the
animals in question.[34] Once this development has taken place it is, says
Smith, 'a matter of no great difficulty to extend this from one subject to
another, from herds and flocks to the land itself'.[35] But already in the
shepherd stage further extensions of another kind take place: not only the
idea of what can be the subject of property claims changes, but also the
idea of how property can legitimately be acquired. The most basic concept
of accession– to milk and offspring – arises naturally once property in
animals is recognized.[36] Also, simple natural principles of succession become recognized and form the basis for legal succession.[37] But there is no
idea of testamentary succession, nor of contracts, nor does the law deal
with marriage settlements.[38] Throughout the development of shepherd

society there is, as already mentioned, a growing tendency to recognize rights arising from delict – or to punish, rather than arbitrate and procure compensation. This takes its beginning in the area of 'public law', with punishment for offences against the society ('treason'), and is gradually transferred to punishment for grave offences against individuals until, in the maturity of this form of society or its transition to agriculture, a fairly fixed system has been worked out. What happens is that the public authority when it intervenes in a private dispute protects the offender against the resentment of the injured party and his family in order to set a standardized punishment which the latter can inflict on the former, and for this service it requires some compensation in the same proportion. This is the beginning of the long process which will make punishment solely a matter for the government.[39]

While government will gain strength and become more articulated in its judicial functions in shepherd society, it will be a long way off from that 'very great refinement of government' which consists in legislating.[40] Its executive power will soon be absolute and the strength which it can command will become overwhelming if it is a nomadic shepherd society. By moving around according to the grazing, it will be possible to maintain many more people. and at the same time the group will be nearly as mobile as hunters in military operations. Since nomads do not defend a particular land area but carry all they own to the field, their battles usually result in the total subjection and absorption of the losing party and its belongings, thus further strengthening the victorious side. With strong leadership from its chieftain, a nomadic shepherd society is therefore often a formidable force, and we find history full of examples of how such societies have overrun settled societies, the most significant being the overthrow of the Roman empire. Nomadic societies were still prevalent in Africa and Asia in Smith's time, and both the Arabs and the Tartars were of significance; of the latter, Smith remarked, 'we find that more of the great revolutions in the world have arose from them than any other nation'.[41]

4 Greece and Rome

Nomadic societies like the ones mentioned existed in areas of the world where the soil does not naturally lend itself to anything but pasture. But in Europe, and first of all in Attica, two conditions coincided which eventually made it possible to go beyond this stage. Not only were the soil and the climate so good that it was possible to cultivate the land, but the country was comparatively easily defended against invading shepherd societies. This coincidence of circumstances makes Smith's story a distinctively European one. Some time after the Trojan wars, first Attica and then other parts of Greece were settled as agricultural societies, and their easy communication by sea with neighbouring societies fairly soon spurred the development of some commerce as well – a process which spread to the rest of the Mediterranean area. Hand in hand with this went the development of 'the severall arts and sciences and manufactures', rendering these societies rich and civilized and a natural object of envy for other less developed societies. The consequent problem of defence was gradually solved by living in fortified cities, and this led to significant political changes. While the movement into the cities took place under the leadership of chieftains who remained from the shepherd society, this form of government would soon decline. The closeness of city life would spur the natural envy and rivalry between the chief and the other nobles, and would make it easier for the latter to exercise influence on the popular assembly. In this way a republican form of government which was half democratic and half aristocratic would arise.[42] These governments were in effect elective aristocracies since only those of noble birth could be elected, but they retained their democratic element and in fact tended increasingly in a democratic direction. This happened in both Athens and Rome. The crucial factor in this was the institution of slavery, for as long as production was taken care of by slaves, all freemen could participate in the political life and at the same time the poor amongst them (the *plebs*) would not be dependent upon the rich and powerful for employment. Consequently, there would be a large group who would try to improve their condition by clamouring for political power. This contrasts markedly with modern society, where there are no slaves, where the poor have little or no time or inclination to participate in politics because they are working, and where they have some *moderate* dependence upon and deference for the rich and powerful. So while the effect of commerce is always to dissolve the power of a hereditary nobility, as we shall see, this happened much more quickly in ancient times than it did, and does, in modern commercial society.[43] With the increasing influence of the popular assembly, the way to political power was to support the demand of the poor for public subsidies,[44] and this policy aggravated a defence problem which was already growing.[45] While society remained basically agricultural the bulk of the population was fitted for war by its labour, although perhaps not so well as during the hunting and shepherd stages; and even though they were significantly less mobile and only able to be away from home for part of the year, they would still constitute a good army.[46] But when people become employed in manufacture and commerce this changes completely: their employment and income stop immediately they are away. To the extent that freemen were involved in these enterprises in Athens and Rome their ability and willingness to join the army therefore dwindled.[47] And although the fact that so much work was carried out by slaves delayed and blunted this effect, it eventually had its impact. Furthermore, the greater degree of luxury which followed upon commerce made people much less fitted for war and also much less inclined for it – and this tendency was increased by the 'democratic' subsidy policies. At the same time, both the art of war and the technology of war machines became much more sophisticated, the former leading to longer campaigns and thus to some dependence upon (foreign) mercenaries, the latter making cities harder to defend and requiring professional skills.[48] The result as far as Athens and Greece were concerned was that the Macedonians found them easy victims.[49] But while the 'defensive' Greek republics were given the final stroke from outside, the expansionist, 'conquering' republic of Rome was led by these developments to internal dissolution. When the armies upon which it depended had their recruiting ground narrowed down to 'the lowest of the mob', especially freed or runaway slaves, these armies would no longer be the tools of the government, but of the general upon whom they depended. Because of this dependence and because of the long and hard campaign against the Carthaginians, these armies changed from militias into professional standing armies, thus forming a power base from which the general would try to make himself dictator. These attempts finally succeeded with Caesar,[50] and the same would have happened at Carthage if Hannibal had not been beaten. The resulting 'military monarchy' sustained and expanded the Roman empire for a long time because of the strength of its standing armies. But when they were allowed to degenerate into poor militias, at least in the border provinces, and when mercenary troops from neighbouring barbaric nations began to be relied upon, the empire was weakened and the way prepared for the men from the North.[51]

During the long development of republican government, the ultimate power in all areas remained with the people as a whole, but as the extent and difficulty of both judicial and executive business grew, more and more of it was discharged by the elected assembly. But while the Athenians never firmly established a separation of the judicial and the executive functions from each other,[52] the judicial business became so specialized in Rome that the courts and the office of the praetor had to be completely separated from the Senate and from the office of the consuls. In Smith's opinion the Romans even for a while 'laid aside' the fundamental idea that the ultimate appeal 'in all matters of moment' was to the people.[53] This period also sees the beginning of the 'very great refinement of government' which consists in laying down formal laws. 'This was the case at Athens, Sparta, and other places where the people demanded laws to regulate the conduct of the judge.'[54] This new function, however, was not put in the hands of a separate branch of government but remained with the people until the military monarchy of the emperors replaced the republic.[55] Then the legislative power was nominally transferred to the Senate – but the senators were 'intirely the creatures of the prince', who held the executive power.[56] The ultimate appeal in judicial matters also eventually fell to the emperor,[57] but this only really mattered in cases involving himself and his interests.[58] In all other cases it was in the interest of the emperor to adhere to the established system of justice and leave it to be administered as strictly as, or even more strictly than, under the republic. And this was the case even under the worst of the emperors. In order to underline his point that 'A military government allows the strictest administration of justice',[59] and thus that individual liberty and political liberty are entirely separate issues, Smith makes a dramatic comparison between the achievements in this respect of the Roman emperors and of Cromwell, and he similarly contrasts the Western empire with the military governments of the East, where the rulers were princes of 'Tartarian' descent who had no knowledge of regular justice.[60]

The system for the administration of justice which was in this way preserved under the rule of the emperors had undergone very significant developments at Athens and Rome. At Athens the large popular Assembly of Five Hundred functioned as a court. Because of its size it was impossible to call anyone to account for its sentences, nor was it willing to pay any attention to precedents, and the consequences were a high degree of arbitrariness in its procedures and the lack of a systematic body of law. This changed dramatically in the Roman republic, where the courts were small and the office of judge was made a separate profession. As a consequence the judges were easily accountable and they therefore covered themselves by using precedents. This 'necessarily formed the Roman law into that regular system in which it has been delivered down to us', and it made the study of law a separate science which was cultivated in particular families who took pride in their profession.[61] The importance of this difference between the Athenian and the Roman system is also underlined by drawing modern parallels – such as the difference between the large assemblies of the Parlement of Paris and the House of Commons when they functioned judicially, and English judges.[62] But the importance of the difference goes much further than that, for it is 'in a great measure' due to their administration of justice that the Romans maintained their republic 'in its grandeur for above 500 years'; while the fact that the Greek orators were able to manage 'the Courts of Judicature in the same manner as the managers of a play-house do the pit', along with the other factors we have seen, meant that 'The Athenian state did not continue in its glory for above seventy years.'[63] Similarly, 'The superiority of character in the Romans over that of the Greeks' was probably due more to 'the better constitution of their courts of justice' than to anything else![64]

In all areas of the law great developments took place in the period under consideration. First of all the concept of property was extended to land, which 'is the greatest extension it has undergone'.[65] Originally property in land was collective, and here Smith lets the spectator apply a very basic Humean law of association: people 'would not easily conceive a subject of such extent as land is, should belong to an object so little as a single man'.[66] In this system the land was allocated for use every season, but once the population – or at least the rich and powerful – had concentrated in cities, a fixed allocation emerged as the most convenient, and accordingly in most of the ancient republics there was enacted 'an Agrarian law, which divided the publick territory in a certain proportion among the different citizens who composed the state'.[67] With the establishment of private property in land went a great extension of accession – first to whatever would grow on the land, afterwards to whatever was under the surface in the form of minerals, etc.[68] The law of prescription changed, too, lengthening significantly the required period, though never to the same lengths as later law.[69] The principles of succession changed extensively, particularly at Rome, and Smith goes to great lengths to explain how the law adjusted gradually to the changing family patterns. Thus the sons who had left the family, daughters who had married, and children who had been given away in adoption, no longer got a share in the inheritance. And the growing independence of women – financially and otherwise – led to new forms of marriage contracts which again affected the succession.[70] Most importantly, however, both Athens and Rome reached the 'considerable refinement in humanity' of respecting the will of the dead and hence began – albeit slowly – to recognize succession by testaments. And although this never came as far as the recognition of entails, it came near enough to it to suggest the idea to the Christian clergy later on – with dire consequences.[71] The development of the rest of the area of real rights in ancient times is only touched upon briefly by Smith, but we are told that servitudes became very numerous and that some of them changed from being considered as personal rights to being considered as real rights.[72]

With the growth in commerce, the various solemn ceremonies which at first provided the only means of entering into something resembling contracts had to be relaxed. And in response to specific needs the number of forms of contract recognized by the law became large and in some measure comparable to modern contract law – a further sign of the strength of government.[73] The other main source of personal rights, namely delict, is not traced systematically by Smith for the period in question, although we find a number of specific forms of punishment referred to. He makes it clear, however, that government gained sufficient strength to abolish the system of merely exacting compensation for offences between individuals, and instead to impose actual punishment. At first 'a crime was considered in two lights, as committed against the family injured and against the peace',[74] and for the latter reason nearly all the crimes in which the public took an interest were treated as treasonable and punished with corresponding harshness. 'But afterwards the praetors changed these punishments into milder ones, more suited to naturall equity', as did Solon in Athens.[75]

The history of ancient marriage law is basically the history of how women, from having no rights against the husband, came to have near equal status. Originally the wife had more or less the same status as a better slave, mainly because she had no property to bring into the marriage. But with the growth in wealth women would become property owners through inheritance, though naturally not through work or the holding of offices. As a consequence both they and their families required separate ownership in what they brought into the marriage and the same right as the husband to terminate the relationship. Many marriages were therefore established on a purely contractual basis with equal right in both parties to divorce. The effect upon the morals and manners of the time was noticeable, and 'there is hardly a great man in the end of the Republick who is not a cuckold upon record'.[76] This state of affairs lasted from late in the republic – with a few modifications – until first the Northern backwoodsmen and then the Christian clergy spoiled the fun.[77]

The father's authority over the children in early society was as absolute as that over the wife; he could expose them, sell them, marry them to whom he wanted; their possessions were his property, and he had complete jurisdiction over them. Although the exposure of children was never completely stamped out until Christianity gained force, all these things were greatly changed by the gradual intervention of the law and the recognition of some independent rights in children. As in the case of marriage, this took its beginning from the intervention of the rest of the family, especially the wife's family.[78] This could not take place, however, with regard to the relationship between the master and his servants; the latter had no one to intervene on their behalf and their history remains one of power and violence, rather than of rights: the history of slavery. As the Roman republic grew in opulence, the number of slaves increased, making harsher discipline necessary; and this was further reinforced by the widening social gap which weakened or stopped whatever sympathetic communication there might have been at an earlier and poorer stage. The Roman republic is the clearest illustration of the rule 'that slavery is more severe in proportion to the culture of society'.[79] And a comparison of the republic and the empire shows with equal clarity that as long as slave owners are legislators there is no hope for the slaves, whereas an absolute government like that of the emperors may at least ease the burden slightly.[80] Strong government is not necessarily strong enough government in all respects.

5 The emergence of modern Europe

The causes which led to the dissolution of the Roman empire were many
and complex, but in the end it came to a problem of defence, and that
problem was exploited by a number of tribal societies which invaded from
the North. These 'German and Scythian nations' were at a transitional
stage between shepherds and husbandmen, for although they were
obviously very mobile they also had the idea of property in land and some
understanding of agriculture. The clash was therefore between a fairly
advanced commercial society and one or more societies which were only
about to embark upon the settled life of farmers. It is hardly surprising
that 'the confusions which followed so great a revolution lasted for several
centuries',[81] and in fact a number of the basic features of European
history right up until Smith's own time were fixed by this event. In the
first place, manufacture was to a large extent spoiled and the communica-
tions system broke down, thus making commerce impossible. The whole
basis for extensive cities was in this way undermined. At the same time the
various chiefs and lords of the invading nations divided the land between
them, and the result was that life in a great part of Europe became completely localized in more or less isolated and self-contained rural communities, which made up a county or the like, the counties again making
up a kingdom. The land was owned by the king and the great lords,
making everyone else dependent upon them to an even greater degree
than they had been during the shepherd stage. At first there was a natural
community jurisdiction in local affairs, while county assemblies took care
of disputes between communities, and the king and national assembly
adjudicated in disputes between counties and functioned as ultimate
courts of appeal. Alongside this hierarchical system there was the jurisdiction of the great lords, who in their own areas were a law unto themselves, the king and everyone else being too weak to intervene with
them.

In time, however, every semblance of popular jurisdiction succumbed
to the constantly growing power of the lords, and the forces which led to
this also dissolved the old allodial form of government.[82] The lords were in
a similar, though aggravated, situation to that of the shepherd chiefs:
being without any real manufacture of 'luxury' goods and without commerce, society provided them no other outlet for their riches than to keep
ever larger numbers of dependents. This gave them complete power over
everyone in their area, but at the same time they could only maintain
this power externally in so far as they could depend upon their tenants.
Consequently they were led to grant the tenants longer and longer terms
for the land and eventually tenancy became hereditary (held as *feuda*). In
return each new tenant had to pay a sum in order to take over the land

('relief') and had to give military service and other work. The land
returned to the lord if duties were not discharged or if there was no heir.
The lord had wardship over the tenants and vassals, and could determine
marriages; he could coin money for his area, and he generally had complete jurisdiction. The same problem of defence which spurred the institution of feudal arrangements downwards from the local lord also led it
upwards: the inferior lords were in need of protection and hence agreed
to hold their land feudally of some superior lord in return for his protection, and the same mechanism led even the great lords to hold their
extensive properties feudally of the king in the country concerned.[83] But
while the king and lords might need each other for defence purposes and
while the king always pressed for extensions of the feudal system, this had
little impact upon the power of the lords in their own areas, where they
remained in effect as absolute as ever. As far as the relationship between
king and lords is concerned, feudalism is therefore in Smith's view not to
be seen as a successful attempt by the lords to grab new land and power,
but as an unsuccessful attempt by the king to curb the lords in what they
had already got. In terms of national government, the result was the
sovereignty of an aristocratic assembly, led by the king as the greatest of
the lords.[84]

Power was concentrated not only in the temporal lords, but also in the
lords of the spirit. The Christian church had early been organized into a
tightly knit hierarchy which soon became international and was 'formed
into a sort of spiritual army, dispersed in different quarters', but under
very central leadership. The 'mistaken piety...of princes and private
persons' had led them to donate huge areas of land to the clergy, and
these riches were further augmented by the right to tithes. The clergy in
each country was therefore as rich as, or even richer than, the feudal lords,
and being in the same position as these, they had enormous numbers of
tenants and retainers dependent upon them, and derived further support
from the fact that they alone took care of all poor relief. In addition to all
this, they had two great advantages over the temporal lords. First, while
the latter were always fighting each other and the king, the clergy had a
high degree of mutual loyalty imposed upon them by their common task.
And secondly, their office was surrounded with all the mystery of sacred-
ness and special connections in another world. The result was that the
clergy were even better able to resist the power of the king than anybody
else – so strong in fact that they managed to avoid being under any other
jurisdiction than their own internal one, thus enjoying 'the benefit of
clergy' and securing the very strong influence of canon law in Europe. All
in all, 'the constitution of the church of Rome may be considered as the
most formidable combination that ever was formed against the authority
and security of civil government, as well as against the liberty, reason, and

happiness of mankind, which can flourish only where civil government is able to protect them'.[85]

Just as the feudal policies of the king could not break the power of the secular lords, so neither the king nor 'the feeble efforts of human reason' were any match for the clergy's 'ties of private interest'. Change came – though slowly – from entirely different and less obvious quarters. There were two other, ignoble classes of people, the villeins in the country and the burghers in the towns. The villeins were in a condition of slavery somewhat milder than the ancient form and they were kept in it for some time yet. But the condition of the burghers changed, and that had significant effects. After the fall of the Roman empire the cities and towns were drastically reduced in size and importance and their inhabitants, the small tradesmen and 'mechanicks', were so dependent upon the king or neighbouring great lord that in effect they were villeins too. But the alliance between monarch and slaves which Smith considers more or less natural soon had its effects. The king would grant various privileges of free trading, first to individual burghers, afterwards to burghers as such; and he would grant them a measure of self-taxation with consequent self-government. Furthermore, he would soon use this policy in his constant struggle with the great nobles, weakening them by freeing the burgher-villeins and thus forming an alliance against them. Both the nobility and the clergy tried to undermine the authority of the king, but by granting the cities the right, not only to internal self-government, but also to self-defence by means of city walls and city militias, he ensured that a growing part of the population became independent of his rivals. The result of this policy was that the cities became 'a sort of independent republicks' within each country, and in some countries, such as Italy and Switzerland,[86] they even became completely independent states. The cities were based upon manufacture and commerce and they had therefore to live by a system of justice which would make the necessary division of labour effective. 'Order and good government, and along with them the liberty and security of individuals, were, in this manner, established in cities at a time when the occupiers of land in the country were exposed to every sort of violence.'[87] However, this imbalance could not last.

The cities created a market for the raw produce of the neighbouring country and they established international trading links. They contributed directly to the improvement of the land, as merchants began to channel some of their profit into this – in so far as they could. But most importantly they created a new outlet for the wealth of the lords, temporal *and* spiritual, for whom the cities provided a market in which they could exchange their raw products for manufactured goods. However, it was not only their wealth that they spent but also their power. When the products which had hitherto maintained a large number of dependents were sent to town, the retainers had to be dismissed, and of the tenants some had to go the same way, while others were squeezed for higher rents in return for greater independence. Thus,

the great proprietors were no longer capable of interrupting the regular execution of justice, or of disturbing the peace of the country. Having sold their birth-right, not like Esau for a mess of pottage in time of hunger and necessity, but in the wantonness of plenty, for trinkets and baubles, fitter to be the play-things of children than the serious pursuits of men, they became as insignificant as any substantial burgher or tradesman in a city. A regular government was established in the country as well as in the city, nobody having sufficient power to disturb its operations in the one, any more than in the other.[88]

This development, which cleared the way for absolute monarchy, took place in most of Europe, but not in the German area where the estates of the nobility were so considerable that not even the lures of the cities could absorb them. Hence they remained self-contained small states and the emperor became a weak elective monarch.[89] With Germany in this condi-tion, and Switzerland and Italy more or less divided into small republics, the other main nations of Western Europe – Spain, Portugal, France, and England – became absolute monarchies. According to Smith, the church had spent much of its wealth and, being increasingly unable and unwilling to provide charity and other traditional social services, its spiritual leader-ship over the bulk of the people declined. In this situation both the French and the English monarchs could re-establish some influence over it.[90] Compared to the king, the lords were becoming impoverished and could no longer muster a militia. So the only one who stood outside the more and more graduated ladder of wealth along which luxury could 'creep' uninterruptedly was the king.[91] Only he was rich enough to have offices to dispense and to maintain an army. And here the problem of defence comes up again. With the growing number of people employed in manufacture and commerce it became more difficult to raise militias, and at the same time the progress in technology made soldiering much more of a specialized profession. The solution to the defence problem was therefore standing professional armies, and once one nation had embarked upon that course, the others had to follow suit.[92] With one exception: England. Because of her geographical position, she had no defence problem – except from the Scots, and that was conveniently solved by the union of the Crowns and later of the Parliaments. Furthermore, the Crown had little revenue, and since Elizabeth for her own personal reasons sold her demesne land the monarch was financially far too weak to maintain a standing army without raising taxes. Taxes, however, could not be raised without the approval of Parliament which had had the opportunity to grow strong. So while continental kings could perpetuate their absolute govern-ment with the support of their armies, English monarchs were put under more and more pressure by Parliament – a process which culminated in the execution of Charles I. After the Restoration it was more a lack of 'vigour' in the monarchs than a lack of funds which saved the British from absolutism; while the Revolution established 'upstarts' on the throne who were heavily dependent upon Parliament.[93]

Of the two Houses of Parliament, it was of course the Commons which became so important in Britain. Originally all owners of an estate had the right to sit in the national assemblies and be heard by the king in important matters, not least money matters. But with the proliferation of minor nobility it became necessary that the insignificant lords should only send local representatives. At the same time the cities became such important sources of revenue that the king had to grant them the right to send representatives to be heard in a separate assembly. And these two groups of representatives were eventually merged into one body, which became more and more mighty as it represented an ever higher proportion of all possible tax revenue. The power of the Lords did, however, dwindle so rapidly that even Britain had a taste of absolutism under the Tudors before the Commons could exert its full power.[94] But once it did so, the balance of the constitution was very much changed. After the Revolution, the king was reduced to having only the choice of assent or veto on legislation emanating from Parliament; financially he was greatly dependent on the voting of the civil list; and although a standing army had come in, this was financially dependent upon Parliament, and many of its officers were, as great landowners and/or Members of Parliament, independent of the king. Similarly the House of Lords was reduced *vis-à-vis* the Commons. The latter was a more numerous and vigorous body, broadly representative of the people and representing as much property as the Lords, or more. Because of the fairly frequent elections the Commons was more accountable and was consequently trusted more with business; it took nearly all legislative initiatives and it had the sole initiative with money bills. The result was that sovereignty no longer belonged to the king but was divided in such a way that the British constitution became a peculiar mixture of the three classical forms of government. The legislative power was overwhelmingly with the Commons, but the king retained a stake in it; the executive power was with the king, but was conducted by ministers who were impeachable by Parliament; and although the king could still be said to be 'the fountain of justice' in as much as he had the appointment of all regular judges, these judges could be independent of him, being appointed for life; the king himself had no judicial power, and the highest court of appeal, the House of Lords, was independent of the monarch both in regard to appointment and to procedure. All these constitutional arrangements of the relationships between the various branches of the sovereign power tended to secure the citizens' rights against the sovereign power as a whole, and this security was further increased by two direct means, namely the Habeas Corpus Act and the fairly frequent elections by electorates which in England – but not in Scotland – were from reasonably broad sections of the populace.[95]

Smith naturally paid very great attention to the special case of Britain but it is of importance to notice that he sets his discussion in a total European framework and makes it largely comparative. With the exception of Germany (apart from the German free cities) all of Western Europe had one basic experience in common: that the fall of the feudal lords led to *strong* government. The close tyranny of the local lord was in effect exchanged for the distant tyranny of an absolute monarch, and the distance was of the greatest importance everywhere, irrespective of whether the monarchical form was subsequently changed or not.[96] The distance between sovereign and subject meant that close 'supervision' became impossible and that the judicial business, greatly augmented by the growth in commerce, took on such proportions for the ruler that he tended more and more to relinquish it into the hands of independent courts and judges.

When Smith talks of this separation of the judicial power, he talks in terms of modern Europe.[97] But in the specific turn which the development of the judicial power took, special attention again had to be paid to England, partly because of Smith's audience in his lectures and for his planned discourse, and partly because circumstances made the English experience different from that of the Continent and Scotland. The emergence of independent courts simply happened earlier in England than anywhere else, presumably because trade was further advanced,[98] and their jurisdiction was wholly based on common-law principles. But in continental Europe and in Scotland this development came so late that the required courts did not evolve in response to specific needs, and had to be instituted directly by the sovereign. The lateness of this development also meant that the law which came to be administered was based on the Roman civil law system and on canon law, instead of being indigenous common law. As we have already seen, 'New courts and new laws are... great evils', because they lack that concreteness and precision which distinguish a common-law system like the English.[99] In Smith's view use of precedent was reinforced by the circumstance that in the early stages of the development of independent courts the judges 'were generally of the meanest sort of no fortune or rank' – often clergymen.[100] Such people were even more exposed than their early Roman counterparts, and they therefore protected themselves even more carefully by the strict application of precedents. Later, when the judges had gained strength, the legislative power would keep them to the strictest observance of precedent for fear of the arbitrary power they could otherwise exercise. And here the 'punishment for unjust punishment' principle which we discussed in an earlier chapter was certainly put into use.[101] So strict was the observance of precedents that the common-law courts did not have the flexibility often associated with them, and they had difficulty accommodating a number of the new claims which needed legal recognition as rights in order for a commercial society to develop. This occasioned the evolution of a whole new court out of the Chancery. Originally the clerks of the Chancery only prepared briefs (writs) for the other courts; in order to meet the new demands, the Chancellor was then allowed to let them prepare briefs out of two or more approximate precedents; and finally the Chancery began to judge in its own right in matters not covered by common law, especially regarding contracts, trusts, and testaments.[102]

It is hardly surprising that the philosopher of impartial spectating should stress the importance of another product of the early strength of the English courts: the jury system. The feature of the modern jury which Smith emphasizes is exactly that it is likely to function as an impartial observer and hence to curb 'the power of the judge', because of the elaborate procedures for its selection. He credits Henry II's legislative wisdom with the organization of this system, for before then the jury was simply an elaboration of the old compurgation system which had existed all over Europe.[103]

Smith also goes into considerable detail in accounting for the separation of the various courts – of King's Bench, of Exchequer, and of Common Pleas – and their functions, but the only thing which needs notice here is his (mistaken) idea that the court dealing with criminal cases, which eventually became the Court of King's Bench, was the first to become separate. The feeling of resentment and the craving for retaliation are so much more acute in criminal than in civil cases that the former require prompt trial and judgement. And since that could hardly be achieved as long as the original 'Grand Justiciary' had to follow the itinerant king, criminal cases had to be tried at a separate court at Westminster.[104]

6 The development of modern law

Smith tells us how both ancient philosophy and science were taken over and developed by the Arabs, who eventually conveyed them to Western Europe; and the generous role he allots the Arabs adds an interesting dimension to his general treatment of the Middle Ages.[105] But as far as the law is concerned he never presents a systematic explanation of the influence which ancient, and especially Roman, law had on the body of law which grew up after the fall of the empire. That set-piece, the recovery of a copy of Justinian's *Pandects* at Amalfi, is mentioned in passing, but not given any exaggerated role. It is, however, quite clear both from his discussion of the development of law courts, as outlined above, and from his account of the evolution of the various areas of law, that he saw a significant influence from Roman law – not least when it had been transformed into canon law. In fact it seems as if Smith saw the church as the main preserver of ancient law: 'The cannon law when it took place was dictated by ecclesiastics, who on most occasions copied the Roman law, as they were the only persons that understood Latin, and among whom the remains of literature were preserved.'[106]

The changes in the individual branches of the law between the settlement of the allodial governments after the fall of Rome and the commercial societies of eighteenth-century Europe were of course enormous. So is the extent of Smith's discussion of them, and we shall here limit ourselves to those he considered most important. In the area of property law he explains how the feudal lords tried to cover their encroachments upon what in natural justice was 'common', such as game and fish, under the principle of property by occupation.[107] And he shows how the lengths of prescription to some extent changed as the varying social and political conditions changed people's ideas of the 'reasonable expectation' of possessing moveable and immoveable goods.[108] But by far the most important changes here were to the laws of succession. As far as legal succession to moveables was concerned the changes were slight. The law continued to rest on the same natural principles as in Rome, distributing the inheritance to both wife and children – with a third part for the deceased which was at first given to the church, as this was thought to aid his business in afterlife, and was later allowed to be disposed of by testament. The main difference between modern and Roman law was derived from the circumstantial factor that the wife now was a more substantial figure, due to the basic indissolubility of marriage; consequently, she had a more substantial share in the inheritance.[109]

It was with regard to succession to land that the modern world revolutionized the law by introducing the right of primogeniture. Smith makes it quite clear that in his opinion this was a simple consequence of the form of government which followed upon the defeat of Rome by the Northern tribes. Whatever order and stability there were depended wholly upon the strength of the local lord, especially after the feudal arrangements began, and it was therefore absolutely necessary for everyone's interest to secure the basis for this strength, namely extensive landholding. Landed estates thus became indivisible, passing on from father to eldest son, and after many and long contests between the interests of younger sons and the interests of the children of their eldest brother, succession of minors by representation became accepted.[110] But although primogeniture was a product of the feudal form of government, it did not disappear with that institution. Security for property and all other rights was now derived from a civil government which was not dependent upon big landholdings for its authority, and which was strong enough to protect properties irrespective of how insignificant they were. Yet primogeniture was still pervasive.[111]

The law of succession also changed in another respect. The Germanic invaders of Rome and its provinces had no idea of testamentary succession, but this was reintroduced by the clergy, partly as a practical effect of the Christian belief in the immortality of the soul, and partly because the clergy knew the Roman laws of testaments and could adapt them to the new circumstances. At the same time this gave the clergy in many parts of Europe the important judicial function of executing wills, and in England this contributed to the development of the Court of Chancery. The Chancellor was generally a clergyman and he therefore came to judge in the new 'conscience' cases, such as testaments and contracts.[112] At first only that third of the property which 'belonged' to the deceased – the other two-thirds belonging to the wife and children – was open to disposal by testament. But with the introduction of primogeniture the idea of disposing of the whole estate by testament came in, in the sense that a testament could lay down a particular line of succession so that no subsequent heir could alienate the property by sale or otherwise. Although this system of entail, which is the 'greatest of all extensions of property', was originally a further attempt to secure feudal estates and thus the feudal form of government, it was still continued and entails were for instance by 'a statute in the time of James the 2^d...made altogether binding, and are so at this day'.[113] In general the 'common law of England ...is said to abhor perpetuities', and yet she has her share of entail. And in Scotland 'more than one-fifth, perhaps more than one-third part of the whole lands of the country, are at present supposed to be under strict entail'.[114]

Smith presents a wealth of material about the development of the remaining real rights; property by voluntary transfer, servitudes, pledges and mortgages, and exclusive privileges. In the present context it is enough, however, to notice two things. In Smith's view the feudal duties 'were all properly speaking servitudes, and make by far the greatest and most important parts of the servitudes in use in this country', that is, Scotland.[115] Secondly, Smith deals with a large number of exclusive privileges, and especially monopolies and privileges of corporations. These were all 'police' measures and had generally been introduced early in the development of manufacture and commerce before the market was strong enough to carry a complete division of occupations in a given city, province, etc. 'But as this end is now fully answered, it were much to be wished that these as well as many other remains of the old jurisprudence should be removed.'[116]

The most fragile of all rights, those arising from promises and contracts, were at length reintroduced into the law of Western Europe, although this happened late as far as the more abstract forms of contract were concerned. There were two main factors which brought about the recognition of contractual rights: the needs of growing commerce and the influence of the Christian clergy. Anything but the most elementary barter needed the legal protection of contracts and, developing from agreements solemnly entered into before a court, normally an ecclesiastical one, a system of real contracts for the lending of money, security for debt, borrowing of goods, and custody of goods came into use. Later consensual contracts about buying and selling, letting and hiring, partnership, and commission were recognized. The whole process was aided by the influence of the clergy who could again apply their knowledge of the Roman law and who at the same time considered contracts as matters of conscience which had to be as it were religiously observed. Smith is very emphatic about the influence of the church in this matter, suggesting that it here was very much the protector of the poor against the rich, and although he is not specific about this, it would seem that he must also have had in mind the relationship between small tenants and landlords.[117] The church has also put a further stamp upon modern contract law. Because the clergy considered contracts as matters of conscience, the courts eventually came to consider the contractual obligation to be the full performance of the specific thing promised, whereas previously – and naturally[118] – it was enough if the obligated party paid the loss if he did not choose to perform.[119] Finally, it should be remarked that in England the common-law courts were so well-developed at an early stage that they were not influenced by the church in contract matters, and instead the Court of Chancery as a separate English 'court of conscience' took on contract cases.[120]

In the most primitive society crime and punishment is purely a matter between the injured and his family and the offender and his family. For good reasons, only serious infringements of the most basic natural rights are acted upon – at any rate, they are the only ones which will make the surrounding society venture to intervene. In so far as disputes are settled, they are settled with a material compensation. As government gains strength in shepherd society, the chieftain can enforce such reconciliation and in return for his trouble he will begin to ask for a part of the compensation, in proportion to the severity of the crime. At the same time people will begin to consider crime under two aspects, partly as an injury to the victim and partly as an injury to the peace of society. As governmental authority becomes absolute, the latter aspect is the only one that matters, and via a graduated scale of bodily retaliation all crimes come to be considered treasonable and capital. As the Germanic nations which overran the empire settled in Western Europe and developed strong jurisdictions first at the more or less local level, later on the national level, they took this last step. Smith's account of the development of punishment in the major part of our period is, therefore, the story of how the government, far from seeing itself as an impartial spectator, came to consider itself the major party in every dispute, with the result that the ladder of punishment had very few steps indeed – in most cases only one. For the later part of the period he then goes on to show that government eventually becomes so strong that it can allow itself to soften this attitude, considering only actions directly against the state as treasonable and allowing the now independent courts to bring more natural ideas of justice to bear on all other crimes. And we have already looked at Smith's own contributions to this process.[121]

The clergy opposed the introduction of capital punishment from the beginning and maintained that this was inconsistent with the demands of the Christian religion – whereas their real motive, according to Smith, was pure conservatism.[122] Although they could not prevent this innovation, their influence had two effects. First of all this was the occasion for the introduction of the benefit of clergy, whereby not only the clergy but all those somehow associated with the church were made exempt from the jurisdiction of the civil courts.[123] And secondly, the courts eventually began to distinguish between murder and manslaughter and to consider the latter as less than capital.[124]

It was also the clergy who worked the changes in marriage law. After the fall of the empire the form of marriage was the old one where all power rested with the husband, the government having neither power nor mind to intervene in domestic matters. But the clergy were considered with 'superstitious veneration', and that gave them significant influence on people's private lives. They created formal equality in marriage and made divorce equally impossible for both parties; and the ecclesiastical courts were at first the only ones which would consider domestic disputes.[125] In the relationship between parents and children the main novelty in modern law is the enforcement of the most basic 'mutual good offices' – once government gained the strength to do so.[126]

In all the cases in which Smith ascribes a significant influence to the clergy the concern with religion is only part of their motivation, whereas church policy or private interest in one form or another are always driving forces. In the *Lectures on Jurisprudence* the Christian clergy is allotted an important role in the history of the abolition of slavery in Western Europe and the motivation is explained as pure power politics.[127] He does, however, seem to have had second thoughts about their importance, for in *The Wealth of Nations* he specifically plays it down.[128] But in so far as the church did have any influence in the matter it coincided with that of the king, which Smith always maintained was decisive. Slavery was in Smith's view bound to be universal in all early societies simply because the government was too weak to intervene in the relationship between a master and his servants, and this relationship was therefore left to that 'love of domination and authority over others' which Smith was 'afraid is natural to mankind'. In fact, the only way in which some sort of order could be maintained was through private jurisdiction. In the case of wife and children this gradually changed because there were people in a natural spectator situation who had an interest in getting domestic rights recognized and who could get this realized as government grew in strength. Those spectators were the surrounding family – especially the wife's family – and their interest increased with the women's fortunes. But there were no such influential spectators in the case of servants, and they would therefore remain slaves. This was the situation in the ancient world, but it changed to some extent with the emergence of the Christian clergy.[129] In contrast to the ancient religions, the Christian religion was universal for all human beings. This obviously appealed to those who were worst off and who were not recognized as belonging to any of the old, 'localized' religions. At the same time it enabled the clergy to act, or present themselves, as the spectators of slaves and lords alike and thus gain the trust of at least the slaves. This they could use in their constant struggle for power over their temporal counterparts by trying to strengthen the position of the slaves against the masters. In this the church had the same interest as the king, whose first efforts were to 'free' those villeins who were already least in the power of the lords, namely the burghers.

Already in early modern times the villeins, even on the land, were somewhat better off than they had been in ancient times, in as much as they had some slight legal protection for a few basic rights. There was in principle *some* punishment for murdering or maiming them; they could marry; and they could only be sold along with the estate.[130] They could not own property, but that privilege was gradually introduced. Maybe under some influence from the clergy, certainly under pressure from the king, and maybe because they saw the greater return that resulted, the landowners would begin to allow the villeins to retain a certain proportion of the produce farmed by them. This tendency to turn the villeins into tenants, and afterwards to improve the terms of tenancy, was of course greatly reinforced by the same need to keep the estates together which in time created the feudal system. All the various reasons – and not least among them the tenant's growing ability to pay and the landowner's need to be paid – changed the system, 'though by very slow degrees', and made the tenants 'farmers properly so called'. While the poorest form of let, the old 'metayer' or steelbow systems, according to Smith still were very prevalent on the Continent and could be found in various places in Scotland,[131] in parts of Europe and in England the tenants were allowed to farm the land with their own stock, paid rent to the landlord, and got longer and longer leases on the land. At first these leases were very insecure but as government got the strength, they were given better and better legal protection, and particularly in England this created a significant yeomanry, which gained political importance when leases of a certain size for life became recognized as freeholds with a right to vote for Members of Parliament.[132]

Smith kept a very clear perspective on the state of the slavery problem. While the abolition of it in Britain made his contemporaries 'apt to imagine that slavery is entirely abolished at this time', this is in fact only the case in a 'very small corner of the world', namely a 'corner of Europe'.[133] But 'all over Muscovy and all the eastern parts of Europe, and the whole of Asia..., all over Africa, and the greatest part of America, [slavery] is still in use'.[134] Moreover, in the colonies slavery was being maintained by the very nations which had abolished it at home, and in Scotland the well-known salters and colliers constituted a few 'vestiges of slavery'.[135] And finally, in the major parts of those countries where slavery has disappeared, apart from England and to some extent Scotland, improvements on the early form of tenancy have been small and very slow in coming. Still, the steelbow system, 'tho... the worst of any by free tenents, was greatly preferable to that by slaves'.[136]

CHAPTER EIGHT

Natural jurisprudence in the face of history

The history of law and government which Smith presents was meant to convey some lessons in law which we have already tried to learn in earlier chapters. But at the same time it was undoubtedly meant to, and certainly likely to, give a view of the historical process which would underline the purpose of his whole intellectual enterprise. The question is: what view? The obvious parallels between the three great attempts by mankind to live in commercial societies, in Greece, in Rome, and in modern Europe, may well suggest a cyclical view of history. And this impression is certainly reinforced by the fatalistic notes Smith on occasion strikes. In the *Lectures on Jurisprudence* he thus prefaces his explanation of how the military government of the Roman emperors came to an end with this remark: 'We come now to shew how this military monarchy came to share that fated dissolution that awaits every state and constitution whatever'; for 'this government, as all others, seems to have a certain and fixed end which concludes it'.[1] And in discussing the 'enormous debts' which modern governments have contracted in order to maintain their standing armies, he notes that these public debts 'will in the long-run probably ruin, all the great nations of Europe'.[2]

The problem with such a view is that the cycle has never gone full circle, so to speak, and that the parallels are better seen as contrasts. Both Greece and Rome left huge legacies, and although heavy duties had to be paid to history, there was enough left significantly to influence posterity. This would in general tend to turn the cycles into a spiral. And the parallels are, I suggest, drawn in order that we may learn from their limitations. The central point of comparison is the problem of defence to which commerce tends to lead. With the growth of commerce, fewer and fewer men are available for militia service and defence devolves upon a standing army, which will tend to be recruited amongst 'the lowest sort' and hence the most unreliable sort, and it may even be necessary to recruit it from foreign mercenaries. This will make defence increasingly expensive and the expense will be greatly added to by the improvement in weapons and equipment, thus ensuring that the army is as badly off for money as it is for men. On these points the parallel between the ancient and the modern world is clear enough. However, despite Smith's occasional fatalistic mood, he obviously did not think that these problems should necessarily produce the same results as in the past. There was a whole complex of policies which would meet these problems, some of which, as it happened, had already been realized, and the rest of which could be realized. Whether they *would* be realized, Smith was too wise to speculate publicly.

The reliability of the standing army had in Smith's view already largely been secured by making sure that a great number of its officers were land-owners and therefore often Members of Parliament. They were independent of the king, and quite apart from all the other ways in which the British constitution limited the king's authority, it was thus almost impossible for him to exploit the problem of defence internally in the way that Caesar had done.[3] This could be further secured by providing the poorest with that minimum of education which would enable them to understand that they have a stake in their country: they would then be able and willing to join a militia, which would make possible a smaller standing army and at the same time provide an extra check on it, although in modern conditions a militia could never *replace* a standing army altogether.[4] Foreign mercenaries are hardly a problem in the modern world, and although there is certainly the kind of international dependence by which the richer nation seeks to maintain a network of allies by supporting the poorer of them financially, this has become more and more a diplomatic game of maintaining an over-all European (and colonial) balance of power.[5] The nations involved in this balancing game were all 'civilized' or commercial ones, or else they were on the verge of becoming so. This is a significant difference from the situation of ancient Rome, for the nations upon which she became dependent towards the end of the empire were all 'barbarous' ones whose militias could only be resisted as long as she maintained her own standing army. Now, Smith distinguished between two very different kinds of violent change in the world. 'The ordinary revolutions of war and government', and 'those more violent convulsions occasioned by the depredations of hostile and barbarous nations continued for a century or two together; such as those that happened for some time before and after the fall of the Roman empire in the western provinces of Europe'.[6] The latter kind of upheaval is not likely to disturb Europe again simply because the invention of modern weaponry has given commercial society the decisive edge over less developed societies.[7]

This means that the problem of defence in modern Europe is a matter of a power balance between commercial societies, and that means a matter of wealth – wealth to maintain alliances, wealth to maintain a standing army with modern weapons. There are two ways in which this is connected with Smith's jurisprudence. First, the shorter and more obvious connection: the commerce upon which wealth so much depends is an international phenomenon, and Smith is in a way saying that the more we trade with our enemies, the better we shall be able to defend ourselves against them.[8] And such trade is better regulated by laws of justice than by the laws of police which institute monopolies and all the rest. At the same time free trade is more likely than anything else to further that integration between nations which tends to make their relations more a matter for diplomacy than for the military.[9] This approach is perhaps best summed up when Smith takes a truly global perspective:

Hereafter, perhaps,...the inhabitants of all the different quarters of the world may arrive at that equality of courage and force which, by inspiring mutual fear, can alone overawe the injustice of independent nations into some sort of respect for the rights of one another. But nothing seems more likely to establish this equality of force than that mutual communication of knowledge and of all sorts of improvements which an extensive commerce from all countries to all countries, naturally, or rather necessarily, carries along with it. (WN, iv, vii, c. 80)

The second way in which justice is at stake is no less important, but seems to have been less obvious. Smith thought that commercial nations would generally get into debt over the defence issue and that their defence capacity therefore depended upon their ability to sustain such public debt.[10] It has been pointed out that Smith on the one hand expresses strong concern over the tendency for public debt to grow, but on the other hand treats it with a certain complacency, suggesting various ways in which the debt could be reduced.[11] The concern arises not only from the size and nature of the debt itself, but from the fact that a large and increasing part of the basis for public borrowing is extremely insecure. This part consists of all the capital which is acquired by commerce and manufactures: such capital is very easily transferred from one country to another, a circumstance of which there are many examples in history; and it is only if part of a merchant's or manufacturer's capital is tied up in land and its improvement that he becomes a citizen of a 'particular country' rather than of 'the world'.[12] And here is certainly a problem of natural justice: sufficient land for this purpose can only become available if land is freed from the feudal restrictions of primogeniture and entail, and is put on the market for circulation. Because Europe got out of the feudal form of government by developing commerce before agriculture – contrary to 'the natural course of things'[13] – she had not managed to relinquish the feudal arrangements in regard to a very large part of her farmland, and the result was that the problem of defence had become a significant problem of justice. A task for a legislator if ever there was one!

The other main focus for contrast between the ancient and the modern world was of course the slavery issue. This is perhaps best approached through its connection with the problem of defence. Both Greece and Rome show that commercial society can derive a certain military advantage from carrying out the major part of its manufacture and commerce by means of slaves, rather than by freemen. This will make it possible for freemen 'of honour' to take care of the defence of the country without production breaking down.[14] But both nations also show that this benefit will not endure for ever, partly because freemen will in time become more and more involved in commerce anyway, and partly because production and trade by slaves, as far as the example of Rome is concerned, will create a dangerous class of poor freemen.[15] This class of people will be excluded from maintaining themselves by regular employment in manufacture and commerce and thus from bettering themselves. The difference between rich and poor will therefore remain extreme, turning the poor freemen into a socially and politically free-floating body who inevitably become a tool for unsettling the balance of power.[16] In modern Europe, as slavery disappears and production and commerce are carried out by freemen, the problem of defence is certainly present; but quite apart from the measures already discussed, the problem will be further mitigated – as compared with the ancient world – by the much greater opulence which production by freemen leads to. The full benefit of this form of production, however, is only achieved if it establishes a graduated ladder of ranks through which wealth and luxury can spread, and which will make it possible for people to work their way up – or at least to think that they can do so – instead of resorting to adventurous political means.[17] However, such a ladder will only establish itself if people's work and business are not hindered by such laws of 'police' as those Smith criticizes in *The Wealth of Nations*, but are regulated by laws of justice. Not only the defence of modern commercial society, but its political and social stability, are therefore dependent upon the establishment and maintenance of a regular system of justice.

These very general reflections locate the fundamental role of Smith's natural jurisprudence. But the question arises whether the historical process, as he saw it, was of such a nature as to allow room, after all, for natural jurisprudence as one of its formative factors. Here we inevitably come into conflict with a view of Smith which for many years has been very widely accepted; according to this view he 'founds...a new interpretation of society which is undoubtedly materialistic'; and his idea of the development of society in four stages is, according to this view, '*a*, if not *the*, materialist conception of history'.[18] For, it is suggested, 'Throughout all these successive stages...the way in which people get their living is conceived to determine the main lines along which they think and behave.'[19]

This 'materialist' or economic interpretation of Smith's view of history would seem to be inconsistent with the proposal that a normative discipline of natural jurisprudence could have an important influence on the direction of history, if properly applied. The problem is that there is a certain vagueness in this interpretation. Apart from the formulation quoted at the end of the previous paragraph, where the relationship between economic factors and the rest of human life is said to be one of determination, this central relation is normally described in rather unspecific terms, such as 'reciprocal interconnection', dependence, and correspondence. A recent formulation is, however, very suggestive for the kind of questions we should ask in order to clarify the issue and thus, perhaps, Smith's view. It has been proposed that Smith 'would appear to come close to Engels's general position in arguing that the economic finally asserts itself as the "ultimate", rather than the sole, determining factor'.[20]

It would seem that the basic question to be asked here is whether the ultimacy of 'the economic' means that all social phenomena can be explained as ultimately determined by economic factors, or whether it means that economic factors are always, or normally, amongst the determinants of social phenomena and hence ultimately have to be referred to in social explanations. The line of argument to be pursued here is that the former view is untenable as an interpretation of Smith and that the latter, while perhaps largely true, can only misleadingly be described as an economic, or 'materialist', view of society and history.

We can take it as a starting point upon which everyone agrees that, according to Smith, economic factors can only be socially determining through their influence on individuals. One supra-individual social phenomenon does not bring about another without the intervening activity of particular persons. This does not, of course, mean that individuals consciously and intentionally work to bring this about. On the contrary, society in general and morality and law in particular are, as we have seen in the preceding pages, the unintended results of individual human actions. In this sense Smith is a 'methodological individualist' but, as we know from our discussions of *The Theory of Moral Sentiments* and the *Lectures on Jurisprudence*, this does not prevent the motives and behaviour of individuals from being explained with reference to a social framework. What is excluded is ultimate explanation in terms of social 'wholes' alone and explanations in terms of individuals alone. It should be clear, then, that the whole discussion of Smith's alleged 'materialism' must be conducted in terms of human motivation. It would seem that 'materialism' here can mean two things. Either it can mean that the motives behind the behaviour which shapes society and its development must ultimately be 'economic' or 'materialist'. Or it can mean that only the 'economic' or 'material' factors in the situation of the individuals determine their motivation and hence their behaviour when they act in ways which are decisive for the form and development of society. In either sense I think that it is a mistake to call Smith's view of society and history 'economic' or 'materialist'.

Smith's ideas of basic human motivation seem far from 'materialist'. It is not the procurement of the necessities for subsistence which motivates man to create an existence which is distinctively human. The necessities are in general provided for him by nature and what distinguishes him above the rest of the animal creation is rather a certain 'delicacy', or taste, as far as both body and mind are concerned.[21] But just as man is motivated to rise above the other animals, not by material need, but by delicacy and taste, so he tries to rise above his fellow men for reasons quite other than those concerned with his subsistence. As far as subsistence is concerned, all men are roughly equal: 'The rich...consume little more than the poor', for the 'desire of food is limited in every man by the narrow capacity of the human stomach'.[22] Much the same applies to all the necessities of nature: 'The wages of the meanest labourer can supply them. We see that they afford him food and clothing, the comfort of a house, and of a family.'[23] Therefore, 'In ease of body and peace of mind, all the different ranks of life are nearly upon a level, and the beggar, who suns himself by the side of the highway, possesses that security which kings are fighting for.'[24] It is not economic needs which motivate men to make the world go round. It is rather an aestheticized version of the taste and delicacy which raised men above the rest of the animal creation:

The pleasures of wealth and greatness...strike the imagination as something grand and beautiful and noble, of which the attainment is well worth all the toil and anxiety which we are so apt to bestow upon it. – And it is well that nature imposes upon us in this manner. It is this deception which rouses and keeps in continual motion the industry of mankind. (TMS, IV, 1, §§ 9–10)[25]

Combined with this aesthetic motivation is *vanity*, the real or imagined pressure of the gaze of society upon us which is received and internalized through sympathy.[26] The resulting race of man's life inspires Smith to some of his most eloquent and ironic observations:

From whence, then, arises that emulation which runs through all the different ranks of men, and what are the advantages which we propose by that great purpose of human life which we call bettering our condition? To be observed, to be attended to, to be taken notice of with sympathy, complacency, and approbation, are all the advantages which we can propose to derive from it. It is the vanity, not the ease, or the pleasure, which interests us. (TMS, I, iii, 2, § 1)

And hence it is that 'place, that great object which divides the wives of aldermen, is the end of half the labours of human life'![27] Taste and vanity constitute the 'invisible hand' that leads and directs all the individual human lives into a more or less orderly social process, and 'first prompted [men] to cultivate the ground, to build houses, to found cities and commonwealths, and to invent and improve all the sciences and arts, which ennoble and embellish human life'.[28]

Perhaps the most spectacular demonstration that it is not economic motives which in general give form to a society is to be found in Smith's insistence that only rarely in the history of mankind is such motivation the basis for political and, in general, social authority. It is true that in the nomadic stage of society the bulk of the population is directly dependent upon the wealth of the chiefs. But beyond that, it is not the economic motives of dependents which create political power and authority, 'for in general the poor are independent, and support themselves by their labour, yet, though they expect no benefit from [the rich], they have a strong propensity to pay them respect'.[29] The explanation of this remarkable phenomenon is men's aestheticizing participation in the lives of the rich through sympathy, whereas hopes of personal gain play little or no role.[30]

In saying that the human motivation which is operative when social change takes place consists of taste and vanity, Smith is only speaking of the general form of motivation. He is clearly not saying anything about the specific content of human motives, but rather about the principles in accordance with which they are formed. The specific content is filled in according to the situation in which man finds himself and since men through the ages are to be found in a multiplicity of situations they will be acting on a multiplicity of motives, as we shall see below. This point is also important in relation to a proposal about how Smith, after all, could be seen to find one specific motive behind all human activity which, although it is not in itself 'economic', is more easily turned into 'economic' motivation proper than are motives formed in accordance with the principles of taste and vanity. I am thinking of the suggestion that, according to Smith, man 'is self-regarding in all spheres of activity', and that this explains 'his pursuit of security, wealth, and that form of satisfaction on which the development of productive forces may be seen to depend'. In other words, 'man is motivated by a desire to seek pleasure and to avoid pain'.[31] It should be clear, however, that this attempt to unify all human motivation does not work as long as a multiplicity of things can create pleasure and pain. Motivation cannot be understood simply by reference to pleasure and pain.[32] And furthermore, Smith is – as we have just seen – emphatic that in connection with 'that great purpose of human life which we call bettering our condition...[it] is the vanity, not the ease, or the pleasure, which interests us'.[33]

It seems safe to conclude that Smith's view of society and its development was not 'materialist' or 'economic' in the sense that he held human motivation to be ultimately of that nature. The alternative understanding of this interpretation of Smith would be that the situational factors which influence mankind as far as the maintenance and development of society

are concerned are 'material' or 'economic'. I suggest that this is not a
tenable view either, for throughout Smith's account of the development
and function of society we have met a large number of non-economic
factors with determining influence. First of all there is the range of problem situations which are relevant, and they include in prominent places
military, political, religious, judicial, and intellectual problems – as well as
economic ones. And in each of these kinds of problem situation there is a
multiplicity of relevant factors. The problem of *defence* is a matter of
geography, as evidenced by the settlements in Attica in ancient times and
by the development of modern Britain. And as we have seen, it is a matter
of civic morality and education, of organization, of political institutions,
of international relations, of technology, of particular individuals – such
as Philip of Macedon, Caesar, or Cromwell – and, of course, a matter of
wealth. *Political* problems are defined by military and economic ones, but
also by the state of a large number of institutions such as the organization
of sovereignty, including the position of, say, Parliament and the law
courts, the hereditary or elective nature of a monarchy, etc.;[34] by such
institutions as the church and slavery; and individuals will also exert their
particular influence in this area, as is shown by Elizabeth I's sale of Crown
lands or the preference shown by Charles II and James II for luxury
rather than military expenditure. We have seen how *religious* problems
mingled with various other concerns to shape the whole form of domestic
law and, not least, the slavery issue; and we have seen how ancient intellectual traditions were conveyed as an active force to the modern world.
Finally, the responses to *legal* – and behind them *moral* – problems have
been the objects of our particular attention and we have seen how they
took the form of new laws and new institutions.

All these considerations make it abundantly clear that the situational
factors facing men at the various stages of social development include a
large number of non-economic and particularly institutional ones –
including the law. But let us face squarely the central issue at stake in the
discussion of a materialist conception of history, that of determinism.
Perhaps the best way to a properly balanced view of this matter is to start
with some antidotes to a simple deterministic interpretation. Smith in
various connections allows for pure chance as a factor in history. The all-
important securing of English liberty through the development of independent and professional law courts had a large element of chance in it:

it may be looked upon as one of the most happy parts of the British Constitution,
though introduced merely by chance and to ease the men in power, that the
office of judging causes is committed into the hands of a few persons whose sole
employment it is to determine them. (LRBL, 170)

Equally it seems hard to find the law of history which would determine that Elizabeth I, rather than one of her predecessors, 'sold the royal demesnes' in 'order to supply her exigencies' and because she had no off-spring, thus decisively weakening the Crown for future generations.[35] Further, it would seem simply a matter of good luck that both Charles II and James II were so lacking in 'vigour' and so given to luxury and extravagance that they spent the huge revenue settled upon them in pur-suit of pleasures rather than on a standing army.[36] And the restoration of the British monarchy after the Civil War was itself a matter of 'such a concurrence of accidental circumstances as may not...ever happen again'.[37] To such cases we may add examples of the importance of con-sidered political interventions, such as those of Caesar and Cromwell, or the deliberate support by both the monarchy and the church for the development of the cities in feudal Europe and for the emancipation of the slaves. And we must of course mention the Union between England and Scotland – which Smith thought could provide a model for America and Ireland as well.

All this should bring us sufficiently near to meeting one caricature with another. And I hope it will have made it clear that the choice between determinism and indeterminism in history, as far as Smith is concerned, is a false alternative – if by indeterministic we understand 'arbitrary'.[38] As a good Newtonian Smith, of course, did not believe that there existed any arbitrary or undetermined events, if this is taken to mean that there is no more reason why event x should happen than why non-x should happen. This does not, however, mean that someone with Smith's views is forced to adopt a 'hard' determinism. With phenomena as complex as those of human society there will nearly always be a number of directions in which things can develop, and which direction is taken will depend upon a multi-plicity of factors, ranging from 'hard' determining ones, like the absence of sea transport for a country, to 'soft' determining factors, like an indi-vidual's decisions about how to act. This means that although in our social and historical explanations we shall often be unable to point out the necessary and sufficient conditions of events, we shall yet be able to make these events intelligible by pointing out some of the more or less necessary conditions.

These ideas are very carefully explained by Smith in the *Lectures on Rhetoric and Belles Lettres*. First with regard to the central issue of the 'soft' determining influence of human motives. Without distinguishing explicitly between the epistemic (or methodological) and the ontological sides of the problem,[39] Smith makes in effect the following points about them: although we can take it that motives are the causes of human actions, for epistemological reasons we cannot ascertain that a particular action was caused by a particular motive; and even if we could know that a particular motive was present, this would not be proof that a particular action followed from it, because in the flow of events human actions are open to many other causal influences besides motives.[40] Consequently when we try to understand human behaviour we shall have to have recourse to the circumstances, to the general character of the person or persons concerned, and to the motives which we should sympathetically impute to such a person in such circumstances.[41] And since each individual's motives, as we know, are formed through the volatile medium of mutual sympathy with the motives of other people in more or less similar situations, we can see how the motivational factor in the shaping of behaviour really forms a huge social network which both influences and is influenced by the external world – but which in each individual instance of behaviour is neither completely determined by, nor completely determining for external events.

In view of this it is not strange that Smith is very critical of the medieval Schoolmen's attempt to deal with the human mind in the same way as the physical world, as a matter of ontology. This turned the subject into a 'doctrine of spirits, of which so little can be known', in contrast to 'the doctrine of bodies, of which so much can be known'.[42] Certainly, 'There are two different sorts of facts: one external, consisting of the transactions that pass without us, and the other internal, to wit, the thoughts and sentiments or designs of men which pass in their minds.'[43] But in so far as we want to deal with the latter exclusively, we shall have to do so by drawing in the circumstantial factors. Or to put it in modern jargon, we shall have to turn psychology into a social science.[44] And in so far as we want to do social science we shall have to do so at least partly historically by joining the two sorts of facts,[45] so that through sympathy we gain an understanding of particular actions by understanding their circumstances. It is by this composite method that we shall understand historical events, and this dictates the way in which history has to be written:

Events...may be described either in a direct or indirect manner...in most cases the indirect method is much preferable, even when the objects were inanimate. Much more, then, will it be to be chosen, when we describe the actions of men, where the effects are so much stronger, as the actions themselves are more interesting. 'Tis the proper use of this method that makes most of the ancient historians, as Thucydides, so interesting, and the neglecting it that has rendered the modern historians for the most part so dull and lifeless. The ancients carry us, as it were, into the very circumstances of the actors; we feel for them as if it were for ourselves. (LRBL, 90–1)[46]

Whether and in what way this approach will lead to a theoretical social science is a further issue, but it is this method of understanding actions – and thus events – sympathetically through the circumstances which makes Smith's science into what was later called conjectural history. And it is exactly this approach which is behind Smith's repeated emphasis on the educational value of history: when through sympathy we understand a past pattern of reaction to certain kinds of circumstances, this can influence the wisdom with which we ourselves react to similar sets of circumstances.[47] This is the general background to the care and detail with which Smith draws up the parallels and the contrasts between mankind's three great attempts to live by laws of justice in a commercial society. The situations had to be drawn up in both their similarities and their dissimilarities so that we could see how pluralistic and open-ended the historical process is.

If we have to choose between the view that 'the economic' is a necessary and sufficient condition for historical change, and the view that it is merely a necessary condition, we can safely say that the former was not Smith's view. But the latter is obviously true in the sense that certain broad, general conditions of an economic kind are necessary for certain broad, general kinds of social and political organization. This gives Smith the four stages theory – but he never mistakes taxonomy for explanation.[48]

Smith's view of history is especially suited to showing all the balancing acts a would-be legislator has to consider. It shows all the multifarious obstacles to a system of justice, but at the same time it demonstrates the task for such a system. It is, as we have seen, a very heavy task, and in order to keep a proper perspective on Smith's intention it is of decisive importance always to think of it in terms of that concept – a task. Few of Smith's expressions have been as misleading as his insistence on the importance of a 'regular *administration* of justice'. The regular administration is a guiding ideal, an ideal of perfection, which can lead and direct a political process; but given the usual condition of human society, it will necessarily turn out to be less a realized ideal than a rough approximation. It is therefore a genuine misreading of Smith if his concept of a system of natural justice is taken as merely an 'administrative' matter, and his 'science of a legislator' thus seen as an impoverishment of political theory. The system of natural jurisprudence was in itself a *political* challenge, and Smith had no illusions about its magnitude. We have repeatedly seen how he perceived both the geographical and historical dimensions of the problem. Slavery and feudal or semi-feudal institutions were still prevalent in the world, and it was only in a 'corner of Europe' that men had begun to live by laws of justice – and here only fairly recently and very imperfectly. But furthermore, now that Europe – and particularly Britain – had embarked upon the venture, her very livelihood depended on a steady extension of the system.[49]

The view of natural jurisprudence as a political task is put forward in a general manner when Smith lists the factors which commonly shape the course of positive law and make it deviate from natural justice:

Sometimes what is called the constitution of the state, that is, the interest of the government; sometimes the interest of particular orders of men who tyrannize the government, warp the positive laws of the country from what natural justice would prescribe. In some countries, the rudeness and barbarism of the people hinder the natural sentiments of justice from arriving at that accuracy and precision, which, in more civilized nations, they naturally attain to. Their laws are, like their manners, gross, and rude, and undistinguishing. In other countries, the unfortunate constitution of their courts of judicature hinders any regular system of jurisprudence from ever establishing itself among them, though the improved manners of the people may be such as would admit of the most accurate. (TMS, vii, iv, § 36)

At the same time as the study of these failings throughout human history can show the character and the magnitude of the task for natural jurisprudence, it can also suggest to a philosopher like Smith the foundation of such a discipline in the ideal impartial spectator, and thus inspire him 'to give an account of the general principles of law and government'. When the principles are applied to the task, the contemplation of a philosopher turns into the science of a legislator.

Notes

I INTRODUCTION

1 See Duncan Forbes, *Hume's Philosophical Politics* (Cambridge, 1975).
2 Donald Winch's *Adam Smith's Politics* (Cambridge, 1978) is particularly suggestive about the relationship between Smith's jurisprudence and his politics. See also Duncan Forbes, 'Sceptical Whiggism, commerce, and liberty', in A. S. Skinner and T. Wilson (eds.), *Essays on Adam Smith* (Oxford, 1975), pp. 179–201. Hans Medick's *Naturzustand und Naturgeschichte der bürgerlichen Gesellschaft* (Göttingen, 1973), is interesting because of its stress on the importance of history for Smith's jurisprudence; the work does not, however, offer any suggestions about the normative background to Smith's critical intentions and is hampered in its appreciation of the significance of these by its preoccupation with *Ideologiekritik*.
3 See pp. 150–1, below.
4 In addition there were second-hand reports, most notably in Dugald Stewart's 'Account of the Life and Writings of Adam Smith, LL.D.', in EPS, pp. 269–351.
5 Adam Smith, *Lectures on Justice, Police, Revenue, and Arms*, ed. Edwin Cannan (Oxford, 1896).
6 But for an attempt in a broader context, see K. Haakonssen, 'Natural Justice: The Development of a Critical Philosophy of Law from David Hume and Adam Smith to John Millar and John Craig', Edinburgh University Ph.D. thesis, 1978.
7 See the editorial introduction to this edition, containing details about both sets of notes and about the relationship between them.
8 The new set of notes takes up close on 400 compact pages, twice as many as the set published by Cannan.
9 These are the so-called Anderson notes which Smith's later colleague John Anderson entered in his Commonplace Book. Probably he copied them from a student's notes. For this text, as well as an interesting discussion of it, see R. L. Meek, 'New light on Adam Smith's Glasgow Lectures on Jurisprudence', *History of Political Economy*, vol. VIII, 1976, pp. 439–77.
10 Adam Smith, *Lectures on Rhetoric and Belles Lettres*, ed. J. M. Lothian (London, 1963).
11 It should be noted that in quotations from the lecture notes I do not reproduce the variations, corrections, etc., which are minutely recorded by the editors. Nor do I make any attempt to celebrate the innumerable cases of faulty spelling, grammar, etc., with 'sic!'.

2 HUME'S THEORY OF JUSTICE

1 *The Letters of David Hume*, ed. J. Y. T. Greig (Oxford, 1932), vol. I, p. 32; and cf. T. 620–1.
2 Hume, *Letters*, I, p. 33; and cf. T. 621.
3 See especially: R. D. Cumming, *Human Nature and History* (Chicago and London, 1969), vol. II, chapter 13, esp. pp. 170ff.; N. Capaldi, *David Hume: The Newtonian Philosopher* (Boston, 1975), pp. 179–87; J. T. King, 'The place of the language of morals in Hume's second *Enquiry*', in D. W. Livingston and J. T. King (eds.), *Hume: A Re-evaluation* (New York, 1976), pp. 343–61.
4 Cumming, *Human Nature and History, loc. cit.*
5 *Ibid.*, esp. pp. 172–4.
6 E. 219–20, note.
7 The following short sketch of Hume's moral theory, needless to say, does not pretend to any completeness nor to any originality. Its only purpose is to set the scene for Hume's theory of justice. I owe much in this introduction to Professor P. S. Ardal's interpretation in his *Passion and Value in Hume's Treatise* (Edinburgh, 1966); cf. also his introduction and notes to his edition of *Treatise*, Books II and III.
8 See Ardal's treatment of sympathy in chapters 3 and 6 of his *Passion and Value*.
9 This idea permeates large parts of the *Treatise*, and it is difficult to single out any passage in particular. But the whole passage T. 584–7 must be one of the clearest. Also its use of the example of the 'building [which] seems clumsy and tottering to the eye' (T. 586) provides an interesting reference-through-contrast to one of the early treatments of sympathy, the house with 'the little room lost in the stairs, antichambers and passages'! (T. 363–4).
10 Again there is an absolute abundance of clear and quotable passages all through the *Treatise* to illustrate this, and again I will refer especially to Book III, Part iii, Sect. 1 (T. 580–4).
11 Hume gives this division in the *Treatise* on pp. 589–90. It is not necessary for my purposes to argue that sympathy is involved in our evaluation of all four kinds of qualities. But see Ardal, *Passion and Value*, pp. 152–6.
12 T. 590.
13 T. III, ii, 1: 'Justice, whether a Natural or Artificial Virtue?'.
14 T. 479.
15 T. 480.
16 *Ibid.*
17 T. 480–1.
18 T. 481.
19 T. 481–2.
20 T. 482.
21 T. 482–3.
22 This and some of the subsequent quotations from Hume's *Treatise* incorporate minor changes and additions which Hume made in the margin of one of his own copies of the book. These are all given in P. H. Nidditch's revised edition.

23 T. 483; my italics.
24 K. Haakonssen, 'Hume's social explanations: the case of justice', *Danish Yearbook of Philosophy*, vol. 12, 1975, pp. 114–28.
25 See Duncan Forbes's treatment of this in the first two chapters of his *Hume's Philosophical Politics*.
26 T. 484.
27 T. 485.
28 T. 486.
29 T. 492–3.
30 T. 488–9.
31 See e.g. T. 489.
32 T. 487.
33 E. 184; cf. T. 495.
34 E. 185–6; cf. T. 495.
35 E. 187–8.
36 T. 493–4; E. 188–9. In *Treatise*, 493, Hume says that the state of nature can be very useful and a legitimate *methodological* device, enabling one to treat the emotional side of human nature in abstraction from the 'understanding', i.e. social restraint (a point which incidentally shows his social conception of reason).
37 It is in connection with Hume's account of the origin of justice that R. D. Cumming in *Human Nature and History* sees a difference between the *Treatise* and the *Enquiry*: in the *Treatise* justice is mainly seen to alleviate the miseries of mankind; in the *Enquiry* it is regarded more as an instrument that creates 'abundance'. But this does not seem to be very persuasive, for just as Hume in the *Enquiry* points out how by 'art, labour, and industry' in society we can create our enjoyments in 'great abundance' (E. 188), so in the *Treatise* he points out, not only that it is 'by society all [man's] infirmities are compensated', but also that 'tho' in that situation [society] his wants multiply every moment upon him, yet his abilities are still more augmented, and leave him in every respect more satisfied and happy, than 'tis possible for him, in his savage and solitary condition, ever to become' (T. 485). And Hume then goes on to point out the arrangement which really makes society advantageous: the division of labour. On the other hand, Hume also says in the *Enquiry* that 'few enjoyments are given us from the open and liberal hand of nature', etc. (E. 188). In both works, justice thus has a backward-looking as well as a forward-looking aspect, which is hardly surprising since the two aspects are complementary. And I fail to see any significant difference in the stress put on them in the two works.
38 E. 195, T. 492.
39 Concerning Hume's theory of the calm passions, see Ardal, *Passion and Value*, chapter 5, esp. pp. 104–6.
40 T. 536–7.
41 T. 490; cf. E. 306.
42 The treatment of the matter on p. 498 of the *Treatise* is at least as ambiguous. For a discussion of the conventional institution of justice very similar to the present one, see P. S. Ardal, 'Convention and value', in G. P. Morice (ed.), *David Hume: Bicentenary Papers* (Edinburgh, 1977), pp. 51–68.
43 See e.g. T. 497 and 531–3.

44 I take it as self-evident that Hume is talking of the extension of justice to more and more people, not the extension of the concept of justice to new areas, such as contracts, or the extension of, say, the concept of property from cattle to land. There is no indication that anything like the latter was in his mind in the paragraphs of the *Treatise* with which I am dealing here.

45 T. 498.

46 E. 192.

47 T. 489.

48 E. 195.

49 On the low level of rationality, see also T. 492 and 526.

50 See also e.g. T. 497 and 531–3, E. 304–6.

51 T. 488.

52 The points about the artificiality of justice are discussed at pp. 21–6 below. Here the passage is only quoted at length for the sake of comprehensibility.

53 And that is said explicitly elsewhere, at T. 495; cf. T. 499.

54 On the traditional reading of Hobbes!

55 See the criticism of such moral and legal positivism at T. 500, 521, 578–9; E. 214.

56 We still have to see how justice becomes obligatory.

57 This seems to me the most fitting label for Hume's position. For the message of his discussion of determinism seems to be distinctly methodological, rather than metaphysical, namely: don't be an indeterminist, for that is to abdicate the very hope of finding an explanation by means of causation, whereas determinism is a way of keeping the hope up.

58 Cf. T. 475, 477, 484, 493; E. 307.

59 Hume goes on to oppose 'natural' to 'miraculous', to the 'rare and unusual', to 'artificial', to 'civil', and to 'moral' (T. 474–5); and the first three comparisons reappear in the *Enquiry*, pp. 307–8, note.

60 T. 474, and E. 307.

61 E. 308.

62 Hume, *Letters*, vol. I, p. 33. This was not the last time Hume had reason to be annoyed that people misunderstood him on this point. When he came to write his own 'reference' for the Edinburgh chair, he had to do it in the form of an anonymous defence of the *Treatise*. One of the last points he makes is this: 'When the Author [i.e. Hume himself] asserts that Justice is an *artificial* not a *natural Virtue*, he seems sensible that he employed Words that admit of an invidious Construction; and therefore makes use of all proper Expedients, by *Definitions* and *Explanations*, to prevent it. But of these his Accuser [identity not established] takes no Notice. By the *natural Virtues* he plainly understands *Compassion* and *Generosity*, and such as we are immediately carried to by a *natural Instinct*; and by the *artificial Virtues* he means *Justice, Loyalty*, and such as require, along with a *natural Instinct*, a certain Reflection on the general Interests of Human Society, and a Combination with others. In the same Sense, Sucking is an Action natural to Man, and Speech is artificial. But what is there in this Doctrine that can be supposed in the least pernicious? Has he not expressly asserted, that Justice, in another Sense of the Word, is so natural to Man, that no Society

of Men, and even no individual Member of any Society, was ever entirely devoid of all sense of it?' (*A Letter from a Gentleman to His Friend in Edinburgh*, ed. E. C. Mossner and J. V. Price (Edinburgh, 1967), pp. 30–1).

63 For discussions of this tradition and its relevance to social and political philosophy, see F. A. von Hayek, *Law, Legislation, and Liberty*, 3 vols (London, 1973–9), vol. 1 (esp. pp. 20–1), as well as the literature referred to there (*ibid.*, pp. 150–1), and Popper, *The Open Society and Its Enemies*, 2 vols (London, 1966), vol. 1, chapter 5.

64 As Professor D. D. Raphael has suggested in his 'Obligations and rights in Hobbes', *Philosophy*, vol. 37, 1962, pp. 345–52.

65 It is undoubtedly this last circumstance which leads Hayek to say that Hume actually did revise the traditional distinction (*Law, Legislation, and Liberty*, vol. 1, p. 20).

66 T. 527–8.

67 E. 199.

68 See above, pp. 18–21.

69 T. 579.

70 T. 577.

71 T. 532–3.

72 T. 495.

73 T. 496, my italics.

74 E. 183.

75 See above, pp. 16–18.

76 T. 490–1.

77 T. 502; E. 192–3.

78 T. 502.

79 E. 193–4.

80 Hume also makes the point that the necessary subordination in society requires inequality: E. 194.

81 T. 505–7.

82 E. 196.

83 T. 514–16; E. 195.

84 T. 516ff.; E. 195.

85 See below, pp. 104–14.

86 T. 518.

87 T. 516–18.

88 T. 519.

89 T. 520.

90 Cf. E. 199–200, note.

91 As Ardal rightly points out, this is in a way an anticipation of J. L. Austin's view 'that "I promise" is a performance, and not a statement about a mental act'. See Ardal's note 39 to his edition of *Treatise*, Books II and III, p. 347. Cf. Ardal, 'And that's a promise', *The Philosophical Quarterly*, vol. XVIII, 1968, pp. 225–37.

92 See below, pp. 112–14.

93 T. 498.

94 When Hume deals with obligation in the section on promises in the *Treatise* he says explicitly that the reasoning is the same as for 'justice in general' (T. 518).

95 T. 518.
96 See above, pp. 7–9.
97 See above, pp. 7–9.
98 On this point, see Ardal's introduction to his edition of *Treatise*, Books II and III, p. 28.
99 This is of course the main theme of 'A Dialogue'.
100 See Forbes's exposition of this in *Hume's Philosophical Politics*, chapter 4.
101 T. 499–500.
102 See above, pp. 7–8.
103 There is at least one other place where Hume hints that actions rather than motives can be the important thing in seeing how obligation comes about; see *Treatise*, p. 479, on obligation, where he ends by saying, 'Actions are at first only consider'd as signs of motives: But 'tis usual, in this case, as in all others, to fix our attention on the signs, and neglect, in some measure, the thing signify'd.'
104 Apart from obligation in the sense dealt with in this section, Hume also frequently talks of 'natural obligation'. Concerning this, see Haakonssen, 'Hume's obligations', *Hume Studies*, vol. IV, no. 1, 1978, pp. 7–17 (pp. 14–17).
105 TMS, I, i, 3, § 8.
106 T. 551.
107 E. 210–11.
108 T. 326.
109 T. 531–2.
110 T. 530, and cf. the whole paragraph, pp. 529–31.
111 T. 491.
112 I am here reflecting points made by Duncan Forbes; see *Hume's Philosophical Politics*, pp. 26–7 and 59ff. (especially p. 61, note 1).
113 Cf. T. A. Roberts, *The Concept of Benevolence* (London, 1973), p. 103.
114 T. 502.
115 Hume does not, like Smith later, go into the development of the idea of property in any systematic way, but he does at least once mention three of the famous four stages: Hume, 'Of Commerce', in *Essays*, vol. I, p. 289.
116 E. 214–15.
117 It is difficult not to read this as a reference to the work of Mandeville.
118 Forbes, *Hume's Philosophical Politics*, p. 119. The whole of his chapter 4, 'Social experience and the uniformity of human nature', is highly relevant for the points made here.
119 Cf. also the parallel case of international law, T. 567–9. This theme becomes of the very greatest importance in Adam Smith, where the only thing which can override justice is defence. See below, pp. 94–5.
120 Cf. T. 500–1; E. 214.
121 E. 193.
122 T. 499.
123 I owe this formulation in terms of the distinction between means-utility and end-utility to Hayek's *Law, Legislation, and Liberty*, vol. II, pp. 17ff.; and cf. the very interesting note 14, *ibid.*, p. 155.
124 E. 219, and cf. pp. 7–9 above.
125 E. 186.

126 I think that this argument can be extended to the whole of Hume's moral philosophy, but that is outside our concern here.

127 This latter point is worth noting, for it suggests that not all the aims are equally important or equally close to human nature, and hence do not have the same value in the test of maximization of compatibility of aims. Hume does not have any very specific theory on this point. But in suggesting the primacy of the prevention of the negative (injustice) over the promotion of positive valuations, he approaches a distinction between negative and positive values, of which the former are basic to the very existence and well-being of men and consist in not suffering one or another form of harm. This is taken up and worked out in some detail by Smith as part of the foundation of justice, and in this form it is akin to negative utilitarianism. See below, pp. 83–7.

128 See for example: F. A. von Hayek, *Studies in Philosophy, Politics and Economics* (London, 1967), pp. 99–107, 111, 160; H. B. Acton, 'Prejudice', *Revue internationale de philosophie*, 1952, pp. 323–36. For general treatments of Hume on the one hand, and the Common Law and Whig traditions and Burke on the other, see J. G. A. Pocock, 'Burke and the ancient constitution: a problem in the history of ideas', in Pocock, *Politics, Language, and Time* (London, 1971), pp. 202–32; and cf. also Forbes, *Hume's Philosophical Politics*, pp. 260–307. For the Common Law tradition in particular, see J. G. A. Pocock, *The Ancient Constitution and the Feudal Law* (New York, 1967).

129 T. 526.

3 SMITH'S MORAL THEORY

1 See for example his contrast between 'Philosophers' and men in 'common life', TMS, I, i, 3, § 8.

2 In this chapter I do not aim at discussing Smith's moral theory as a whole, but only at giving the background to his theory of justice.

3 TMS, I, i, 1, §§ 6–9.

4 TMS, I, i, 1, §10.

5 Cf. Hume: 'we blush for the conduct of those, who behave themselves foolishly before us; and that tho' they shew no sense of shame, nor seem in the least conscious of their folly' (T. 371). This is to Hume 'a pretty remarkable phenomenon' (T. 370).

6 TMS, I, i, 1 §§ 11–13.

7 TMS, I, ii, 2, § 2.

8 This is in a way the main point of the whole Section, but it forces Smith to treat of the theme we are interested in here, i.e. the accessibility of the various kinds of passions.

9 See J. R. Lindgren, *The Social Philosophy of Adam Smith* (The Hague, 1973), pp. 21ff.

10 TMS, VII, ii, 3, § 21.

11 For a very strong expression of this need for identification, see TMS, VII, iii, 1, § 4. The expressions are particularly strong here because Smith is trying to refute the suggestion that the act of sympathizing is in the end egoistic. For a similar, but more detached, refutation, see TMS, I, i, 2, § 1,

where he points to the spontaneity, as opposed to the reflectiveness, of the pleasure of sympathy and the pain of antipathy.

12 Cf. TMS, VI, ii, 1, § 1: 'Every man feels his own pleasures and his own pains more sensibly than those of other people. The former are the original sensations – the latter the reflected or sympathetic images of those sensations. The former may be said to be the substance – the latter the shadow.'

13 It is particularly unfortunate that Lindgren chose to call this 'aesthetic sympathy' since Smith's whole point is that no sympathy is involved. This leads to various curious mistakes in his treatment. See Lindgren, *Social Philosophy of Adam Smith*, pp. 23–5. The need for sympathy when we try to understand human beings is a fundamental problem when we make *them* the objects of a science: see pp. 80–2 below.

14 TMS, I, i, 4, §§ 5–6.

15 TMS, I, i, 4, § 7.

16 *Ibid.*

17 While Smith was preparing a second edition of the TMS Hume sent him some criticism on this point. See Hume, *Letters*, vol. I, pp. 311–14.

18 From the second edition till the fifth, Smith continued the note with the following analogy: 'Two sounds, I suppose, may, each of them taken singly, be austere, and yet, if they are perfect concords, the perception of their harmony and coincidence may be agreeable.'

19 These distinctions should make it futile to take any more rides on that old hobby-horse 'sympathy v. self-interest' in Smith.

20 TMS, I, i, 2, §§ 1–6.

21 See my summary of Hume's argument, at pp. 7–9, above.

22 TMS, I, i, 4, § 7.

23 TMS, III, 1, § 5.

24 *Ibid.*: 'We begin...to examine our own passions and conduct, and to consider how these must appear to [others], by considering how they would appear to us if in their situation.'

25 TMS, III, 1, § 3. The idea that the mutuality of sympathy with sentiments creates awareness of the sentiments is closely parallel to Smith's treatment of the tactile sense in his essay on the external senses. There he singles out the tactile sense as unique because it alone is able to create an awareness of itself. If one part of our body touches another, this other part will, so to speak, answer back, and in this way we become conscious of our body as one large tactile sense in contrast to the rest of the world. External Senses, 5.

26 Smith gives this explanation of propriety in contrasting it with our judgement of actions and their motives according to *merit*. We shall deal with merit below, since Smith's viewpoint is that merit is in a sense dependent upon or derivative from propriety.

27 Cf. LJ(A), iii, 5, and LJ(B), 102.

28 TMS, III, 2.

29 TMS, III, 2, §§ 4 and 11, respectively for praise and blame.

30 TMS, III, 2, §§ 5 and 9–10, respectively. There is a strong asymmetry between the positive case, praise, and the negative, blame, which is of great importance in Smith's theory and to which we shall return at pp. 83–7, below.

31 TMS, III, iii, § 4.

32 TMS, vi, iii, § 11.

33 TMS, iii, 3, § 2.

34 TMS, iii, 2, §§ 6–7. Cf. again Smith's account early in the TMS of how both the sentiment of the agent and of the spectator must be changed in order to get 'such correspondence with one another as is sufficient for the harmony of society' (TMS, i, i, 4, § 7).

35 See also all the other examples of adjustment in TMS, iii, 3; and LJ(A), iii, 5; LJ(B), 102.

36 Cf. TMS, iii, 3, § 38: 'The man within the breast, the abstract and ideal spectator of our sentiments and conduct, requires often to be awakened and put in mind of his duty, by the presence of the real spectator: and it is always from that spectator from whom we can expect the least sympathy and indulgence, that we are likely to learn the most complete lesson of self-command.'

37 TMS, v, 2, § 9. The whole of v, 2 is relevant.

38 TMS, v, 2, § 13.

39 At the end of the quotation Hume is referring to Montesquieu.

40 See WN, i, ii, 4, and v, i, f. 51.

41 LJ(B), 326–7. We return to the whole problem of situationally determined selection of behaviour in various contexts; see especially the discussion of Smith's views on history in chapter 8 below, pp. 186–8.

42 TMS, iv; cf. TMS, v, i, § 1.

43 TMS, iii, 4, § 7.

44 TMS, iii, 5, § 7.

45 Concerning Hume's theory, see pp. 31–5 above; see also below, pp. 112–13.

46 See below, pp. 79–82.

47 TMS, ii, i, 1.

48 TMS, ii, i, 1, §§ 5–6.

49 TMS, ii, i, 2, §§ 1–3.

50 TMS, ii, i, 4, §§ 1 and 3.

51 TMS, ii, i, 5, §§ 1–2 and 5.

52 TMS, ii, iii, 1, § 7.

53 See LJ(A), ii, 118–20; LJ(B), 188–9. Cf. pp. 119–20 below.

54 It is interesting in this connection to notice that when Smith comes to show how society's, or the spectators' reactions to us are internalized by mutual sympathy (in TMS, iii, 2), he combines the present issue with his sharp distinction between the positive and the negative in human morality (see pp. 83–7, below): praise is rarely internalized unless there are praiseworthy motives behind our behaviour (TMS, iii, 2, § 4); but *blame* is always received and internalized, both when there are blameworthy motives behind our behaviour and when there are not (TMS, iii, 2, § 11, and cf. TMS, iii, 2, § 29).

55 Cf. pp. 114–20, below.

56 TMS, iv, 1, §§ 1–2.

57 See pp. 40–1, above.

58 TMS, iv, 1, §§ 4–6.

59 Lindgren, *Social Philosophy of Adam Smith*, esp. pp. 16 and 74–8.

60 TMS, iv, 1, §§ 8–10.

61 This is a reference to TMS, vi, ii, 2, §§ 15–18.

62 TMS, iv, 2, § 3.

63 This is interestingly reflected in Smith's ideas of how to describe a person: 'The character of a man is never very striking nor makes any deep impression: it is a dull and lifeless thing, taken merely by itself. It then only appears in perfection when it is called out into action. We are not then generally to begin our panegyric with a character of the man whose reputation we are to raise, but are rather to begin with an account of his...actions' (LRBL, 128).

64 Cf. also E. 213, note. In a note to TMS, IV, 2, § 3, the editors, Professors Raphael and Macfie, point to this note in the second *Enquiry*, saying that 'Hume must have had an objection of this character put to him, for he attempts to reply to it in a footnote appended to *Enquiry concerning the Principles of Morals*, V, i, first paragraph...'. As shown in the text above, however, Hume deals very clearly with this issue already in the *Treatise*: pp. 471–2 are particularly clear. The *Enquiry* does not add anything new to this.

65 T. 472.

66 See TMS, VII, iii, 2, §§ 7–9.

67 T. 472.

68 Although Hume despairs of a full explanation at T. 617, he does, of course, characterize the difference between the pleasure/pain of moral approval/disapproval and other kinds of pleasure and pain. Apart from what is quoted and mentioned in the text above, he invokes his theory of the indirect passions of pride and humility, love and hatred which attend moral judgement (T. 473, 574–5, and 614). I do not think that Smith takes an explicit position on this theory.

69 TMS, IV, 2, §12.

70 TMS, IV, 2, § 5.

71 TMS, IV, 2, §§ 7–11.

72 TMS, IV, 2, § 3.

73 TMS, I, i, 4, § 4.

74 TMS, IV, 2, § 11.

75 *Ibid.*; and cf. e.g. TMS, VII, iii, 1, § 2.

76 See e.g. TMS, II, ii, 3, § 8; and IV, 2, § 7.

77 TMS, VII, iii, 3, § 16.

78 See e.g. TMS, III, 5, § 8; VII, ii, 2, § 13; VII, iii, 1, § 2; VII, iii, 3, § 16.

79 TMS, VII, ii, 2, § 13.

80 TMS, V, 2, §§ 12–16; and III, 5, § 8.

81 TMS, III, 2, § 32; and II, iii, 3, § 6.

82 TMS, III, 2, § 33; and VII, ii, 1, § 45.

83 TMS, III, 5, § 13. This is a frequently recurring theme in the TMS; e.g. II, ii, 3, §§ 11–12; III, 2, § 12, §§ 33–5; III, 5, §§ 7, 12–13.

84 TMS, VI, ii, 3, § 2.

85 See below, pp. 79–82.

86 This occurs in connection with the laws relating to succession, contracts, slavery, homicide, marriage, parental authority, etc. Smith's statement about the ceremony necessary to mark the assumption of the duties of marriage is typical of the tone in which he deals with these matters: 'This differs in different countries, but in general is connected with religion, as it is *supposed to make the greatest impression*' (LJ(B), 105; my italics). The height of 'scientific' detachment, however, is reached when Smith debates

religion as a social and political phenomenon with Hume. He quotes one-and-a-half pages from Hume's *History* in which it is argued that the clergy ought to be on the public payroll 'to bribe their indolence', thus 'rendering it superfluous for them to be farther active, than merely to prevent their flock from straying in quest of new pastures'. To which Smith in effect answers that while this may be right in theory, in practice those who command the payroll will just use religion to stay in command. Instead, he prefers to leave the clergy like 'the hussars and light infantry of some armies; no plunder, no pay'. While making them more active, it will make them more responsive to the particular wishes of their followers, thus dividing them into many small sects which are morally more valuable to the individual – and of no political consequence! WN, v, i, g. Quotations from paragraphs 6 and 2.

87 It is altogether amazing how frequently and easily religion and superstition are bracketed together.

88 TMS, vii, ii, 1, § 46.

89 Cf. vii, ii, 1, §§ 45–7.

90 TMS, iii, 2, § 34.

91 See E. 270, and Hume, 'A Dialogue', in E. 340–3. And cf. WN, v, i, f. 30: 'when moral, as well as natural philosophy, came to be taught only as subservient to theology, the duties of human life were treated of as chiefly subservient to the happiness of a life to come. In the antient philosophy the perfection of virtue was represented as necessarily productive, to the person who possessed it, of the most perfect happiness in this life. In the modern philosophy it was frequently represented as generally, or rather as almost always inconsistent with any degree of happiness in this life; and heaven was to be earned only by penance and mortification, by the austerities and abasement of a monk; not by the liberal, generous, and spirited conduct of a man.' Cf. also the significant quotation from Massillon, TMS, iii, 2, § 34.

92 Cf. R. H. Popkin, 'Hume and Kierkegaard', *Review of Religion*, vol. 31, 1951, pp. 274–81.

93 TMS, ii, ii, 3, § 5.

94 TMS, ii, i, 5, § 10.

95 See WN, v, i, f. 25; and LRBL, 51.

96 Astronomy, ii, 8. Smith is here mainly concerned with physical phenomena, but his description applies generally. Sections i and ii of the essay on astronomy provide the longest and most detailed discussion of the function of surprise and wonder in human knowledge. But the theme appears very frequently in the TMS, where some of the more significant uses of it are at: i, i, 4, § 3; i, i, 5, §§ 6–8; i, ii, 1, § 12; i, iii, 1, § 13; ii, ii, 1, § 6; iv, 2, §§ 8 and 11; vi, ii, 2, § 2; vi, iii, esp. §§ 5, 9 and 11. Cf. also WN, v, i, f. 24; LRBL, 64–5, 87, 93–4, 100, 107, 118, 127, 167, 172; Ancient Physics, 2. Very often 'admiration' is associated with surprise and wonder, but that is of no importance here.

97 Astronomy, ii, 4.

98 Astronomy, iii, 3. Smith does say in the *Lectures on Jurisprudence* that 'Geometry, arithmetick, and writing have all been invented originally to facilitate the operation of the severall arts' (LJ(A), vi, 18; cf. LJ(B), 210). But the whole point here is that these are 'subsidiary arts' to some of the

'thousand arts' which have been invented to satisfy that 'delicacy of man' which inspires him to what we might call aesthetic pursuits in food, lodging, clothing – and knowledge; all of which go beyond his 'natural wants'. Cf. the editorial note 14 to WN, v, i, f. 24.

99 See WN, v, i, f. 25.

100 TMS, VII, iii, 2, § 5.

101 LRBL, 87–8.

102 See Smith's strictures on casuistry, his commendation of 'Ethics' as an exhortative discipline like 'criticism', and his outline of a system of natural jurisprudence in TMS, VII, iv.

103 Astronomy, IV, 19. Cf. Ancient Physics, 9: 'As soon as the Universe was regarded as a complete machine, as a coherent system, governed by general laws, and directed to general ends, viz. its own preservation and prosperity, and that of all the species that are in it; the resemblance which it evidently bore to those machines which are produced by human art, necessarily impressed those [ancient] sages with a belief, that in the original formation of the world there must have been employed an art resembling the human art, but as much superior to it, as the world is superior to the machines which that art produces. The unity of the system, which, according to this ancient philosophy, is most perfect, suggested the idea of the unity of that principle, by whose art it was formed; and thus, as ignorance begot super-stition, science gave birth to the first theism that arose among those nations, who were not enlightened by divine Revelation.'

104 Astronomy, IV, 35.

105 Astronomy, IV, 67–76. See also Ancient Physics for a very similar story.

106 Astronomy, IV, 76.

107 Cf. WN, v, i, f. 26: 'Speculative systems have in all ages of the world been adopted for reasons too frivolous to have determined the judgment of any man of common sense, in a matter of the smallest pecuniary interest. Gross sophistry has scarce ever had any influence upon the opinions of mankind, except in matters of philosophy and speculation; and in these it has fre-quently had the greatest.'

108 TMS, VI, ii, 2, § 18.

109 WN, IV, v, b. 43. Cf. WN, II, iii, 28, 36; III, iii, 12; IV, ix, 28.

110 Cf. TMS, VII, ii, 1, § 44: 'By Nature the events which immediately affect that little department in which we ourselves have some little management and direction, which immediately affect ourselves, our friends, our country, are the events which interest us the most, and which chiefly excite our desires and aversions, our hopes and fears, our joys and sorrows.'

111 The further question of how the individual efforts even come – or can come – to form a *system* would need an additional discussion of Smith's political economy – which is not part of the present design.

112 WN, v, i, f. 30.

4 SMITH'S THEORY OF JUSTICE AND POLITICS

1 See e.g. TMS, I, iii, 1, § 7; and IV, 1, § 10: 'In ease of body and peace of mind, all the different ranks of life are nearly upon a level, and the beggar,

who suns himself by the side of the highway, possesses that security which kings are fighting for.'

2 TMS, ɪ, iii, ɪ, §§ 7–8; ɪ, iii, 2, §§ ɪ and 8; ɪv, ɪ, §§ 8 and 10.

3 See Astronomy, ɪ, 6, for this elaboration of the idea.

4 TMS, ɪ, iii, ɪ, § 3. Cf. TMS, ɪɪɪ, 2, § 15: 'Pain...is, in almost all cases, a more pungent sensation than the opposite and correspondent pleasure. The one almost always depresses us much more below the ordinary, or what may be called the natural state of our happiness, than the other ever raises us above it.' The theme also appears in LRBL, especially p. 80; and it seems to be clearly reflected in the very first thing John Anderson entered in his Commonplace Book: 'To deprive a man of life or limbs or to give him pain is shocking to the rudest of our species when no enmity or grudge subsists, i.e., where no punishment is due or danger apprehended' (Anderson Notes, ɪ). It is interesting that when Anderson began his notes he obviously intended to order them in numbered principles, the present one being the first, and the spectator-cum-labour theory of property (see pp. 106–7, below) being the second, but he did not continue this system for the rest of the notes. This makes it clear that the numbered principles probably were Smith's and not Anderson's: since he did not take notes from the full course, he could not use the system. It therefore seems likely that Smith at one stage structured his jurisprudence lectures by means of a set of numbered principles, of which the first seems to have been the primacy of the negative.

5 LRBL, 80–1.

6 TMS, ɪ, iii, ɪ, §§ ɪ, 3, 5 and 9. And cf. LRBL, 81, for a general statement of the point. It should be noticed that it is in this connection that Smith, in answer to Hume's criticism, clarifies the various layers in the whole sympathetic process and points out which is pleasant in itself, and which follows the quality of the original feeling (TMS, ɪ, iii, ɪ, § 9 note). Cf. the discussion at pp. 50–1, above.

7 TMS, ɪ, iii, ɪ ,§ 2.

8 TMS, ɪɪɪ, 2, § 15, and ɪ, iii, ɪ, § 8.

9 TMS, ɪ, iii, ɪ, § 8.

10 TMS, ɪ, i, 2, § 3.

11 TMS, ɪ, i, 2, §§ 12–15.

12 The idea of the 'negative' (i.e. of pain, misery, unhappiness) as, in a sense, of primary importance in morals has been rediscovered in our century in the form of so-called negative utilitarianism. See K. R. Popper, *The Open Society and Its Enemies*, vol. ɪ, chapter 5, note 6, and chapter 9, note 2. Also K. E. Tranöy, 'Asymmetries in ethics', *Inquiry*, vol. 10, 1967, pp. 351–72; and F. A. Hayek, *Law, Legislation, and Liberty*, vol. ɪɪ, pp. 35–42, and 162–4, where most of the relevant literature is referred to. For an interesting criticism of 'negativism' in morals, see J. Griffin, 'Is unhappiness more important than happiness?', *Philosophical Quarterly*, vol. xxɪx, 1979, pp. 47–55.

13 TMS, ɪɪ, ii, ɪ, § 3.

14 Cf. Smith's speculations about this in LRBL, 80–1.

15 TMS, ɪɪ, ii, ɪ, § 7

16 TMS, ɪɪɪ, 6, § 10.

17 TMS, ɪɪɪ, 6, § 11.

18 TMS, ii, ii, 3, §§ 1–2.

19 E. 305.

20 It is this very basic agreement on the absolute utility, public (i.e. means) utility of justice plus Hume's well-known formulation that the strength of obligation follows the extent of utility (in the above sense), which keeps a little doubt lingering in my mind as to the identity of the 'author of very great and original genius', referred to in TMS, ii, ii, 1, § 5. Professors Raphael and Macfie maintain (p. 80, note 1 of their edition of TMS) that it must be Kames, and their most weighty argument seems to be that Kames stressed the stricter obligation of justice as compared with benevolence. But the same seems to be the case with Hume.

21 TMS, ii, ii, 3, § 6.

22 See pp. 117–18, below.

23 See TMS, ii, ii, 3, § 8.

24 Cf. pp. 35–6, above.

25 He thus talks of the pain produced by injustice as 'real and positive hurt to some particular persons' (TMS, ii, ii, 1, §§ 3 and 5). And in LRBL he mentions that 'a debate concerning peace or war..., though very important, will never affect the passions so highly as the distress of a single person or indignation against the crimes of an individual' (LRBL, 181).

26 In External Senses, 7, Smith maintains that this basic fellow-feeling extends 'not only towards all other men, but (though no doubt in a much weaker degree) towards all other animals'.

27 See pp. 79–82, above.

28 TMS, vi, ii, 2, §§ 12–18. The whole of Part vi was added in the sixth and final edition of the book in 1790.

29 TMS, vi, ii, 2, § 15.

30 'The man of system...is apt to be very wise in his own conceit, and is often so enamoured with the supposed beauty of his own ideal plan of government, that he cannot suffer the smallest deviation from any part of it' (TMS, vi, ii, 2, § 17).

31 TMS, vi, ii, 2, § 17.

32 See e.g. WN, iv, ii, 10: 'What is the species of domestic luxury which his capital can employ, and of which the produce is likely to be of the greatest value, every individual, it is evident, can, in his local situation, judge much better than any statesman or lawgiver can do for him.' And *ibid.*: 'the law ought always to trust people with the care of their own interest, as in their local situations they must generally be able to judge better of it than the legislator can do'. And cf. similarly WN, i, x, c. 12 concerning freedom of employment (apprenticeship laws).

33 Such a view would seem to imply that the sovereign's knowledge could, so to speak, be equal to the sum of that of the citizens.

34 Cf. also WN, iv, ii, 10.

35 Cf. pp. 67–8, above. For the machine analogy, see also TMS, vii, iii, 1, § 2.

36 TMS, iv, 2, § 11.

37 See WN, i, xi, pp. 7–10.

38 WN, v, i, f. 61.

39 The whole of WN, v, i, f. is relevant for Smith's argument.

40 TMS, iv, 1, § 11.

41 TMS, vi, ii, 2, § 18.

42 WN, iv, ii, 39.

43 TMS, vi, ii, 2, § 18.

44 See TMS, vi, ii, 2, §§ 15 and 18 respectively.

45 Hume, *Essays*, vol. i, pp. 480–1.

46 The fruitfulness of this perspective on both Hume and Smith has been demonstrated in the works of Duncan Forbes and Donald Winch.

47 WN, v, iii, 68. The main sources for Smith's ideas about union with America are WN, iv, vii, c. 77–9 and his 'Thoughts on America' (Corr., pp. 380–5).

48 WN, iv, vii, c. 77.

49 WN, iv, ii, 43.

50 WN, iv, ix, 51. Concerning each of these, see WN, v, i, 1, 2 and 3.

51 TMS, ii, ii, 1, § 8.

52 See pp. 123–7 and 144–5, below.

53 See WN, v, i, f. 61: 'Though the state was to derive no advantage from the instruction of the inferior ranks of people, it would still deserve its attention that they should not be altogether uninstructed.' The preceding discussion shows how strongly Smith felt about the issue.

54 See WN, v, i, e. 4. For other examples of intervention in free trade justified by concern for defence, see WN, iv, ii, 23ff. (the Navigation Act): WN, iv, v, a. 27 (fishing bounty); WN, iv, v, a. 36 (regulation of export of strategic materials).

55 See Donald Winch, *Adam Smith's Politics*, chapter 5. The integration between the various parts of Smith's politics is well brought out in Winch's study.

56 TMS, iv, 1, § 11.

57 WN, iv, ii, 30. Cf. also the parallel cases referred to in note 54 above.

58 See pp. 155–9, below.

59 LJ(A), i, 7; cf. LJ(B), 6. Concerning Hume, see pp. 39–40, above.

60 LJ(A), i, 1 (cf. 9), and LJ(B), 5. Smith is thus more accurate in his formulation of his priorities in WN, as quoted above, p. 93.

61 TMS, vii, iv, § 37.

62 See LJ(A), i, 1–2; and vi, 1; LJ(B), 203; and cf. LJ(B), 5. In WN, see e.g. i, vii, 20; i, vii, 29; i, xi, p. 8.

63 LJ(B), 203; cf. LJ(A), vi, 1.

64 LJ(A), i, 1–4; vi, 1–7; LJ(B), 5–6; 203–5.

65 LJ(A), i, 6–8; vi, 1; LJ(B), 5.

66 See LJ(A), i, 5–6; LJ(B), 313; WN, v, ii, b. 4–6. Revenue consisting in rent of Crown land tends to take and keep away land from the market: LJ(A), i, 5.

67 WN, v, 1.

68 See LJ(A), i, 8–9; LJ(B), 6, and 339–58. In LJ(A), 1, Smith is reported as intending to incorporate the laws of nations under 'Arms', but since these notes do not extend to the 'Arms' section of the lecture course, we do not know how literally to take this. Smith obviously saw a close connection between the problem of defence and the conduct of foreign policy, and maybe that is all he meant to indicate in this passing remark.

69 LJ(B), 5.

70 LJ(B), 1. Cf. LJ(A), i, 1: 'Jurisprudence is the theory of the rules by which civil governments ought to be directed.' And in TMS the discipline is referred to as 'a system of what might properly be called natural jurisprudence, or a theory of the general principles which ought to run through and be the foundation of the laws of all nations' (TMS, vii, iv, § 37). This is repeated at the end of the section.
71 The laws of nations constitute an analogical extension of the general laws of justice.
72 Cf. J. Viner, 'Guide to John Rae's *Life of Adam Smith*', in John Rae, *Life of Adam Smith* (New York, 1965), pp. 30–1. And for the best general discussion of the legislator, see Winch, *Adam Smith's Politics*, pp. 159–60, and 170–3.
73 WN, iv, ii, 39.
74 TMS, vi, ii, 2, § 16. Sections 14–18 should be read together.
75 WN, iv, ix, 28.
76 TMS, vi, ii, intro. § 1.
77 By Winch's *Adam Smith's Politics*, which replaces most of the earlier scholarship in the area.

5 SMITH'S ANALYTICAL JURISPRUDENCE

1 See especially TMS, vii, ii, 1, § 10; LJ(A), i, 15; and the manuscript printed in Appendix ii to the Glasgow Edition of TMS, p. 390.
2 TMS, Appendix ii, p. 390. Smith also points out that 'justice' is sometimes used in so broad a sense that it becomes identical with 'propriety', and as such it encompasses both positive and negative virtues: TMS, vii, ii, 1, § 10.
3 TMS, vii, iv, § 36.
4 Except in passing, as at the beginning of ii, ii, 1, § 7.
5 LJ(A), i, 14–15, and cf. LJ(A), i, 1 and 9.
6 LJ(A), i, 9. The whole of the introductory part of the lecture course is relevant: see LJ(A), i, 1–25 and LJ(B), 5–11. Cf. also LJ(B), 340.
7 LJ(A), i, 10. Cf. LJ(B), 6.
8 LJ(A), i, 10.
9 These basic divisions of the law are introduced at the beginning of both sets of lecture notes: LJ(A), i, 10–11; LJ(B), 6–7. And see Fig. 1, p. 105, below.
10 The distinction between natural and acquired rights is dealt with or referred to in the following places: LJ(A), i, 12 and 24; ii, 93; LJ(B), 8, 9–10, 11, 149, 182. In the first two places in LJ(A) the student has obviously been confused, taking Smith to be saying that natural rights were identical with the whole area of private law, including property law. But at ii, 93 he has got it right, and the student writing LJ(B) seems to have had no difficulties with the distinction.
11 See LJ(A), i, 24 and LJ(B), 11 and 149.
12 LJ(B), 11. And cf. WN, v, i, b., especially § 2.
13 See TMS, v, 2, § 15.
14 TMS, vii, ii, 1, § 28.
15 The 'weakness' of contract rights as compared with property rights is explained at length in LJ(A) at ii, 44–5 and 62–3, and in LJ(B) at 176; and

it is shown how this was determining for the lateness of the recognition of the former rights as part of law. Cf. pp. 113–14, below.

16 See the beginning of LJ(A), i, 25.

17 See pp. 13–14, above.

18 See pp. 21–6, above.

19 See p. 120, below.

20 See LJ(A), i, 12–13, and 24; LJ(B), 7 and 11.

21 LJ(A), i, 13–14 and 24; LJ(B), 7 and 11. It is a fairly typical example of Smith's somewhat mischievous sense of humour that he illustrates this last point in the following way: 'We do not injure Sir Isaac Newton..., when we say that Sir Isaac was no better philosopher than Descartes' (LJ(B), 7).

22 Smith's course also contained shorter sections on 'Police, Revenue and Arms' – material which to a large extent went into *The Wealth of Nations*.

23 LJ(B), 11.

24 See LJ(B), 8, and LJ(A), i, 16.

25 For Smith's own survey, see LJ(A), i, 16–20 (real rights), 21–3 (personal rights); and LJ(B), 8–10 (real rights), 10–11 (personal rights).

26 LJ(A), i, 25–6; LJ(B), 149.

27 LJ(A), i, 35–6. The editors of these lecture notes quite rightly give a specific reference toTMS, ii, ii, 1, § 5.

28 The general spectator account of occupation is to be found in LJ(A), i, 35–7, and LJ(B), 150.

29 See pp. 79–81, above.

30 Smith goes through the problems concerning the beginning and the end of occupation in LJ(A), i, 38–42, and LJ(B), 150. The gradual extension of property is treated in LJ(A), i, 42–53, and LJ(B), 150–1.

31 See LJ(A), i, 60–3; LJ(B), 152.

32 See LJ(A), i, 53–60; LJ(B), 152.

33 WN, I, x, c.12.

34 The editors of the *Lectures on Jurisprudence* in the Glasgow Edition seem to see one sentence in LJ(A) as Lockean: see LJ(A), i, 37, and editorial note 17. But they rightly indicate a contrast here with Smith's better established view. The passage in question will be dealt with below.

35 These critical points are well made by Donald Winch in *Adam Smith's Politics*, pp. 58–9.

36 In other words, they should be read, 'just as..., so', not 'because..., so'.

37 Anderson Notes, 1. My italics.

38 It so reminded the editors of the lectures; see note 34 above.

39 See LJ(A), i, 63–76, and LJ(B), 152–4. Smith also summarizes the traditional disputes about ownership in cases where the accession is the work of one person, but the 'subject' in which it is worked is the property of another: LJ(A), i, 70–6, LJ(B), 153–4. In this, as generally in his lectures on property law, Smith is very close to Hume's sketches in the *Treatise*, iii, ii, 3.

40 LJ(A), i, 66.

41 And in case the students should be in doubt, a utility foundation is explicitly ruled out. What the spectators perceive in disregard of the principle of accession is 'the impropriety that appears in it rather than any inconvenience' (LJ(A), i, 64).

42 See for example the following: 'the young even for some time after its birth

as well as the milk for ever seem to be a part and but a small part of the mother, and accordingly goes to the proprietor of the whole as a part of it' (LJ(A), i, 65).

43 LJ(A), i, 64.
44 LJ(A), i, 62–3, and cf. LJ(B), 152.
45 LJ(A), i, 68–9, and LJ(B), 152–3.
46 LJ(A), i, 100. The passage as recorded by the student is ungrammatical; it is a general comment on the concrete argument, written on the otherwise blank verso page of the manuscript.
47 See LJ(A), i, 76–90 and LJ(B), 154–5.
48 LJ(A), i, 77.
49 LJ(B), 154.
50 There is explicit use of the spectator in LJ(B) too, but it is mainly in connection with the theory of punishment.
51 Intermingled with these are a number of more 'rationalistic' sounding phrases, of which we have already noticed 'reasonable expectations' in connection with occupation above. In the discussion of accession Smith also uses 'foundation in reason' and 'agreeable to reason' (LJ(A), i, 74). For comments on these, see pp. 136–7, below.
52 See especially lectures No. 13 and No. 16 (pp. 63–8 and 80–3).
53 LRBL, 81, and cf. LRBL, 82.
54 See earlier, pp. 79–80, and pp. 186–8, below.
55 For succession by law, see LJ(A), i, 90–148 and LJ(B), 155–64. For succession by testament, see LJ(A), i, 149–ii, 1, and LJ(B), 164–9.
56 LJ(A), i, 90–2; LJ(B), 155–6.
57 See pp. 104–7, above.
58 Cf. LJ(B), 156: 'As the father and sons lived together and were joint acquirers of any property they had, when the father died the children had a joint right to the goods not so much on account of their relation to the father as on account of the labour they had bestowed on acquiring them. The mother and the children would therefore continue in possession.' And the Anderson Notes, 4: 'Children succeed to the goods of their *intestate* father, not on account of the *parental relation*, but on account of their connection with his goods, etc., i.e., they succeed by the 2d principle' – and 'the 2d principle' is exactly the labour-cum-spectator principle which we quoted above at note 37.
59 See references in note 55, above.
60 See LJ(A) i, 104–15, and LJ(B), 158–9.
61 LJ(A), i, 150.
62 LJ(B), 164.
63 See p. 46, above.
64 LJ(B), 165; and cf. LJ(A), i, 150–1.
65 LJ(A), ii, 1–13; LJ(B), 169–71.
66 See T. III, ii, 4.
67 See pp. 112–13, below.
68 Servitudes: LJ(A), ii, 14–19; LJ(B), 172–3. Pledges: LJ(A), ii, 19–26; LJ(B), 173–4. Exclusive privileges: LJ(A), ii, 27–41; LJ(B), 174–5.
69 LJ(A), ii, 28; cf. LJ(B), 175.
70 Cf. LJ(B), 175. Concerning contracts, see LJ(A), ii, 41–84; LJ(B), 175–80.

Quasi-contracts: LJ(A), ii, 85–8; LJ(B), 180–1. Delict: LJ(A), ii, 88–180; LJ(B), 181–201.
71 For this discussion, see LJ(A), ii, 59–60.
72 LJ(A), ii, 59.
73 LJ(A), ii, 58–9.
74 LJ(A), ii, 56. Cf. LJ(A), ii, 43–4; and LJ(B), 175: 'That obligation to performance which arises from contract is founded on the reasonable expectation produced by a promise, which considerably differs from a mere declaration of intention.'
75 LJ(A), ii, 56–7.
76 Concerning Smith on general rules, see pp. 61–2, above. Concerning Hume's theory, see pp. 31–5, above.
77 Actual or potential relations – *vide* his treatment of 'virtue'.
78 LJ(A), ii, 46. Cf. also LJ(A), ii, 48.
79 'Breach of contract is naturally the weakest of all injuries because we naturaly depend more on what we possess than what is in the hands of others' (LJ(B), 176) – 'the injury done by the breach of a contract is the slightest possible; at least the slightest one can well account to require any satisfaction...One never has so great dependence on what is at the mercy or depends on the good faith of another as what depends only on his own will. The spectator can not think he has so good a ground for expectation of the possessing it' (LJ(A), ii, 44–5).
80 LJ(A), 57–8.
81 See pp. 173–4, below.
82 See p. 123, below.
83 LJ(A), ii, 88. Concerning delict, see LJ(A), ii, 88–180 and LJ(B), 181–201.
84 Cf. LJ(B), 181.
85 LJ(B), 181 and 183.
86 TMS, Appendix ii, p. 390. This Appendix reprints the text of the early manuscript and contains a most interesting discussion of it by D. D. Raphael.
87 See Raphael in TMS, Appendix ii, p. 393.
88 LJ(B), 201.
89 See pp. 174–5, below.
90 See pp. 127–32, below.
91 Concerning Habeas Corpus and bail, see LJ(A), ii, 127–30, 133–5; LJ(B), 191.
92 Cf. pp. 88–9, above.
93 Professor Raphael, in TMS, Appendix ii, p. 394, sees this issue as connected with a difficulty in the general theory of justice, arising out of a particular example ('the sentinel case'). I do not believe, however, that there is any difficulty – see my suggestions below at pp. 120–3.
94 See pp. 87–9, above.
95 The case is also used in LJ(B), 182, and WN, iv, viii, 17.
96 LJ(A), ii, 92, and LJ(B), 182. The sentinel case also figures in TMS, ii, ii, 3, § 11, and has a further significance, as we shall see immediately below.
97 Smith refers to 'Grotius and other writers' (sc. Pufendorf).
98 LJ(A), ii, 92–3.
99 TMS, ii, ii, 3, §§ 7 and 8. In the lectures Smith also said that Grotius's three utility considerations 'will no doubt have an effect...also': LJ(A), ii, 171.

100 Cf. Fig. 1, p. 105, for Smith's general system of rights.

101 See below, pp. 120–1.

102 See pp. 127–32, below.

103 LJ(A), ii, 78 and 88; LJ(B), 181.

104 See LJ(A), ii, 94–127, and LJ(B), 182–91, for Smith's discussion of punishment for bodily injury.

105 Smith refers to the TMS at LJ(A), ii, 78, and cross-refers to this at ii, 88.

106 See the discussion of this at pp. 64–6, above.

107 See TMS, ii, iii, 2, §§ 8–10; LJ(A), ii, 118–20; LJ(B), 188–9.

108 '...as far as I know there is no country where the attempt to committ a crime is punished with the same severity as the actuall committing it. The resentment of the party injured is not...so great; and it is on this...that the punishing of criminalls is founded' (LJ(A), ii, 175). See LJ(A), ii, 174–7; LJ(B), 201; TMS, ii, iii, 2, § 8. Smith takes it as a confirmation of his theory and a further argument against Grotius and Pufendorf that he can explain this feature of the law: on the utility view the person who attempts a crime is just as much in need of correction and deterrence as the person who also succeeds!

109 LJ(A), ii, 94–144 and LJ(B), 182–94. By comparison punishment of crimes against 'estate' rights take up LJ(A), ii, 144–74, and LJ(B), 194–200.

110 This is why these rights require more explanation of a direct kind: 'It does not at first appear evident that, e.g. any thing which may suit another as well or perhaps better than it does me, should belong to me exclusively of all others barely because I have got it into my power' (LJ(A), i, 25).

111 See pp. 113–14, above.

112 See pp. 93–8, above.

113 Cf. the parallel passage in the early manuscript: 'Upon some occasion indeed we punish meerly from a View to the general interest of Society which...we imagine cannot be otherwise supported. The punishments, for Exemple, which military discipline prescribes are all inflicted from this motive' (TMS, Appendix ii, p. 389).

114 LJ(A), ii, 92, and TMS, ii, ii, 3, § 11. Apart from these two, the sentinel case occurs in LJ(B), 182, and the early manuscripts, TMS, Appendix ii, p. 389.

115 See LJ(A), ii, 91–2; LJ(B), 182; WN, iv, viii, 17.

116 See WN, v, ii, k. 64.

117 My italics. Cf. LJ(B), 343.

118 TMS, ii, ii, 3, § 11.

119 LJ(A) ii, 91.

120 WN, v, ii, k. 64.

121 TMS, ii, ii, 1, § 8.

122 See pp. 94–5, above.

123 TMS, ii, ii, 3, § 11. In LJ(A), ii, 92, he is even more hesitant: 'we may perhaps approve of the sacrificing one person for the safety of a few' (in TMS and the early manuscript it was, more accurately, 'a multitude' and 'thousands', respectively).

124 Concerning revenue laws, see also WN, v, ii, k. – especially 64 and 75.

125 See pp. 93–4, above.

126 Such as the Navigation Act: WN, iv, ii, 24–30.

127 Such as some parts of domestic law; see pp. 124–5, below.

128 See WN, v, i, f. 61. And cf. pp. 93–4, above, and Winch, *Adam Smith's Politics*, pp. 103–20.

129 WN, v, i, f. 61.

130 Professor Raphael suggests that Smith's use of this expression is a confirmation that he was in difficulties with the sentinel case. On Raphael's interpretation, this case constitutes a utilitarian exception to Smith's general theory of punishment. Raphael does not, however, connect the theory of punishment and the distinction between laws of justice and laws of police, and consequently he does not see the systematic difference between the two systems of punishment. See Raphael's very thorough discussion in TMS, Appendix II, pp. 394–5. For the difficult passages in Smith, see TMS, II, ii, 3, § 11; early manuscript, TMS, Appendix II, p. 389 (here 'Nothing can be more just' than the sentinel's punishment); and LJ(B), 182 (where it is simply 'just').

131 LJ(B), 343. It is perhaps worth noting that in the TMS passage it is equally the *necessity* which prompts Smith momentarily to extend his concept of justice (TMS, II, ii, 3, § 11).

132 LJ(A), ii, 158. See LJ(A), ii, 158–60 and LJ(B), 197–8.

133 Smith only mentions two other cases: piracy, where the impossibility of enforcing the law necessitates other ways of protecting it (LJ(A), ii, 156); and a historical case relating to theft, though the real rationale here seems to be the legal value of consistency (LJ(A), ii, 150–1).

134 See pp. 113–14, above.

135 LJ(B), 179. Cf. LJ(A), ii, 49.

136 For each of these, see LJ(A), iii, 1–77, 78–87, and 87–147; and LJ(B), 101–126, 126–30, and 130–48.

137 LJ(A), iii, 15–16; LJ(B), 102–3. In LJ(A) Smith only treats of fidelity in connection with divorce. Cf. also TMS, VII, iv, 21: 'breaches of the rules of chastity…in all grosser instances are real breaches of the rules of justice'.

138 LJ(A), iii, 16. It is typical, in more than one respect, that Smith should rest his explanations on the situation rather than the qualities of the clergy.

139 LJ(A), iii, 16, and LJ(B), 148.

140 LJ(B), 112; cf. LJ(A), iii, 23–5.

141 See LJ(A), iii, 23–48 (summary at 48–52); LJ(B), 111–17.

142 LJ(A), iii, 23–4; LJ(B), 111–12.

143 LJ(A), iii, 24.

144 LJ(A), iii, 50.

145 LJ(A), iii, 58–69; LJ(B), 120–3. Smith also gives a brief, descriptive account of the effect of marriage on the property rights of the parties: LJ(A), iii, 52–8; LJ(B), 118–20.

146 LJ(A), iii, 58–9; LJ(B), 121. But even here Smith finds an exception which, however, derives from 'the delirium of superstition': LJ(A), iii, 60.

147 LJ(A), iii, 59–60; LJ(B), 121.

148 LJ(A), iii, 66. The space after 'naturall' is actually blank in the manuscript, but the editor's guess that 'law' is meant is fairly obvious from the context.

149 LJ(B), 122. By 'political views' Smith means regard to public order.

150 See LJ(A), iii, 61–2. It is perhaps significant that the lonely reference to reason occurs in a summary of past lectures.

151 LJ(A), iii, 63–4; LJ(B), 121. There is also some little obscurity here: contrast LJ(A), iii, 63 (at the end) with 66.

152 LJ(B), 122–3; LJ(A), iii, 66–9. Smith's exegesis of Leviticus 18:18 in the light of Jewish customs is particularly subtle: LJ(A), iii, 67.

153 TMS, ii, ii, 1, § 8. The parent–child relationship is dealt with in LJ(A), iii, 78–87, and LJ(B), 126–30.

154 LJ(A), iii, 86.

155 *Ibid.*

156 LJ(B), 145. There is no specific discussion of the principles of contemporary law in this area in the report in LJ(A).

157 See LJ(B), 145–6. Smith also mentions the mutual obligations in apprentice-ship relations.

158 See chapter 7 below, pp. 176–7. Smith discusses slavery in LJ(A), iii, 87–147, and LJ(B), 130–45.

159 The former is dealt with in LJ(A), v, 54–86, and LJ(B), 78–86; the latter in LJ(A), v, 102–49 and LJ(B), 91–9.

160 The latter comprising aristocratic and democratic governments.

161 LJ(A), v, 54, and LJ(B), 79.

162 LJ(A), v, 59. Cf. LJ(A), v, 60, and LJ(B), 79.

163 See the interesting contrast between treason and ordinary crime in a republic in LJ(A), v, 57: when the citizen of a republic engages in treasonable activity, 'he sets himself above the authority of the people and above the laws. A murtherer tho he breaks the laws does not set himself above them, but one who by a *sort of authority* puts one to death plainly does' (my italics).

164 TMS, ii, iii, 2, § 4.

165 LJ(A), v, 62 and 63; LJ(B), 80. While Smith in the TMS clearly had a monarchical sovereign in mind when making this point, his formulation in the lecture reported in LJ(A) is generalized so that it can cover republican forms of government as well. This is an interesting detail, for Smith makes the general point in a discussion of the specific laws of treason in England – a 'mixed' government. LJ(A), v, 62: 'In the injuries of private persons the publick enter only by sympathy, but in the case of the sovereign they punish the injuries against themselves, and for this reason injuries against the publick are always more highly punished than those of individualls.'

166 See LJ(A), v, 72–3.

167 LJ(A), v, 61–4; LJ(B), 80–1.

168 See pp. 145–6, below.

169 See LJ(A), v, 102–49, and LJ(B), 91–9.

170 LJ(A), v, 102–4; LJ(B), 91.

171 LJ(A), v, 103–4.

172 LJ(A), v, 104–11; LJ(B), 92–3.

173 Concerning authority, see LJ(A), v, 119–20, and 129–32; LJ(B), 12–13 and 93. Concerning utility, see LJ(A), v, 120–2, and 129–32; LJ(B), 13–14 and 93.

174 This is the basis for Smith's well-known theory of the distinction of ranks. See TMS, i, iii, 2.

175 This doctrine occurs, with variations, in WN, v, i, b. 4–8; LJ(A), v, 129; LJ(B), 12. As far as the first kind of quality is concerned, see also LRBL, 168.

176 LJ(A), v, 123–4; LJ(B), 14–15.

177 LJ(A), v, 120.

178 LJ(A), v, 123–4; LJ(B), 14–15.

179 LJ(A), v, 122; LJ(B), 93.

180 LJ(A), v, 132.

181 See LJ(A), v, 114–19; 127–8; 134–8; LJ(B), 15–18; 93–6. Apart from Locke, Smith also mentions Sidney (LJ(A), v, 114) and, as indicated by the editors, he also has Pufendorf, Cocceius, and Hutcheson in mind in some of his more specific criticisms of the consent idea (LJ(A), v, 135–8; LJ(B), 95–6).

182 See particularly his detailed arguments against the supposed necessity of consent to taxation, to alienation of territories, and to changes in the line of succession: LJ(A), v, 134–8; LJ(B), 94–5.

183 LJ(A), v, 125. Smith's ideas on the right of resistance are to be found in LJ(A), v, 124–7, 132–4; LJ(B), 93 and 94.

184 LJ(A), v, 126.

185 LJ(A), v, 140. Cf. LJ(A), v, 102–3: 'There is…no authority sovereign to the sovereign.' (LJ(A), v, 113–14: 'In whatever place there is a sovereign, from the very nature of things the power must be absolute; and no power regularly established of calling the sovereign to account.' LJ(B), 91: 'To suppose a sovereign subject to judgement, supposes another sovereign.')

186 LJ(B), 91.

187 For Smith's general treatment of the division of powers, see LJ(A), v, 104–11, 138, 141–2; LJ(B), 92–3, 96. And cf. WN, v, i, b. 25; and LRBL, 170.

188 LJ(B), 98.

189 Cf. LJ(B), 96.

190 See e.g. LJ(A), v, 138: 'With regard to governments where the supreme power is divided amongst different persons, there is no great difficulty in ascertaining when any one transgresses the limits of his power.'

191 See WN, v, i, f. 61.

192 For a discussion of this aspect of Smith's politics, see Winch, *Adam Smith's Politics*, pp. 168–71.

193 WN, v, i, f. 61.

194 Cf. pp. 91–3, above.

195 Concerning both the historical and the geographical aspect, see below, pp. 170–1.

196 For a detailed discussion of this, see Forbes, 'Sceptical Whiggism, commerce, and liberty', pp. 187–91.

197 LJ(A), v, 15, 108–11; LJ(B), 92–3.

198 See pp. 148–9, below.

199 Cf. LJ(A), v, 113: 'the question is, when is it lawfull or allowable to resist the power of the king and Parliament. They would never have any thoughts of making any laws which should tell us that, when they went beyond such and such limits, the people were not bound to obey them but might resist.'

200 LJ(A), v, 102.

201 LJ(B), 339; cf. LJ(A), v, 102. Smith deals systematically with the laws of

nations in LJ(B), 339–58. The incomplete notes in LJ(A) do not cover this part of his lectures.

202 TMS, III, 3, § 39.

203 TMS, VI, ii, 2, § 3. TMS, III, 3, § 39, and VI, ii, 2, §§ 3–5 are important supplements to LJ(B) concerning the laws of nations.

204 Smith deals with this under public law in connection with citizenship: LJ(A), v, 86–102; LJ(B), 88–91.

205 Smith discusses these two questions in LJ(B), 340–1 and 342–50, respectively. He also considers the relationship between warring and neutral nations and the status of ambassadors (LJ(B), 351–2 and 353–8). The latter discussion is interesting for its stress on the necessity of diplomatic missions to maintain the trade relationships between commercial societies, and – not least – for its demonstration of *how* international Smith's outlook was.

206 LJ(B), 340. The only exception to this general rule is that violations of quasi-contractual rights are not clear enough injuries to provide a justification for war: LJ(B), 341.

207 LJ(B), 342.

208 LJ(B), 343: 'This can by no means be founded upon justice and equity properly so called; it must be upon necessity, which indeed in this case is a part of justice.' In this context Smith criticizes the following theory put forward by Francis Hutcheson: if a war is justly instigated because some injury has been done by the government of another nation, it is justified to treat all the individual citizens of that nation as enemies, because they must be presumed to have given their government a tacit consent to its behaviour, as long as they do not overthrow it. Smith's criticism is simply that if this were to have any jurisprudential point, there would have to be a regular, well-established right of resistance – which there is not. (See pp. 129–30, above.)

209 LJ(B), 345.

210 LJ(B), 344. Cf. TMS, VI, ii, 2, § 3.

211 TMS, III, 3, § 42.

212 *Ibid.*

213 *Ibid.*

6 SMITH'S CRITICAL JURISPRUDENCE

1 W. C. Swabey, *Ethical Theory from Hobbes to Kant* (London, 1961), p. 179.

2 T. D. Campbell, *Adam Smith's Science of Morals* (London, 1971), p. 51.

3 *Ibid.*, p. 219; and cf. *ibid.*, p. 52.

4 See pp. 67–74, above.

5 See pp. 79–81, above.

6 See pp. 61–2, above.

7 TMS, II, ii, 2, § 4, and LJ(A), ii, 90. This mixed terminology is present throughout the TMS and the jurisprudence lectures, but it is used particularly extensively in Smith's spectator account of conscience (see especially TMS, III, 2, § 32).

8 LRBL, 170. Concerning the relationship between case and statute law, see pp. 151–3, below.

9 TMS, III, 5, § 6, and LJ(A), iv, 35. Cf. LJ(B), 22–3.

10 For other examples of this, see also LJ(A), i, 148; ii, 136–40; iii, 58ff.

11 The principles are in obvious accord with Smith's general speculations about knowledge, as outlined at pp. 79–81, above. Concerning the primacy of the negative, see also pp. 83–7, above.

12 WN, iv, v, b. 16.

13 WN, i, x, c. 12.

14 WN, i, x, c. 59. Cf. *ibid*.: 'There is scarce a poor man in England of forty years of age, I will venture to say, who has not in some part of his life felt himself most cruelly oppressed by this ill-contrived law of settlements.'

15 WN, iv, viii, 47.

16 WN, iv, viii, 17. This form of criticism recurs frequently in Book iv.

17 WN, iv, viii, 30.

18 TMS, vii, ii, 1, § 28.

19 WN, iv, vii, b. 54, and LJ(A), iii, 111.

20 LJ(B), 138: 'It is almost needless to prove that slavery is a bad institution even for freemen.' Cf. WN, i, viii, 41; WN, iii, ii, 9; WN, iv, ix, 47; LJ(A), iii, 111–14; LJ(B), 138–40, 290, 299–300.

21 LJ(A), iii, 130. Cf. LJ(A), iii, 114; LJ(B), 134; WN, iii, ii, 10.

22 See pp. 167–8, below. The countries of that corner of Europe, however, were still happy to maintain slavery in their colonies – a fact to which Smith was anything but blind; see WN, iv, vii, b. 53–6; LJ(A), iii, 101, 127–8, 132, 110; LJ(B), 137.

23 For these arguments, see WN, iv, vii, b. 54; LJ(A), iii, 101–5, 114–17; LJ(B), 134–6. (Quotations are from WN, iv, vii, b. 54; LJ(A), iii, 101–2.)

24 See WN, iv, vii, b. 53–4.

25 Cf. LJ(A), iii, 116–17.

26 LJ(A), iii, 105–11; LJ(B), 136–8. The point about sympathy is well made in LJ(A), iii, 109: 'Those persons most excite our compassion and are most apt to affect our sympathy who most resemble ourselves, and the greater the difference the less we are affected by them.'

27 See LJ(A), iii, 138–9.

28 LJ(A), i, 53 and 56. The argument concerning 'the common' stretches from i, 53 to 63.

29 LJ(A), i, 53–5.

30 LJ(A), i, 55.

31 LJ(A), i, 57.

32 LJ(A), i, 56.

33 LJ(A), i, 57–63. The editors of LJ explain the Franchises of Waifs and of Treasure Trove as the 'privilege of taking stolen goods abandoned by the thief' and 'the privilege of taking any precious metal which had been found hidden in the ground and whose owner was unknown'. See notes 37 and 38 to LJ(A), i, 57–8.

34 WN, iii, ii, 4. Cf. LJ(A), i, 131–40; LJ(B), 161–2. Concerning this historical aspect, see pp. 165–6, below; cf. pp. 109–10, above.

35 LJ(A), i, 116.

36 WN, iii, ii, 3 (my italics). Cf. p. 110, above. It is interesting that Smith pursued the jurisprudential side of the argument in the following way. Once the principle of primogeniture was established, it would under certain circumstances throw the law into further confusion by conflicting with the spectator-based principles of succession. For if a man succeeded to an estate

but died before his son had reached majority, should the *son* or the *eldest brother* (or all the brothers, or children) succeed? The logic of the primogeniture system would lead to the first solution, whereas established spectator principles would tend towards one or another of the other possibilities. Under the pressure of political necessity, and after much struggle, the former won out as succession by representation became established: LJ(A), i, 135–40.

37 Cf. LJ(A), i, 164, and LJ(B), 168.
38 LJ(A), i, 164.
39 Cf. LJ(A), i, 149ff.; and TMS, i, i, 1, § 13.
40 LJ(A), i, 154; 161–3; 164–6; LJ(B), 166 and 168.
41 LJ(A), i, 161–3; LJ(B), 164.
42 LJ(A), i, 165.
43 LJ(A), ii, 30. See also pp. 111–12, above; and LJ(A), ii, 27–41; LJ(B), 174–5.
44 LJ(A), ii, 30–3. Cf. WN, v, i, e. 30.
45 LJ(A), ii, 136–40, and LJ(B), 192. Quotations are from LJ(A), ii, 136–7, 137, and 139.
46 Cf. LJ(B), 196. Much the same goes for house-breaking where nothing is stolen: LJ(B), 196. See also a related historical case in LJ(A) ii, 151–2.
47 See LJ(A), ii, 168–74, and LJ(B), 199–200.
48 LJ(A), ii, 168–9.
49 LJ(A), ii, 165–8. The implication of Smith's remarks at the end of 167 and the beginning of 168 is that something like twenty years might well be enough. Cf. LJ(B), 199.
50 LJ(A), ii, 169–70. Cf. LJ(B), 199–200.
51 LJ(A), ii, 172–4, and LJ(B), 200. Smith's great emphasis on the importance of the whole matter of prescription of punishment for crime is shown by the fact that he argues that even if punishment were based upon Grotius's and Pufendorf's utility principles, rather than on his spectator principles, the conclusion would still be the same: LJ(A), ii, 170–1.
52 See pp. 120–2, above.
53 See the discussion of this at pp. 124–5, above.
54 If they were practised in defiance of laws of police against them, the matter would be complicated by the civil disobedience involved. Hence Smith's caution here.
55 Cf. LJ(B), 111–12.
56 Unfortunately Smith only considered voluntariness on the side of the husband.
57 LJ(A), iii, 37. Cf. LJ(B), 114.
58 LJ(A), iii, 51.
59 *Ibid.*
60 LJ(B), 81. Cf. LJ(A), v, 64–5: 'counterfeiting the king's coin...should naturally be considered not as treason, but as the crimen falsi; and for this reason it is now generally tried as a felony'.
61 LJ(A), v, 67. Cf. LJ(B), 82.
62 LJ(A), v, 71. Cf. LJ(B), 82.
63 LJ(B), 98–9. See LJ(A), v, 138–40, and 142–9; LJ(B), 96–9.
64 Cf. pp. 133–4, above.
65 WN, iv, vii, b. 59. Cf. also WN, iv, vii, c. 80: 'To the natives...both of the East and West Indies, all the commercial benefits which can have resulted

from these events have been sunk and lost in the dreadful misfortunes which they have occasioned...At the particular time when these discoveries were made, the superiority of force happened to be so great on the side of the Europeans, that they were enabled to commit with impunity every sort of injustice in those remote countries. Hereafter, perhaps, the natives of those countries may grow stronger, or those of Europe may grow weaker, and the inhabitants of all the different quarters of the world may arrive at that equality of courage and force which, by inspiring mutual fear, can alone overawe the injustice of independent nations into some sort of respect for the rights of one another. But nothing seems more likely to establish this equality of force than that mutual communication of knowledge and of all sorts of improvements which an extensive commerce from all countries to all countries naturally, or rather necessarily, carries along with it.'

66 WN, iv, vii, a. 15.

67 WN, iv, i, 32.

68 WN, iv, vii, b. 44. The whole of WN, iv, vii is of relevance.

69 WN, v, iii, 88.

70 *The Wealth of Nations* especially is an amazingly critical work from a juris-prudential point of view. It would seem, however, that all the criticism falls within the categories discussed here.

71 The right to protection of reputation is at least a partial exception. It is listed as a natural right, but is obviously to some extent of changing content (cf. p. 103, above). Whether Smith was simply bowing here to tradi-tional divisions of the law, or whether he thought the universal elements more important than the changing ones, we do not know.

72 This criticism is to be found in TMS, vii, iii, 2; while the main source for Smith's jurisprudential programme is TMS, vii, iii, 4.

73 TMS, vii, iii, 2, § 1. Cf. LJ(B), 2–3: according to Hobbes, obedience to the sovereign's will 'constituted civil government, without which there could be no virtue, and consequently it too was the foundation and essence of virtue'. Concerning Hume's similar criticism, see p. 20, above.

74 Nothing could better illustrate how interwoven descriptive and normative theory are for Smith than this extraordinary suggestion that the criticism of the command theory of law is now on a better footing owing to the improve-ment in the science of human nature.

75 TMS, ii, ii, 1, § 7.

76 TMS, vii, iv, § 36.

77 TMS, vii, iv, § 37. Cf. the first sentence in each of the two sets of lecture notes: 'Jurisprudence is the theory of the rules by which civil governments ought to be directed' (LJ(A), i, 1), and 'Jurisprudence is that science which inquires into the general principles which ought to be the foundation of the laws of all nations' (LJ(B), 1).

78 Cf. the early manuscript: 'The rules by which the magistrate in all coun-tries actually regulates all his decisions of this kind [i.e. redress in cases of injury] whether established upon express Statute, upon accidental custom or upon their own evident equity constitute the civil and criminal Jurisprudence of that Country. The Rules by which it is most suitable to the natural principles of Justice, or to the Analogy of those Sentiments upon which our Sense of it is founded [,] that such decisions should be

regulated, constitute what is called Natural Jurisprudence, or the Theory of the general principles of Law. they [sic] make a very important part of the Theory of moral Sentiments' (TMS, Appendix II, p. 389). Unfortunately Smith never returns to the idea that our sense of justice is founded upon an *analogy* of sentiments. Could it reflect some early, Hume-inspired speculations about the 'artificial' character of justice? (Cf. pp. 21–6, above.)

79 Campbell, *Adam Smith's Science of Morals*, pp. 58–9.
80 TMS, VII, iv, § 37.
81 *Ibid.*; and LJ(B), 1–2.
82 TMS, VII, iv, § 37.
83 See the early manuscript, TMS, Appendix II, p. 389, and the Advertisement to the sixth edition of the TMS, p. 3: 'In the last paragraph of the first Edition of the present work, I said, that I should in another discourse endeavour to give an account of the general principles of law and government, and of the different revolutions which they have undergone in the different ages and periods of society; not only in what concerns justice, but in what concerns police, revenue, and arms, and whatever else is the object of law. In the *Enquiry concerning the Nature and Causes of the Wealth of Nations*, I have partly executed this promise; at least as far as concerns police, revenue, and arms. What remains, the theory of jurisprudence, which I have long projected, I have hitherto been hindered from executing... Though my very advanced age leaves me, I acknowledge, very little expectation of ever being able to execute this great work to my own satisfaction; yet, as I have not altogether abandoned the design, and as I wish still to continue under the obligation of doing what I can, I have allowed the paragraph to remain as it was published more than thirty years ago, when I entertained no doubt of being able to execute every thing which it announced.'
84 See the discussion of this at pp. 96–7, above.
85 TMS, VII, iv, § 8. Cf. the general statements about the relationship between natural justice and positive law quoted above on pp. 149–50.
86 Cf. LJ(A), v, 42–3, where Smith also contrasts the law of England with that of France and that of Scotland in very similar terms and concludes that 'The law of England is...of a peculiar nature and well worth the study of a speculative man.'
87 Cf. LJ(A), v, 24–5. And see LRBL, 170, where Smith contrasts proof from common law and from statute: 'The other way to prove anything to be law is to show that it follows from some Statute law by abstract reasoning. The other [i.e. from common law] is always preferred to this, where it can be made use of, as the abstract reasoning renders it [i.e. statute law] less easily comprehended.' (The reporting here is obviously somewhat confused, but the context makes the meaning indicated in square brackets clear enough.)
88 LJ(A), v, 43. Cf. LJ(B), 75: 'All new courts disdain to follow the rules that were formerly established. All new courts are a great evil, because their power at first is not precisely determined and therefore their decisions must be loose and inacurrate.'
89 LJ(B), 74.
90 WN, v, i, f. 44.

91 LJ(A), iv, 35.

92 LJ(A), iv, 35: 'It is a sign of great authority in the government to be able to make regulations which shall bind themselves, their posterity, and even persons who are unwilling.' LJ(B), 22–3: 'It was indeed long before the legislative power was introduced, as it is the highest exertion of government to make laws and lay down rules to bind not only ourselves, but also our posterity, and those who never gave any consent to the making them.'

93 The editorial note says: 'Presumably "extend" was intended.'

94 Cf. LJ(B), 93: 'the legislative power was introduced as a restraint upon the judicial'.

95 Unless, of course, we are dealing with statutes in the areas of 'Police, Revenue, and Arms', in which case the relationship to justice is the more complicated and indirect one discussed above at pp. 93–7.

96 See above, pp. 149–50.

97 Early manuscript, TMS, Appendix II, p. 389; my italics. The passage is quoted in full in note 78 above.

7 SMITH'S HISTORICAL JURISPRUDENCE

1 TMS, VII, iv, § 37.

2 See LRBL, 85–6, 107, and especially 101–2, where this view of the task of history is the ground for his commendation of Thucydides as the first historian proper. Cf. pp. 186–7, below.

3 LJ(A), i, 27. The four stages theory is dealt with or referred to in a number of places, the most important being: LJ(A), i, 26–35; LJ(B), 149–50; WN, v, i, a.–b. The stadial theory is used as a framework for the specific history of law and government in Europe from ancient Greece to Smith's time: LJ(A), iv, 1–v, 54; LJ(B), 18–78; WN, v, i, a.–b.; III, ii–iv.

4 FA 3; LJ(A), iv, 36–7; LJ(B), 27–8.

5 FA 3; ED, 24–7; LJ(A), i, 28; LJ(B), 286–7.

6 WN, v, i, a. 5; LJ(A), iv, 38–9; LJ(B), 28–9.

7 WN, v, i, a. 2; LJ(A), ii, 152; iv, 4, 19, 22, 74; LJ(B), 19, 25, 287–8.

8 WN, v, i, b. 5–6.

9 WN, v, i, b. 7–8.

10 WN, v, i, b. 2; LJ(A), i, 47; LJ(B), 150.

11 WN, v, i, b. 9; LJ(A), iv, 42–3.

12 LJ(A), iv, 19, 33.

13 LJ(A), iv, 4.

14 LJ(A), iv, 22.

15 LJ(A), iv, 4–7, 37; LJ(B), 19, 22.

16 LJ(A), iv, 6.

17 LJ(B), 23, 25.

18 LJ(A), ii, 96–7; LJ(B), 183.

19 LJ(A), iv, 4–5; LJ(B), 19, 23, 26.

20 LJ(A), i, 64 (accession); i, 92 (succession); ii, 46–8 (contract).

21 LJ(A), iii, 6–7; 78–9; 88–90. LJ(B), 105–6; 126–7; 131. It is worth noticing, however, that Smith in LJ(B), 105, remarks that 'Tho' there was little or no regard paid to woemen in the first state of society as objects of pleasure, yet there never was more paid them as rational creatures.'

22 WN, v, i, a. 2, and ii, iii, 34.

23 See e.g. LJ(A), i, 28, and LJ(B), 149, *versus* FA 3, and LJ(A), iv, 36–8.

24 LJ(A), ii, 97.

25 The development from hunting to a fully developed shepherd society is explained in LJ(A), iv, 7–55, and LJ(B), 20–30. The end result is outlined in WN, v, i, b. 7–8, and 10–16. And the development within the particular branches of the law is dealt with at its systematically appointed place in the lectures.

26 See LJ(A), iv, 7, 9–10.

27 LJ(A), iv, 7–13; LJ(B), 20–3; WN, v, i, b. 7.

28 LJ(A), iv, 41–7; LJ(B), 20–1; WN, v, i, b. 7–11. These points are expressed in a number of places.

29 WN, v, i, b. 11; my italics.

30 LJ(A), iv, 33–4; LJ(B), 26.

31 LJ(A), iv, 15–18, 30–5; LJ(B), 25–6.

32 LJ(A), iv, 34; ii, 122–3.

33 LJ(A), iv, 25–7, 30; LJ(B), 23–4.

34 See LJ(A), i, 44–6; LJ(B), 150–1. Cf. the excellent spectator account of the transitional stage in a particular case: LJ(A), i, 47.

35 LJ(A), ii, 97.

36 LJ(A), i, 64.

37 LJ(A), i, 91–2.

38 LJ(A), iv, 10; LJ(B), 25.

39 LJ(A), 97–9, 152–3, iv, 25–30; LJ(B), 183–5.

40 LJ(A), iv, 35.

41 LJ(A), iv, 53. See LJ(A), iv, 35–40, 47–55; LJ(B), 29–30.

42 LJ(A), iv, 65–8; LJ(B), 33.

43 LJ(A), iv, 68–74; LJ(B), 34–6. Cf. WN, iv, vii, c. 77. For a clear summary of the development in Athens, see LRBL, 143–6, and in Rome, LRBL, 149–153.

44 This whole tendency was much more pronounced in Rome than in Athens, because the differences in fortune were very great in the former place, and it did not, like Athens, have a 'middle rank' to 'restrain' rich or poor, as necessary: LRBL, 150–1. In the earlier period of the republic especially much of this high political pressure was reduced by means of colonial expansion and land-grabbing for the poor: WN, iv, vii, a. 3.

45 See especially LRBL, 144–5.

46 WN, v, i, a. 6–7.

47 WN, v, i, a. 8–9, 11.

48 WN, v, i, a. 10; LJ(A), iv, 85–7; LJ(B), 40–1.

49 For the story in Greece, see especially LJ(A), iv, 75–87.

50 For the fate of the Roman republic, see LJ(A), iv, 87–91; LJ(B), 41–3.

51 See especially WN, v, i, a. 30–6; LJ(A), iv, 99–104; LJ(B), 46–9.

52 Except perhaps for 'the areopagite court', LJ(B), 27.

53 LJ(A), iv, 18. Smith does not set out in one particular place his views on the development of the separation of powers in Greece and Rome, but the following passages add up to a fairly full picture: WN, v, i, b. 24; LJ(A), iv, 16–18, 59–60, 96–8, 105–7; LJ(B), 27; LRBL, 168–75.

54 LJ(A), v, 110. Cf. LJ(B), 92.

55 Smith is not at all clear about this. See e.g. LJ(A), iv, 105.

56 LJ(A), iv, 97, 105; LJ(B), 44.

57 LJ(A), iv, 106.

58 LJ(A), iv, 98–9; LJ(B), 45.

59 LJ(B), 45.

60 LJ(A), iv, 97–9, 107–8; LJ(B), 44–6.

61 WN, v, i, f. 44. And cf. LRBL, 168–75. In the *Lectures on Rhetoric* Smith says that the praetor did not pay any attention to precedents (169–70). It would seem, however, that he is thinking mainly of the role of precedents in specific court cases, whereas precedent undoubtedly could play a significant role in the formulation of the annual edicts upon which the praetor acted. At any rate, the formulation in WN is obviously the more considered and the more authoritative.

62 LRBL, 169. The equity of the House of Lords is duly acknowledged as an exception.

63 LRBL, 173.

64 WN, v, i, f. 44.

65 LJ(A), i, 53.

66 LJ(A), i, 49.

67 WN, iv, vii, a. 3. For these developments generally, see LJ(A), i, 48–53; LJ(B), 151. It is worth noticing that the WN passage goes on to point out that attempts to re-establish the original division of land by new agrarian laws, once marriage, succession and *alienation* had 'deranged' it, were unsuccessful. But while land was thus subject to some market-flexibility this had little effect, for the land was worked by slaves, as were manufactures and commerce later, and poor freemen were therefore excluded from the possibility of improving their lot. This contrasts interestingly with modern Europe, where there were no slaves and where people could work themselves up through a graduated ladder of ranks in manufactures and commerce – but where land was stifled by the old feudal laws. See also Anderson Notes, 35–6. Cf. pp. 180–1, below.

68 LJ(A), i, 65–8; LJ(B), 152–3.

69 LJ(A), i, 80–6; LJ(B), 155.

70 For the laws of succession at Rome, see LJ(A), i, 93–104; LJ(B), 155–8. Cf. WN, iii, ii, 3.

71 Concerning the emergence of testamentary succession, see LJ(A), i, 92, 152–160; LJ(B), 156, 164–6. In WN, iii, ii, 5, Smith denies that the Roman *fideicommissum* resembled modern entail.

72 LJ(A), ii, 14–16; cf. LJ(B), 172. Smith is unspecific about the timing of the change.

73 LJ(A), 53–6, 69–73; LJ(B), 176–9.

74 LJ(B), 185.

75 LJ(A), ii, 154.

76 LJ(A), iii, 11.

77 LJ(A), iii, 6–13, 52–4; LJ(B), 106–8, 118–19.

78 LJ(A), 79–85; LJ(B), 127–9.

79 LJ(B), 137; cf. LJ(A), iii, 109, and WN, iii, ii, 8.

80 LJ(A), iii, 115; LJ(B), 135–6; WN, iv, vii, b. 54–5. Concerning ancient slavery generally, see LJ(A), iii, 88–116; LJ(B), 130–7.

81 WN, III, ii, 1. The fall of the Roman empire is dealt with in a number of places by Smith, the main ones being: WN, v, i, a. 36; LJ(A), iv, 99–104, 109–13; LJ(B), 46–9.

82 Concerning allodial government, see LJ(A), 114–24; LJ(B), 49–52. Cf. WN, III, iv, 5–8.

83 It is a very interesting sidelight on Smith's whole perception of the relationship between these feudal developments and his own time that he should remark: 'till within a hundred and fifty years ago their were still some allodial lands' (LJ(A), iv, 131), although he thought that the change from allodial to feudal holding generally took place 'in the whole of Europe about the 9th, 10th, and 11th centuries' (LJ(A), iv, 134), and perhaps was completed even in the tenth century (LJ(B), 55).

84 Concerning these developments of feudalism, see especially, WN, III, ii, 1–3; III, iv, 5–9; LJ(A), iv, 124–41; LJ(B), 52–6. And generally for allodial and feudal forms of government, see also LJ(A), i, 116–48; LJ(B), 159–63.

85 WN, v, i, g. 24. These developments were at their height 'through the greater part of Europe during the tenth, eleventh, twelfth, and thirteenth centuries, and for some time both before and after that period' (*ibid.*), and they are discussed in WN, v, i, g. 20–4.

86 It is interesting to notice that in Italy this was greatly aided by the crusades, of all things: WN, III, iii, 14.

87 WN, III, iii, 12. The rise of the cities is explained in a number of places: WN, III, iii (and iv); LJ(A), iv, 142–5; LJ(B), 57.

88 WN, III, iv, 15. Concerning the fall of the lords, see WN, III, iv; LJ(A), iv, 157–9; LJ(B), 59.

89 For the case of Germany, see LJ(A), iv, 162–4, 166–7; LJ(B), 60–1.

90 WN, v, i, g. 26.

91 See LJ(A), iv, 161–2; LJ(B), 60.

92 WN, v, i, a. 37; LJ(A), iv, 167–70.

93 For these developments, see LJ(A), iv, 167–74; LJ(B), 61–2.

94 Concerning the evolution of Parliament, see especially, LJ(A), iv, 145–8; 151–7; LJ(B), 58–60.

95 Concerning these developments, see LJ(A), iv, 178–v, 12; LJ(B), 61–4.

96 LJ(A), iv, 165–6.

97 WN, v, i, b. 24–5; LRBL, 170; LJ(A), v, 15–16.

98 Smith is not specific; he may also have thought that the decline of the nobles and the rise of the king happened earlier in England; and the break with the Roman church obviously prevented canon law from playing the role it otherwise might have.

99 LJ(A), v, 43; cf. LJ(B), 75. And see pp. 151–3, above.

100 LJ(A), v, 21. The development of the courts is discussed in WN, v, i, b. 17–25 (intermittently); LJ(A), v, 12–45; LJ(B), 64–75.

101 LJ(A), v, 23–4; LJ(B), 67. See pp. 114–16, above.

102 LJ(A), v, 27–32; LJ(B), 69–71.

103 LJ(A), v, 32–41; LJ(B), 71–4.

104 LJ(A), v, 17–19; LJ(B), 65. The separation of the various courts is explained at LJ(A), v, 15–21, 25–9; LJ(B), 64–6, 67–9. Cf. WN, v, i, b. 21.

105 See Astronomy, IV, 21–3.

106 LJ(B), 109; cf. LJ(A), ii, 5–6. Roman civil law was of course not always adaptable to Christian principles – see e.g. LJ(A), i, 85–6.

107 LJ(A), i, 54–9; cf. LJ(B), 151–2. We saw how Smith criticized this above, at pp. 141–2.

108 LJ(A), i, 77–86. The canon law had some influence by its stress on the necessity of *bona fides*, not only at the take-over of property, but forever after: LJ(A), i, 85–6.

109 LJ(A), i, 104–14; LJ(B), 158–9.

110 LJ(A), i, 116–48; LJ(B), 159–63; WN, iii, ii, 2–3. Again, it is very interesting to notice Smith's time-perspective here: primogeniture took its beginning in feudal times and as a consequence of the feudal form of government, but 'in Germany it did not fully take place before the last century' (LJ(B), 161). And concerning succession by representation: 'in time this...has come to be established thro all Europe. But in some places but very late' (LJ(A), i, 139).

111 WN, iii, ii, 4. For Smith's jurisprudential criticism of primogeniture, see p. 142, above.

112 See LJ(A), v, 29–30.

113 LJ(B), 166, and LJ(A), i, 164. Concerning testamentary succession and entail in the modern world, see LJ(A), i, 161–ii, 1; LJ(B), 166–8. For entail, see also WN, iii, ii, 5–6. Smith's jurisprudential criticism of entail was discussed above, at pp. 142–3.

114 WN, iii, ii, 6.

115 LJ(A), ii, 37.

116 LJ(A), ii, 41; cf. LJ(B), 175. We discussed Smith's jurisprudential criticism in this regard at p. 143, above. For the 'police' side, cf. WN, i, x, c.; iv, vii, c.; v, i, e. 30; LJ(B), 306.

117 For the influence of the church, see especially LJ(A), ii, 49–51, 73–5; LJ(B), 178–9. Concerning the modern development of contract law generally, see LJ(A), ii, 48, 49–52, 64–9, 73–84; LJ(B), 176–9, 302–3. Cf. also pp. 113–14, above.

118 See LJ(B), 179.

119 See LJ(A), ii, 73–5; LJ(B), 178–9. See pp. 113–14 and 123, above, where we noted the special status of contractual rights which made contract law open to influences other than those of natural justice.

120 LJ(A), ii, 75; v, 29–30; LJ(B), 70–1, 179.

121 See LJ(A), v, 64–72, and LJ(B), 81–3, for his criticism of various laws of treason; and pp. 143–4, above, for his criticism of the level of punishment for certain crimes. He states his over-all perspective on the development of punishment at LJ(A), ii, 152–5; and LJ(B), 196–7. Cf. also WN, v, i, b. 13–17.

122 LJ(A), ii, 110; cf. LJ(B), 187.

123 LJ(A), ii, 110–12; LJ(B), 187–8; WN, v, i, g. 23.

124 LJ(A), ii, 106–16; LJ(B), 186–8.

125 LJ(A), iii, 12–22; LJ(B), 108–11.

126 LJ(A), iii, 85–7; LJ(B), 130. Cf. TMS, ii, ii, 1, § 8.

127 LJ(A), iii, 117–22; LJ(B), 141–2.

128 WN, iii, ii, 12. Maybe these were also his first thoughts, for in the Anderson Notes the church is not given much credit in this connection: see 32–3. But

the account of the abolition of slavery seems in general somewhat different in the very brief Anderson Notes.

129 The lack of religion for ancient slaves is explained in LJ(A), iii, 96–8; LJ(B), 132–3. The selection of Christianity by the slaves is one of the more extraordinary examples of both Smith's situationist method of explanation (cf. pp. 186–8, below), and of his natural history approach to religion (cf. pp. 74–7, above); see LJ(A), iii, 98–100; LJ(B), 133; Anderson Notes, 31–2.

130 WN, iii, ii, 8; LJ(A), iv, 141–2.

131 WN, iii, ii, 13. 'In France...five parts out of six of the whole kingdom are said to be still occupied by this species of cultivators', i.e. metayers.

132 This long process or parts of it are dealt with in a number of places; see especially WN, iii, ii, 8–21; LJ(A), iii, 117–26; LJ(B), 140–2; ED, 44–8.

133 LJ(A), iii, 101; ED, 45; LJ(A), iii, 117. Cf. LJ(A), iii, 114; LJ(B), 134; WN, iii, ii, 8.

134 LJ (A), iii, 101.

135 LJ(A), iii, 126–30; LJ(B), 138–9; ED, 44.

136 LJ(A), iii, 123.

8 NATURAL JURISPRUDENCE IN THE FACE OF HISTORY

1 LJ(B), 46, and LJ(A), iv, 99.

2 WN, v, iii, 10.

3 LJ(A), iv, 179–v, 1; LJ(B), 337; WN, v, i, a. 41.

4 WN, v, i, f. 59; LJ(B), 338; and concerning Smith's very balanced view of the militia *v.* standing army issue, see the whole of WN, v, i, a.; WN, v, i, f. 59–61; and Corr., 251. (Letter No. 208). And cf. Winch, *Adam Smith's Politics*, chapter 5, pp. 103–20.

5 LJ(A), iv, 112; LJ(B), 353–8; WN, v, i, e. 2.

6 WN, iii, iv, 24.

7 WN, v, i, a. 44: 'In modern war the great expence of fire-arms gives an evident advantage to the nation which can best afford that expence; and consequently, to an opulent and civilized, over a poor and barbarous nation. In antient times the opulent and civilized found it difficult to defend themselves against the poor and barbarous nations. In modern times the poor and barbarous find it difficult to defend themselves against the opulent and civilized. The invention of fire-arms...is certainly favourable both to the permanency and to the extension of civilization.'

8 Cf. TMS, vi, ii, 2, § 3.

9 Smith had a very keen sense of this integration and never demonstrated it better than in his explanation of the development of modern diplomacy in response to the needs of commerce. See LJ(B), 353–8, and WN, v, i, e. 2.

10 WN, v, iii, 4ff.

11 See Winch, *Adam Smith's Politics*, chapter 6, esp. pp. 135–41, for a multitude of perspectives on this very complex problem. The only reason for going over the problem here is the position of the jurisprudential criticism.

12 See WN, iii, iv, 24, and WN, v, ii, f. 6. Cf. WN, ii, v, 14; v, ii, k. 80; and v, iii, 55; LJ(A), v, 47–9.

13 WN, iii, i, 8–9, and iii, iii.

14 LJ(A), iv, 81–5; LJ(B), 39–40.

15 Athens was rather different in this respect: there were not the extremes of rich and poor that there were in Rome, and her institutions were much more democratic. So the way to decay was a set of democratic, all-round subsidies. See LRBL, 144–6.

16 See p. 160, above.

17 LJ(A), iii, 134–44; LJ(B), 138–40. See LRBL, 150–1, concerning the significance of the lack of a 'middle rank' in Rome.

18 R. Pascal, 'Property and society: the Scottish historical school of the eighteenth century', *The Modern Quarterly*, vol. I, 1938, pp. 167–79 (p. 173), and R. L. Meek, 'Smith, Turgot, and the "four stages" theory', *History of Political Economy*, vol. III, 1971, pp. 9–27 (p. 10).

19 R. L. Meek, 'The Scottish contribution to Marxist sociology', in his *Economics and Ideology and Other Essays* (London, 1967), p. 40.

20 A. S. Skinner, 'Adam Smith: an economic interpretation of history', in A. S. Skinner and T. Wilson (eds.), *Essays on Adam Smith* (Oxford, 1975), pp. 154–78 (p. 175). In a note, Professor Skinner refers to the relevant, rather interesting, passage from Engels: 'In a letter to J. Bloch, dated September 1890, Engels wrote that "According to the materialist conception of history, the *ultimately* determining element in history is the production and reproduction of real life. More than this neither Marx nor I have ever asserted. Hence if somebody twists this into saying that the economic element is the *only* determining one, he transforms that proposition into a meaningless, abstract, senseless phrase" (*Marx–Engels, Selected Works* (1958), ii, 488)' (*ibid.*, p. 175, note 53). Professor Skinner has since developed and clarified his interpretation of Smith considerably in a 'pluralistic' direction. See his *A System of Social Science* (Oxford, 1979), chap. 4, pp. 68–103. (This important study of Smith came too late for me to use more extensively, but I am grateful to Professor Skinner for allowing me to read some sections of it in manuscript.)

21 LJ(A), vi, 7–13; LJ(B), 205–9.

22 TMS, IV, 1, § 10, and WN, I, xi, c. 7.

23 TMS, I, iii, 2, § 1.

24 TMS, IV, 1, § 11.

25 The distinction between basic subsistence needs and 'the pleasures of wealth' which we meet in this discussion is obviously closely related to Smith's famous distinction between necessaries and luxuries in WN, v, ii, k. It should not be confused with this, nevertheless, for Smith is very emphatic in the latter discussion that the level of necessaries is *socially* determined. We are thus being presented with an implicit confrontation between something 'artificial' and something 'natural'. The relationship between the two distinctions and their promise of the basic idea behind diminishing marginal utility are outside our concern here.

26 Cf. pp. 52–4, above.

27 TMS, I, iii, 2, § 8. Cf. also the description of 'The poor man's son whom heaven in its anger has visited by ambition': TMS, IV, 1, § 8.

28 TMS, IV, 1, § 10.

29 LJ(B), 12.

30 TMS, I, iii, 2, § 3.

31 A. S. Skinner, 'Adam Smith: an economic interpretation of history', p. 155, and 'Adam Smith. Science and the role of the imagination', in W. B. Todd (ed.), *Hume and the Enlightenment: Essays Presented to E. C. Mossner* (Edinburgh, 1974), pp. 164–88 (p. 165).

32 I owe this point to an unpublished paper by J. F. G. Shearmur. The point that pleasure and pain are not as such explanatory, but are dependent upon the situation in which they occur, is also borne out by the connection with sympathy which, when it is mutual, is the selector of behaviour. See pp. 58–60, above.

33 TMS, i, iii, 2, § i.

34 For some specimens concerning Parliament, see e.g. LJ(A), iv, 159–61, 172–4; WN, iii, iii, 11 (see the excellent editorial note 22). Concerning hereditary *versus* elective monarchy, see e.g. LJ(A), iv, 162–4, 166–7.

35 LJ(B), 61; cf. LJ(A), iv, 171.

36 LJ(A), iv, 173; cf. LJ(B), 62.

37 Corr., 384.

38 Cf. R. L. Meek: 'Everything in society and in history was bound together by a succession of causes and effects...Society developed blindly, but not arbitrarily' – according to Smith ('Smith, Turgot, and the "four stages" theory', p. 9).

39 We could hardly expect this, since Smith presents these ideas within the framework of his discussion of how to give proofs in judicial orations.

40 See LRBL, 165–6.

41 For some of the many formulations of this, see LRBL, 85, 88–9, 90–1.

42 WN, v, i, f. 28.

43 LRBL, 58–9.

44 Smith's idea of how to explain each individual psychological 'item' by reference to both internal and external circumstantial factors is outlined in the following passage: 'The different passions all proceed...from different states of mind and outward circumstances. But it would be endless and useless to go through all these different affections and passions...It would be endless because, though the simple passions are of no great number, yet these are so compounded in different manners as to make a number of mixt ones almost infinite. It would be useless, for though we had gone through all the different affections, yet the difference of character and age and circumstances of the person would so vary the effects, that our rules would not be at all applicable' (LRBL, 65). Cf. also LRBL, 71.

45 Cf. the continuation of the previous quotation in the text: 'The design of history, compounded of both of these, is to state the remarkable transactions that pass in different nations, and the designs, motions, and views of the most remarkable men in those times, so far as they are necessary to explain the great changes and revolutions of states which it is intended to relate' (LRBL, 59).

46 See also LRBL, 88–9, and for just some of the cases where this is the standard by which historians are assessed: LRBL, 102–3, 104, 106, 109. For the general epistemological background to these methodological ideas, see pp. 79–82, above.

47 For a few examples of this, see LRBL, 85–6, 102–3, 107.

48 Smith spells out his view of the place of 'the economic' in history in explicit

terms in the following passage: 'Opulence and commerce *commonly precede* the improvement of arts and refinement of every sort. I do not mean that the improvement of arts and refinement of manners are the *necessary consequences* of commerce, – the Dutch and the Venetians bear testimony against me, – but that [it] is a *necessary requisite*' (LRBL, 131–2; my italics). And in a similar vein he points out that 'Commerce gave the lowest of the people an *opportunity* of raising themselves fortunes, and by that means power' (LRBL, 144; my italics).

49 See above, pp. 179–81. At the same time, of course, the system set certain subsidiary political tasks, notably that of education. See p. 94, above.

Bibliography

A PRIMARY SOURCES

David Hume. *Enquiries Concerning Human Understanding and Concerning the Principles of Morals*, edited by L. A. Selby-Bigge, Oxford, 1902; third revised edition by P. H. Nidditch, Oxford, 1975
Essays Moral, Political, and Literary, edited by T. H. Green and T. H. Grose, 2 vols, London, 1898
A Letter from a Gentleman to His Friend in Edinburgh, edited by E. C. Mossner and J. V. Price, Edinburgh, 1967
The Letters of David Hume, edited by J. Y. T. Greig, 2 vols, Oxford, 1932; reprinted 1969
A Treatise of Human Nature, edited by L. A. Selby-Bigge, Oxford, 1888; second revised edition by P. H. Nidditch, Oxford, 1978
Adam Smith. 'Anderson Notes', from John Anderson's Commonplace Book, vol. I, in the Andersonian Library, University of Strathclyde; printed in R. L. Meek, 'New light on Adam Smith's Glasgow Lectures on Jurisprudence', *History of Political Economy*, vol. VIII, 1976, pp. 439–77
The Correspondence of Adam Smith, edited by E. C. Mossner and I. S. Ross, Oxford, 1977
'Early Draft' of part of *The Wealth of Nations*, in *Lectures on Jurisprudence*, pp. 562–81
Essays on Philosophical Subjects, edited by W. P. D. Wightman and J. C. Bryce; with Dugald Stewart's 'Account of Adam Smith', edited by I. S. Ross; Oxford, 1980
First fragment on the division of labour, in *Lectures on Jurisprudence*, pp. 582–4
An Inquiry into the Nature and Causes of the Wealth of Nations, edited by R. H. Campbell and A. S. Skinner; text edited by W. B. Todd; 2 vols, Oxford, 1976
Lectures on Jurisprudence, edited by R. L. Meek, D. D. Raphael, and P. G. Stein, Oxford, 1978
Lectures on Justice, Police, Revenue and Arms, edited by E. Cannan, Oxford, 1896; reprinted New York, 1964
Lectures on Rhetoric and Belles Lettres, edited by J. M. Lothian, London, 1963; reprinted Carbondale and Edwardsville, 1971
The Theory of Moral Sentiments, edited by D. D. Raphael and A. L. Macfie, Oxford, 1976

B OTHER LITERATURE

H. B. Acton. 'Prejudice', *Revue internationale de philosophie*, 1952, pp. 323–36
P. S. Ardal. *Passion and Value in Hume's Treatise*, Edinburgh, 1966.
'And that's a promise', *The Philosophical Quarterly*, vol. XVIII, 1968, pp. 225–37
Introduction and notes to D. Hume, *A Treatise of Human Nature*, Books II and III, London, 1972
'Convention and value', in *David Hume: Bicentenary Papers*, edited by G. P. Morice, Edinburgh, 1977, pp. 51–68
T. D. Campbell. *Adam Smith's Science of Morals*, London, 1971
N. Capaldi. *David Hume: The Newtonian Philosopher*, Boston, 1975
R. D. Cumming. *Human Nature and History*, 2 vols, Chicago and London, 1969
D. Forbes. *Hume's Philosophical Politics*, Cambridge, 1975
'Sceptical Whiggism, commerce, and liberty', in *Essays on Adam Smith*, edited by A. S. Skinner and T. Wilson, Oxford, 1975, pp. 179–201
'"Scientific" Whiggism: Adam Smith and John Millar', *Cambridge Journal*, vol. 7, 1953–4, pp. 643–70
J. Griffin. 'Is unhappiness more important than happiness?', *Philosophical Quarterly*, vol. XXIX, 1979, pp. 47–55
K. Haakonssen. 'Hume's social explanations: the case of justice', *Danish Yearbook of Philosophy*, vol. 12, 1975, pp. 114–28
'Hume's obligations', *Hume Studies*, vol. IV, no. 1, 1978, pp. 7–17
'Natural Justice. The Development of a Critical Philosophy of Law from David Hume and Adam Smith to John Millar and John Craig', Edinburgh University Ph.D. thesis, 1978
F. A. von Hayek. *Studies in Philosophy, Politics and Economics*, London, 1967
Law, Legislation, and Liberty, 3 vols, London, 1973, 1976, 1979
J. T. King. 'The place of the language of morals in Hume's second *Enquiry*', in *Hume: A Re-evaluation*, edited by D. W. Livingston and J. T. King, New York, 1976, pp. 343–61
J. R. Lindgren. *The Social Philosophy of Adam Smith*, The Hague, 1973
Hans Medick. *Naturzustand und Naturgeschichte der bürgerlichen Gesellschaft*, Göttingen, 1973
R. L. Meek. 'The Scottish contribution to Marxist sociology', in R. L. Meek, *Economics and Ideology and Other Essays*, London, 1967, pp. 34–50
'Smith, Turgot, and the "four stages" theory', *History of Political Economy*, vol. III, 1971, pp. 9–27
'New light on Adam Smith's Glasgow Lectures on Jurisprudence', *History of Political Economy*, vol. VIII, 1976, pp. 439–77
R. Pascal. 'Property and society: the Scottish historical school of the eighteenth century', *The Modern Quarterly*, vol. I, 1938, pp. 167–79
J. G. A. Pocock. *The Ancient Constitution and the Feudal Law*, New York, 1967
'Burke and the ancient constitution: a problem in the history of ideas', in J. G. A. Pocock, *Politics, Language, and Time*, London, 1971, pp. 202–32
R. H. Popkin. 'Hume and Kierkegaard', *Review of Religion*, vol. 31, 1951, pp. 274–81
K. R. Popper. *The Open Society and Its Enemies*, 2 vols, London, 1966

D. D. Raphael. 'Obligations and rights in Hobbes', *Philosophy*, vol. 37, 1962, pp. 345–52

T. A. Roberts. *The Concept of Benevolence*, London, 1973

A. S. Skinner. *A System of Social Science*, Oxford, 1979

'Adam Smith. Science and the role of the imagination', in *Hume and the Enlightenment: Essays Presented to E. C. Mossner*, edited by W. B. Todd, Edinburgh, 1974, pp. 164–88

'Adam Smith: an economic interpretation of history', in *Essays on Adam Smith*, edited by A. S. Skinner and T. Wilson, Oxford, 1975, pp. 154–78

D. Stewart. 'Account of the Life and Writings of Adam Smith, LL.D.', in EPS, pp. 269–351

W. C. Swabey. *Ethical Theory from Hobbes to Kant*, London, 1961

K. E. Tranöy. 'Asymmetries in ethics', *Inquiry*, vol. 10, 1967, pp. 351–72

J. Viner. 'Guide to John Rae's *Life of Adam Smith*', in John Rae, *Life of Adam Smith*, London, 1895; reprinted New York, 1965

D. Winch. *Adam Smith's Politics*, Cambridge, 1978

Index

law(s) *(cont.)*

canon, 152, 166, 170, 172, 222 n. 108

case, 137, 152–3; *see also* common law

civil (as distinct from criminal law), 99, 149, 156

civil (as distinct from natural and ecclesiastic law), 28, 123

civil (Roman), *see* law, Roman

command theory of, 132, 148, 216 n. 74

common, *see* common law

courts, *see* courts of law

criminal, 99, 117, 149, 156; *see also* delict; punishment

criticism of, 1–2; *see also* jurisprudence, critical

of defence, *see* defence

domestic, 94, 96, 100, 103, 105 (fig. 1), 118–19, 123–7, 144–5, 156, 185; *see also* law, family

English, 152

family, 100, 101; *see also* law, domestic

French, 152

history of, 2, 21, 42, 65, 101, 102, 105–6, 110, 111, 113, 115, 119, 126–7, 131, 138, chap. 7, 178, 218 n. 3; *see also* jurisprudence, historical; jurisprudence, natural, and history; justice and history

of justice, 95, 96–7, 101, 114, 119, 120, 124, 126, 140, 143, 144, 151, 180, 181, 188, 205 n. 71, 210 n. 130, 217 n. 83

marriage, 94, 164; *see also* rights of a husband; rights of a wife

of nations, 20, 96, 103, 104, 120, 121, 133–4, 146–7, 204 n. 68, 205 n. 71, 213 n. 205

natural, of nature, 20, 21, 22, 28, 29, 37, 40, 43, 125, 142, 149, 150 (*see also* justice, natural); traditional, 2, 12, 21, 96

origin of, 99

philosophy of, 2, 20, 150

of police, 95, 96, 114, 119, 120, 121, 122, 123, 124, 125, 126, 143, 144, 151, 154, 173, 180, 181, 210 n. 130, 215 n. 54, 217 n. 83, 218 n. 95

positive, 20, 148, 149, 150, 153, 188, 189

private, 103, 113, 115, 118, 119, 127, 128, 139–40, 205 n. 10

public, 100, 101, 103, 115, 119, 127–33, 145–6, 156, 159

of revenue, *see* revenue

and rights, *see* rights

Roman, 103, 104, 152, 162, 170, 171, 172, 173, 174, 222 n. 106

Scots, 152

of settlement, 139, 214 n. 14

statute, 28, 108, 137, 152–3, 216 n. 78, 217 n. 87, 218 n. 95

system of, division of, 95, 96, 97, 100, 105 (fig. 1), 114, 118 (fig. 2), 136, 138, 150, 153, 154, 205 n. 9

traditionalist justification of, 43

written, 153

see also jurisprudence; justice; positivism, legal; rights

'leap-of-faith', 77

legislation, 95, 169

legislator, 37, 97, 135, 164, 180, 188, 203 n. 32, 205 n. 72

legislature, 82, 139, 153

Levellers, the, 27, 40

Leviticus, 211 n. 152

liberty, 94, 96, 97, 103, 118 (fig. 2), 120, 122, 126, 127, 130, 131, 132, 133, 139, 140, 141, 153, 166, 167

English, 185

natural, system of, 93

personal and political, 140

Lindgren, J. R., 196 n. 9, 197 n. 13, 198 n. 59

Locke, John, 106–7, 129, 130, 142, 206 n. 34, 212 n. 181

logic, situational, 64

see also situation, role of in moral knowledge

Macedonians, the, 161

Macfie, A. L., 199 n. 64, 203 n. 20

Mandeville, Bernard, 21, 79, 195 n. 117

manufacture, 95, 160, 165, 167, 168, 173, 180, 181, 220 n. 67

market, the, 93, 120, 173, 180, 220 n. 67

marriage, 124–5, 158, 163, 164, 166, 172, 175, 199 n. 86, 220 n. 67

Marx, Karl, 224 n. 20

Massillon, J. P., 200 n. 91

Medick, H., 190 n. 2

Mediterranean, the, 160

Meek, R. L., 190 n. 9, 224 nn. 18, 19; 225 n. 38

Members of Parliament, 169, 177, 179

mercenaries, mercenary troops, 161, 178, 179

merit, *see* propriety; sympathy

'metayer' system, 176, 223 n. 131

methodology, 6, 11–12, 78, 192 n. 36

see also determinism

Middle Ages, the, 171

virtues *(cont.)*
  see also artifice; justice; obligation;
    promises

waifs, franchise of, 142, 214 n. 33
West Indies, 215 n. 65
Whig(s), Whiggism, 43, 128, 131, 132,
    146, 196 n. 128

will(s), 173
Winch, D., vii, 190 n. 2, 204 nn. 46, 55;
    205 nn. 72, 77; 206 n. 35, 210
    n. 128, 212 n. 192, 223 nn. 4, 11
wonder and surprise, 72, 80, 200 n. 96
wool, export of, 117, 121
works, public, 93
  see also institutions, public